Wild Sweet Notes

Wild Sweet Notes

Fifty Years of West Virginia Poetry
1950 – 1999

EDITED BY
BARBARA SMITH AND KIRK JUDD

PUBLISHERS PLACE

Library of Congress Catalog Card Number: 00-103841
ISBN: 0-9676051-0-5 (Special Edition)
ISBN: 0-9676051-1-3 (Hardcover Edition)
ISBN: 0-9676051-2-1 (Paperback Edition)

First Edition, First Printing

Printed in the United States of America

Design: Mark S. Phillips
Cover Photograph: Vincent James Vendolini
(courtesy Blennerhassett Island Museum)
Drawings: Jan Dickinson
Jacket Copy: John Patrick Grace
Acknowledgements:
Art Stringer and Jeffrey Tutt
(English Department, Marshall University)
Phyllis Moore (research)
Lauretta Gordon (typography)

Publishers Place, Inc.
945 Fourth Avenue, Suite 200A
Huntington, West Virginia 25701

publish@cloh.net

www.publishersplace.org

INTRODUCTION

Alberto Rios in his introduction to *Approaching Poetry*[1] said:

*During brushfires, jackrabbits can get caught in the flames,
no matter how fast they are. And when they're caught
their hair can catch on fire. Of course, they run away
from the flame, but you know what happens—they bring
the fire with them.*

*I think poetry is like that sometimes...catching us...
No matter where you are in your writing (or reading!)...
you may catch on fire...so be warned. But it won't be like
the jackrabbits. It may feel like it, but no flames will come
from your hair.*

Not at first.

As Rios suggests, this may not happen every time we deal
with poetry, but it certainly happened as this anthology came
into being. We, the editors and the publisher, caught fire. And
we're still burning, both with the excitement of the quality of
the material and with the knowledge of and communication
with many, many fine poets in West Virginia.

Early in 1998 Patrick Grace and Mark Phillips of Publishers
Place, Inc., expressed interest in doing a collection of fifty
years of West Virginia poetry. We, Kirk Judd and Barbara Smith,
were asked to serve as editors as well as contributors. We sent
out word via West Virginia Writers, Inc., and other such organi-
zations. We perused lists of poets in the files of literary histo-
rian Phyllis Moore. We talked with established poets in the
state, and we asked members of our Advisory Board to supply
us with names and addresses. The list grew and grew and
grew, to a total of approximately 175 names of poets, living
and deceased, who had written and published within the fifty

---

[1] Schakel, Peter J., and Jack Ridl, eds., New York: St. Martin's Press, 1997.

years between 1950 and 1999. Then we searched for addresses or contacts, and we found approximately 130 of them. Letters of invitation went out to the living poets, and we searched the archives at West Virginia University and the collections of libraries and individuals to be sure that we could include as many of the deceased poets as possible.

We received submissions from approximately 120 living poets, and we selected poems from the publications of approximately 25 deceased poets. The average number of poems in a submission was ten. From the almost 1300 pieces thus collected, we made choices for the anthology. Criteria began with quality. Then we looked for variety of subject and form.

We began burning with the initial concept of the project, but the flames burst forth dramatically when we realized what a treasure we had in our hands. Time after time we commented to each other, "This person ought to have a book published," or, "I wish we could include all of these!" or "Wow! Look at this!" In short, working on this collection has enriched our lives beyond measure.

We apologize to any poets who were inadvertently overlooked. We did our best to include all who would meet the three criteria: 1) the poet must have been born in West Virginia or else have lived here at least five years, 2) the poet must have had work published in at least one publication of national distribution, 3) the poet must be recognized as "established" by at least two West Virginia poets of national reputation.

This collection is a celebration of the quality and quantity of poetry in our beloved West Virginia. It is dedicated to all who have contributed and who will continue to contribute to the remarkable body of poetic work that is part of our Mountain State heritage.

Barbara Smith
Philippi, West Virginia

Kirk Judd
Huntington, West Virginia

DEDICATION

It is a pleasure and honor to support

Wild Sweet Notes:
Fifty Years of West Virginia Poetry

In celebrating the writers herein,
we take special pride in recognizing the dedication
of these West Virginia authors whose writing captures
the spirit of creativity and whose completed work is
among the best to be found.

A heartfelt congratulations to Publishers Place, Inc.
and the editors and designers of this
publication who have produced one of this nation's
great poetry anthologies.

Thank you for allowing us to be a small part
of this wonderful project.

From the Employees and Owners of
MOUNTAINEER RACE TRACK & GAMING RESORT
Chester, West Virginia
March 31, 2000

Wild Sweet Notes

FIFTY YEARS
of
WEST VIRGINIA
POETRY
1950 - 1999

Enigmatic.
How can you find
support with me — . . .
You, who never danced
to wild sweet notes,
Outpouring of
nimble-fingered fiddlers.

— Muriel Dressler
Appalachia
pp 105-106

Elegy for My Father

The spring that I was
four going into five
you sat me on the wooden drag
as the horses stomped nervously.
You stood behind me, tugged the reins,
yelled, "Giddup, Babe, Kate" and
geed and hawed and smiled.
The drag flattened fresh clods of earth
and brown worms fled broken tunnels.

In summer we fished the pond and creek,
I learned to thread a worm onto a hook,
to hold the homemade pole just so,
to grasp the flopping fish behind the gills,
and guide the barbed hook out.
At night you built a fire and showed me
how to stack the wood. "A fire
like everything has to breathe," you said.
Later you scaled the fish, cut away
the parts we would not eat,
rolled the headless body in flour,
sizzled it in an iron skillet.

In autumn we tramped the cornfield,
rustled through the rows until
we found the perfect pumpkin, round and firm.
You cut off the top. I squished bare
hands into seeds and guts, pulled strings
of membrane out, flung it on the ground.
You cut the face true to my lopsided design
and inside cut a niche to fit a candle.

In winter we went to a secondhand store,
bought a sled with rusted runners

and broken boards for fifty cents.
Together we sanded and waxed curved metal,
hammered in new boards, painted them red.
You pulled me down the hill to make a road,
showed me how to steer
and left me alone to learn.

In my teenage years, you yelled and sometimes
cursed, said all my boyfriends were too smooth,
too crude, too handsome. Later you vowed
you had no daughter when nerves
in your brain tangled like pumpkin membrane.
Then you curled like a fetus
around oxygen tank and feeding tube.
What carried me through it all
was the year of four going into five.

At Honanki

At Honanki (the Badger House)
the guide,
Arizona Hopi face
framed by gray braids,
leans against the red cliffs,
points at the pictograph,
and recites, "This is
Kokopelli,
the Sinagua symbol
of fertility,
fertility of soil,
of woman,
of action and thought.
See the raindrops he scatters."

In the partition
beside me, stones
laid precisely front
irregular stones
from two centuries earlier,
each held together
by red earth mixed
with animal blood,
urine and water.
I climb higher
and fit fingers
into prints left
700 years ago.

I see myself
a girl of five
crouched in the shadows,
skin blending with the red walls
of the only home I've known.
In fields far below
corn droops and squash vines
shrivel till they look like
yucca rope. Old men chant
prayers to Kokopelli,
the god who sprinkles rain,
while younger ones whisper
of abandonment.

The guide's scarred boots
crunch gravel beside me.
His hand blends into Sedona stone
as he motions me to the jeep.
My fingers slip down the wall,
and I follow.

GAIL GALLOWAY ADAMS

THREE WOMEN ON A PORCH

The wooden swing sways with a push.
It is not centered.
Fleece slippers skitter on uneven boards
as the chain buckles quick as a fling of hands.
The second rocks straight on,
her bare toes push the floor as if she tested mud.
The third sits in a chair lined to stairs
that are not plumb.
At evening's end she will step into
dark space,
trusting to a sudden blaze to bring her
safely down.
This quiet night is heavy with heat
and the smell of peaches on the ground.
The hum of hearing aids calls crickets home.

The Seabed

My daughter curls toward me
lost in the sea
of my huge bed.
I am a promontory
of the mainland:
my hipbone juts
a fine dark line
above the water;
my arm contains the inlet
beyond my daughter's head.
With my cold foot
I touch her row
of folded toes;
they scuttle
under her nightgown;
her head rears—
turtle mouth, eyes
puffed fetal slits—
sinks down.
Her body coils tighter
moves nearer
my land.
Afloat in the white-quilted
moonlit sea.
I am large but light
and firmly moored:
a mother in her house
in her room
in her bed
her child curling toward her
afloat in sleep.

Red Dress

I want a long

red dress

like a slug

of good bourbon,

a hot

raspy shiver.

I like people

who bite.

Bob Thompson at the Piano

He offers you the melody, like bread
I watched my grandmother lift away from the oven—
a solid, shapely thing, so complete in itself
I could almost forget the way it came about:
the ceremony of the sprinkled yeast,
the necessary bit of something sweet,
the rhythm of the kneading and her voice,
a secret she told about her mother's mother,
who married someone, not the man she loved,
and how *he* came into the hardware store
when both of them were in their seventies
and took her in his arms at last, too late.

He offers you the melody, and then
he seems to simply let it rise, the way
Grandmother put the dough into a bowl,
covered it with a towel, untied her apron,
and told me to go outside, now, and play.
So I went swimming, or maybe I took the canoe
to that quiet cove on the far edge of the lake
where lily pads floated in a trembling layer,
my small heart full of my great-great-grandmother's ache,
crying a dead woman's tears, and wondering who
on earth I would have been, today,
had love prevailed, all those years ago.

He offers you the melody, like bread,
and pours the rest of the song around it, through
the spaces—honey and butter and cinnamon,
and you are a child again, you have nothing to do
except to lose yourself for a little while.
Start out in any direction. Wander. Stray
into the territory of dreams. Stay
as long as you please, and, when you please, return,
for the melody is always there, like bread,

like a woman in a kitchen, telling a story
with no clear lesson, from which a child could learn
the difference between eating and being fed.

Huckleberries

So Dorothy sent us off to Dolly Sods
with a plastic pint container and a lid
and promises of huckleberry muffins
in the morning. We found them where she'd said
we would, in a high and quiet place of spruce
and laurel, bushes as crowded with berries

as a country night with stars. So small. So blue.
Bluer than Prussian, bluer than indigo, bluer than
anything, color that looks right back at you
with the eyes of a long-forgotten, favorite doll.
Tiny as buttons on a doll's dress. So small,
and our fingers grown so clumsy, so fat, so adult.

Picture two middle-aged women, bent over, sweating,
plucking and talking, inhaling spruce and sky.
We grew up together, Julie. You remember
my birthday party the year we both were seven.
Your father used to keep track of us, you told me,
by listening to us, giggling, across the lake.

We didn't even pick a pint of berries,
and of course we stayed too long. The afternoon
went dim. We strayed into a boggy thicket
and lost our way, and blundered in the mud,
and then, like something out of a storybook
with a happy ending, found the path again.

Picture two middle-aged women, hugging and laughing,
telling each other we weren't really scared.
We ran straight down the mountain, ran all the way,

huckleberries bouncing in my backpack,
and leapt from rock to rock across Red Creek,
huckleberries jumping up and down for joy.

Great Aunt Margaret

"There's a name for this disease, but I don't
know what it is," Aunt Margaret said.
"I laugh when other people cry."
To the family, it was
no joke. They couldn't
have her cackling in the pew
when the preacher got to
who gives this woman, and after that
ungodly hoot at Ernie's funeral
she always stayed behind to mind the house.
"One thing about Margaret," everyone said,
"she's got a happy nature."

And needed it. Who else
could put up with boozy Uncle Jack
for all those years, and Wayne
too hateful to bother calling home?
And the way she nursed Louise
after that turnpike wreck?
You had to give her credit, they said.
The kind of life that might have cracked
a smaller woman, Great Aunt Margaret
took in stride, was how they put it.
You had to cut her a little slack:
she laughed when other people cried.

You had to watch her, though. You had
to turn the TV off sometimes.
When they ran that footage of the flood,
for instance. When Kennedy died
she chuckled for days. That time

Marcella's class put on the pageant
in the high school gym, Margaret came,
of course. They'd booked this juggler from
someplace like Hungary, a little fellow,
slim and pretty as a girl. Did his act,
ducked behind the stage, came back
in a costume like a horse. The way
he pranced and tossed that big rear end,
we laughed 'til tears ran down our cheeks,
all of us. Then Billy squawked,
"Looks like she's takin' some kind of fit."

We didn't even get it, at first,
couldn't picture what it'd be like
when the dam inside Aunt Margaret broke.
We had to hoist her down from the bleachers,
lay her flat on the basketball court,
twitching like a Pentecostal
about to speak in tongues,
but it wasn't words came out.

She cried. And not some sniffling little sob
but big, fat, belly-throbbing wails.
Waves and waves! She roared like a bear!
Her housedress heaved and billowed so,
Flo kept having to pull it down.
Somebody ran to get Uncle Jack
and he came, not sober but fairly quick,
and put his hand out and touched her arm.

She seemed to come back a little, then,
raised her face to his,
choked a couple of times, and focused
on that not-quite-steady man.
"Ah, Jesus, Jack, go on. Go back
to the bar. I'm not done."

Querencia

Evenings here, I am touched
by lattice work in shadow
the simplicity of doorways,
what's left at the end of a day
in the yards. How these houses
give off onto fields in back
and the musky smells of gardens,
the new-cut lawns. How the dinner dishes
rustle in various kitchens
like the boats at the docks,
a dull donking in live fog,
in other, fishing, towns at dawn.
Twenty screens glow in twenty living rooms
with news. In some of these houses,
no one's lived for years,
grasses grown high to the porches,
empty of coffee cups and swings,
bare boards and the smeared glass.
How that rusty trumpet mutes in weeds
as the lights come on. In other houses,
curtains are laced even to the attic windows.
And a second floor bedroom, tinted bronze,
holds this last sun
focused. Stuck to that rocking chair
the old dust sifts in its arms.
Tonight the rain glazes
and sharpens the roof tar
and the outline of the chair
seems in silhouette,
as if it's rocking,
as if someone, moving off quickly,
left its fullness
without hesitation
and never came back.

Cucumbers

When they started to grow, there was a long slit, curved,
you could see it widen, in the ground where we had
    dropped
the seeds. It was a mysterious movement of the earth; as if
    we
might be swallowed up. It was late May. By the second
    week
in June, the seam had split, bushy leaves, growing together,
appeared, like a continuous bean plant. There are two and a
half rows. Because I like cucumbers.

In the early mornings, I slither under the leaves to
    search out
mites and yellowness on the underside. I cuddle up next to
them, searching out rot, trying to see into the earth.
Cucumbers smell like copperheads under the rocks by the
river. And I remember why I would never lie down on the
edge of the Cheat to look for crayfish.

Cucumbers contain a small amount of the same poison
    of
copperheads. They are cool in the kitchen, clean, green, and
white; nothing tastes like them; they taste like nothing. They
are wet air with seeds in it. They are copperheads lying
between the rocks, defining where I can walk, making no
    sound.

If you eat enough cucumbers, you will die. If you eat
enough of anything, you will die. If you lie down under a
    row
of cucumber leaves in the early morning, you will never
    want
to get up.

Long Story

To speak in a flat voice
Is all that I can do.
— James Wright

I need to tell you that I live in a small town
in West Virginia you would not know about.
It is one of the places I think of as home.
When I go for a walk, I take my basset hound
whose sad eyes and ungainliness always draw
a crowd of children. She tolerates anything
that seems to be affection, so she lets the kids
put scarves and ski caps on her head
until she starts to resemble the women who have to dress
from rummage sales in poverty's mismatched polyester.

The dog and I trail the creek bank with the kids,
past clapboard row houses with Christmas seals
pasted to the windows as a decoration.
Inside, television glows around the vinyl chairs
and curled linoleum, and we watch someone old
perambulating to the kitchen on a shiny walker.
Up the hill in town, two stores have been
boarded up beside the youth center, and miners
with amputated limbs are loitering outside
the Heart and Hand. They wear Cat diesel caps
and spit into the street. The wind
carries on, whining through the alleys,
rustling down the sidewalks, agitating
leaves, and circling the courthouse steps
past the toothless Field sisters who lean
against the flagpole holding paper bags
of chestnuts they bring to town to sell.

History is one long story of what happened to us,
and its rhythms are local dialect and anecdote.

In West Virginia a good story takes awhile,
and if it has people in it, you have to swear
that it is true. I tell the kids the one about
my Uncle Craig who saw the mountain move
so quickly and so certainly it made the sun
stand in a different aspect to his little town
until it rearranged itself and settled down again.
This was his favorite story. When he got old,
he mixed it up with baseball games, his shift boss
pushing scabs through a picket line, the Masons
in white aprons at a funeral, but he remembered
everything that ever happened, and he knew how far
he lived from anywhere you would have heard of.

Anything that happens here has a lot of versions,
how to get from here to Logan twenty different ways.
The kids tell me convoluted country stories
full of snuff and bracken, about how long
they sat quiet in the deer blind with their fathers
waiting for the ten-point buck that got away.
They like to talk about the weather,
how the wind we're walking in means rain,
how the flood pushed cattle fifteen miles downriver.

These kids know mines like they know hound dogs
and how the sirens blow when something's wrong.
They know the blast, and the stories, how
the grown-ups drop whatever they are doing
to get out there. Story is shaped
by sound, and it structures what we know.
They told me this, and three of them
swore it was true, so I'll tell you
even though I know you do not know
this place, or how tight and dark the hills
pull in around the river and the railroad.

I'll say it as the children spoke it,
in the flat voice of my people:

down in Boone County, they sealed up
forty miners in a fire. The men who had come
to help tried and tried to get down to them,
but it was a big fire and there was danger,
so they had to turn around
and shovel them back in. All night long
they stood outside with useless picks and axes
in their hands, just staring at the drift mouth.
Here's the thing: what the sound must have been,
all those fire trucks and ambulances, the sirens,
and the women crying and screaming out
the names of their buried ones, who must have
called back up to them from deep inside
the burning mountain, right up to the end.

The Only Jazz Bar in Salt Lake

Personal history isn't a once opulent hotel
grown seedy and boarded up for winter, though
most of our language for it is. Wouldn't it be better
to talk about our pasts the way children talk about
the dinosaurs, in esoteric language they love
for its remoteness from their lives? They learn
Latin names for lumbering extinct beasts the way
I've learned the old jazz, what a blue seventh is,
and how to listen for it. They know the brontosaurus
body, free of memory's complication, as I know
Art Tatum's belly at the keyboard, or Chick Webb's
flashy hands when he played at the old Savoy.
Here, in the only jazz bar in Salt Lake,
we're leaning our heads together
in a high wooden booth while a sleepy scat
singer does an old Billie Holiday song
at a wheezy mike, and you're asking me again
if I remember how the coal trucks cool
their brakes at the bottom of the Spall Lick Hill

back home, how ironweed and joe-pye shine across
September fields. We're talking in exaggerated
West Virginia accents, trying to keep them pure
in desert air, though we know how quickly a familiar
speech flattens into mannerism, and all the loved
particulars only make us lonely. Wouldn't it be better
just to make our conversation keep its distance?
All-we've-been-through could become just this bar,
the very way we're sitting now, the smarmy stumble
of that woman's voice. We could tell our history
like stories of the dinosaurs, intricate verbiage,
with no referents anyone has ever seen.

A Place with Promise

Sometimes my affection for this place wavers.
I am poised between a vague ambition
and loyalty to what I've always loved,
kedged along inside my slow boat
by warp and anchor drag. But if I imagine
seeing this for the last time,
this scruff of the borders of West Virginia,
Pennsylvania, and Ohio, shaped by hills
and rivers, by poverty and coal,
then I think I could not bear to go,
would grab any stump or tree limb
and hold on for dear life.

I keep trying to say what I notice here
that's beautiful. There's the evening star
riding the purple selvage of the ridges,
and the flat shine of the Ohio where men
in folding chairs cast their lines out
toward the backwash of the barges.
There are the river names: the Allegheny,
the Monongahela, and the names of the tributaries,

Fish Creek, Little Beaver; the towns named
for function, Bridgeport, Martins Ferry,
or for what the early settlers must have
dreamed of, Prosperity and Amity.

Why can't we hold this landscape in our arms?
The nettle-tangled orchards given up on,
the broken fence posts with their tags
of wire, burdock taking over uncut fields,
the rusted ripples and the mills.
Sometimes I think it's possible
to wash the slag dust from the leaves
of sycamores and make them green, the way
as a child, after lesson and punishment,
I used to begin my life again.
I'd say a little "start" to myself
like the referees at races, then
on the same old scratchy car seat,
with the same parents on the same road,
I could live beyond damage and reproach,
in a place with such promise,
like any of the small farms among the wooded hills,
like any of the small towns starting up along the rivers.

ia Lowku

National statistics indicate
West Virginia has the highest
auto accident fatality ratio
and the lowest crime rate

I take this to mean
that the roads are crooked
and the people are straight.

Richwood

Once I was a grape Nehi
to the woodhicks standing on the porch of the Sportsman
chewing mail pouch tobacco
and spitting into a Heinz pork and beans can…

Just a stripling really—
green and tender as a yearling—
all ears and crewcut and jughead
sent on a mission of milk
but waylaid by words
and stories of wildcats and blizzards,
skid roads and timber it took four tries
with a six foot cross cut
to lay down

on hot days when pulp swelled with puberty
I absorbed the woodgrain of men
who with horses stretched sinews in mud and work—
who dug brogan heels into mountains and shale
and grunted together like primal lovers in suffering sweat;
who filled their nostrils with fog and laurel thickets,
woodsmoke and fresh cut oak;

whose tongues grew fat with Karo syrup
thick as spring sop on biscuits;
who stripped naked and lay down in Laurel Crick
bathed themselves inside and out with moonshine
and gathered pollen from the bodies of young women
sweeter than wild honeysuckle,
who scattered seeds over these hills
that sprouted and prospered safely beneath their canopy...
but now, with the stumps of ancient snags
rotting at my base,
I stand alone in sweetwater and sun
spiraling into an empty sky,
my roots sunk deep into humus, leafmold, and regrets,
richer, for what once thrived here, than death itself.

Poem for my Daddy

Because I sat on a hi-stool and watched over your lean shoulder
as you filled a primed canvas with images of Appalachia:
Two Dogs Bounding Through the Woods
The Cows Coming Home From the Creek,
because you made with the flourish of brush,
chickens cluck, roosters crow, horses kick up their heels,
and snow drift

because you drew the *Turkey in the Straw*
that graced every A&P window from Maine to Virginia—
because it was your Thanksgiving cornucopia of bounty,
your Santa Claus that twinkled in the eyes of all the Christmas kids,
your Easter Bunny and lilies that were the harbinger of spring,
and because you were determined enough to work
your initials into every piece of commercial art
though it was strictly forbidden by company policy

because you have cried and empathized
with those no more pitiable than yourself,

because you didn't go to Paris to study art after the war,
because you moved to Levittown,
the great graddaddy of sub-divisions,
where you planted the first post-war Victory garden
to the dismay of our landscaped neighbors
who were, nonetheless, won over by your tender greenbeans

because your marriage fell apart,
because you fell drunken down the embankment
of the Long Island Expressway
and were hit by a car,
because your famed attempt at hanging yourself in the garage
failed even misery,
because you were committed to Pilgrim State Hospital—
that brick bastille that housed the Empire State's crazies,
because I was too young to visit
and could only wave to your high barred window
from the half-empty Sunday parking lot
my long hollow Appalachian face reflected in pavement puddles,
because you had enough shock treatments
to forget the names of your children
and because you tried to remember

because you are the quintessent hillbilly harmonica player
itinerant whirligig yard art maker
truck patch potato farmer
red-necked drunk
half mean ex-marine
and southern storyteller par excellence

Because we have hoed the same soil
picked the same field stones
and held Henry's vision of Lost Flats
in our hearts and eyes.

because we have marveled at the Sweet Williams
dappled in spring rain

because we both miss Tessie
whose goodness will always surpass our own,

because we are bound for similar dirt on the same hill,
I write you this poem
with tenderness
honor
tinged love
and fierce pride.

Interlocking Circles

I watched the buzzards gliding over Hinkley.
At first it was food they tore from carcasses
After an animal slaughter. Now each year
For decades black wings darken the sun
Like nimbostratus clouds building layers
Across the sky. They seem to float
Over the land, up and down in the air currents,
Their heads tilting back and forth like the loops
They fly. Generations have lived and died
But descendants return each spring,
Flying convoluted, interlocking circles
Over the barren ground.

The Artist's Wife

These summer days I seek the garden's cool
And wander paths where flowers and leaves combine
In perfect harmony of color and shape
And texture and pattern in one glorious landscape.
In sun or shadow he sits there on his stool,
His eyes intent, his brush not just a tool
But the extension of himself, his soul and mind
And deepest longing for something he cannot find.
His brush caresses the canvas with each stroke,
His body sways as the images invoke
Sunlight dancing on a Roman tower,
Athenian warriors wasting Trojan power,
Or Haitian bathers in an aqua sea.
Engrossed, he cannot pause to glance at me.

Breakfast in the Big Scrub

Sunrays sneaking through tall Florida pines
Wake the Big Scrub as a scattered mist
Clears above the trees.
Stretching her arms at the cabin steps,
She listens to the silence of a new day.
She winds a worn path to a rusty well
And splashes cool water on her face,
Tanned by wind and sun.

Pushing back her long, tangled hair,
Cradling her old rifle on one arm,
She heads for the woods to hunt
A rabbit for supper. Six children,
Stretching on their pallets on the cabin porch,
Blink at the sunshine. And wait.

City Darkness

City darkness
is the worst
There are things in the headlight-pierced night
that should breathe only in nightmares;
Yet, they are real,
living in the smog's gloom —
waiting, waiting...
dripping outside my window...
watching, planning...
a thousand footsteps sound
below,
all intruders—all of them—
who walk the streets and
wear the night like a Halloween mask
drinking the neon flowing
like blood through glass veins
conspiring some more against me.
They who will not let me
sleep for the wail of a siren,
the wretching of a dying engine.
With raw ears, dry eyes,
I hide beneath the bed
    and wait,
        and wait
           and then

        I am gone.

Home

imagine

the smell of cookies in the oven
one million miles away,

Home
is where they would be...

and the cat sits in the
window
and the flowers cry for water
and the floorboards ache with silence

No lights warm the heart
of the house in the dark,
Its door unchallenged,
locked.

Mold will take the furniture
before I return
Dust will see that it is safe
to sleep out in the open
now.
The house breathes in upon
itself
until no air is left.

But:

A soul still lives in the silent
house,
walks the carpets,
watches the windows
surrounded by familiar smells
soft, old things she

loves to touch
    Safety to wrap herself
in like a warm blanket

    Her music still lingers,
subdued, where it played
      so much before

She is my soul…and…

    Home is where she
      would be.

Iron Curtains

Miss Yang climbs the thousand steps
of Guilin's mountains

tirelessly

as the Americans
catch their breath
focus their phallic lenses on the beauty
so they can take it home

She does not pause
This is her job, to lead and answer questions
It is not her place to question
(yet she dreams)

She reads George Eliot
and Harold Robbins (a paperback gift from a nice
American lady)
someone laughs and promises her an Agatha Christie
Miss Yang smiles, then asks, "What is America like?"

We sing Simon and Garfunkel songs
        because
they are the last remnants of our country that we
understand.

That night, she asks me again (in the hotel room)
"What is it like, your home?"

My first thoughts are fluorescent nightmares:
        Convenience stores,
Giant neon chickens revolving in the night,
        Golden arches rising up against bulldozed meadows.

A slice of humanity grown fat and pimply
        on grease franchises,
grown rich
        overestimating the vulgarity of the population,
grown simple
        in the opiate glare of game shows and sit-coms.

Family Dinner

The jello salad
came from the June issue of
Good Housekeeping
a cousin in polyester coordinates said
as she swatted
the child's behind.
And what are you doing now?
College? Career?
No, traveling, working on a novel.
Cold stares, cold ham
passed across the table.
Everyone here
(over age 24)

has a degree.
But
a mention of Brautigan or Vonnegut
draws a blank
(they never ask for explanations)
Please pass the rolls,
Uncle Ed belches
It's been so very nice
(what a trite word)
See you next year

AN APRIL EXULTATION

against the lights
I'm crossing streets,
keeping in stride,
perfect timing
(some days are like that)
thinking
who can forget death
once they've read
its calling card,
say,
in a strange lesion
on the tongue
or the smart swelling
of a breast;
or those who simply see it
falling so completely
over the next century?

today, though,
the world is working
in its resurrection
april way;
here, for example,
in lexington
I'm certain
the guardian spirits
are being born
and for that matter,
in rangoon, boston,
and richwood, too;
and one day
they will tell us again

how to forget death
once and for all
and we will remember enough
to at times weep in the night
(and that's okay, too)

this morning the world
is buying flowers
for all the right reasons
and duke willis,
fresh out of jail,
is back on little laurel
making baby dukeys again,
and georgie is in heaven
with edgar bergen
(the world's worst ventriloquest)
and arthur rimbaud
(who no longer dreams of eden)
and hitler will have to be
a better boy next time around,
and by intuition
our destinations
will change trains in aberdeen;

today, joanie is shopping
buying gifts
for the sisters of saint joseph's
because she really loves them
and loves the world,
knowing love
more holy than logic;
crossing limestone
my tie blows wildly
and despite myself
    I find my self whistling

EVERYTHING'S ARRANGED

It is late afternoon in the room of
grandmother's
                        good ghost—
you are alone—
you sit in a deep comfortable chair—
you are facing the clock of the opposite wall—
it is the only sound—
you clasp your hands beneath your chin,
you stare at your shoes
waiting for your feelings
to be defined, to become certain—
a patch of sunlight slides prismatically
                        edged
along the rose petal wallpaper—
the house settles, a stair creaks—
in the china cabinet
poor girls of porcelain
hold up trays of faded pastry—
the years of gentle cooking,
the lingering aromas, settle over you
like an evening—
you do not blink an eye—
a shimmering droplet forms
on the cold lips of the kitchen spigot

John Berryman's Bridge

in minnesota
there is the skeleton
of a rainbow
collapsed across
the mississippi;

you can walk it
from tip to tail
and O mr. Bones
you was right;
no gold at either end

Mars on a Vivid Night

a happy night, a dizzy night
and we lurch cockeyed
from that boothe mountain trailer,
bob snyder and me,
weaving around beneath
the wheeling milkyway;
drinking from one hand
from those old wahoo cups
and with the other
pissing steamy
down November hillside;
and slowly I focus on mars
with its pink and rusty spark,
and think just to be there
and gazing here, so unaware,
of how much woe and rapture,
how much sorrow, how much hope
a tiny star may hold

For Sale: 3/4 ton, 4wd pickup, V8, 4 spd. w/ creeper, positrac., for parts or farm use. Best Offer.

I've spent thousands of dollars on
that clapped out old four-wheel drive vehicle.
It always needs a u-joint and a couple of tires.
It doesn't run worth a damn and
the windshield is smashed.
The right door don't open
and the flat bed is rotting out.
It lurks there in the pasture,
daring me to try to start it.
It thinks I need it to cut firewood.
This is strictly confidential understand,
but someday soon I'm going to pay some fool
to haul it away,
that is of course unless you
want to buy it for parts.
What you got to trade?

- 30

Way too cold for clouds,
moonshine chisels ice prisms into frozen rainbows,
and ridges like rafters run
across hollows shingled with stars.
Before dawn the wind has turned against these
mountains with the essence of the north.
It will not bargain with the sun or the spirits
of woodhicks who curse the cold
in ghost towns on high Cheat, where once,
beneath the sparse blankets they muttered
at the failing stoves in drafty boarding houses.

Their axes idle of a morning too cold for clouds,
too cold for work,
too cold for anything but feeding the horses,
the men,
and the memories.

Allegheny RFD

Somewhere close to home,
a fencepost leans against rusty barbed wire,
heavy with the weight of long forgotten cattle.
I have always welcomed winter,
but today I saw the dozers,
limping across the ridge,
their slag covered treads
splintering young oaks.

Yet I remember nights
winter laid siege to this house,
and you came
greeting the storm along the path.
Until inside the wood,
inside the walls,
we shared luxury conversations,
cast like iron
across a circle,
called as witness to a woodstove.

Each one of us,
inside the myth of this place,
listens for the cry of the panther
above the groaning diesels.
Which leaves me unsure,
as alone,
I sit in the cabin,
tend the fire,
and think of you.

Memorial to my Father, the Miner, from His Child, the Poet

For Fortunato Battaglia
September 2, 1893 - August 9, 1976

Like some giant gnarled oak

you stood

against my masterly bonsai.

Cultured,
formal
perverted nature, I was
humankind civilized,
contained
uniform and almost
cloistered.

You roamed life

in tangle wood
and sagebrush,
torrential fluid fragments.

And now, in the forest by your grave,

I sit, sophisticate, mannequin,

my sad tears
tied,

a taste of ash,

and me,

too fine to spit.

The First Song Dulcinea Sings to Quixote as He Creates Her

And what if I am only Kafka's memory come alive, or,
what if I am some Odysseus, some misplaced sailor
on some mythological wine-dark sea, being born
now in some female form and told
in professional hours
in hoary ironies and studied similes
to the young with concrete ears;

but then,
what if I am not?

Then, what if I am a calligraphic symbol
of some old Chinese sage of the Ming Dynasy,
who loves mint teas and ceremony;
and who dreams me here now in his form,
walking beside some river I can never find the faith
to drown his dream in,

and then,
what if I am not?

Then, what if, finally, I am last night's dream's dream
of a fine gaunt knight in purples
and in mournful countenance,
listening to symphonies being strummed
at the column left of me, becoming,
slowly, in mid dream,
that clock of Dali's.

Oh,
what if
in fact
and
finally,

I am that clock of Dali's
lying limp over bare tree limbs,

or worse,
what if I am not.

Downstairs: 5:30 A.M.

morning is
black coffee
a kitchen

a newspaper
white and banded
waiting on the tiled porch

a rug
soft under bare feet

a back door
open
to screened darkness

upstairs
sleeping children
my husband alone

and down
on summer's last day
you
looking over my shoulder
reading these words
seeing through my back door

the vining wisteria
that clings, to the moonflower

the ripe tomatoes
heavy with seed

Postcards

He loved postcards.

Glossy photos of Niagara Falls
and the Grand Canyon
scrawled with "Having a great time...
wish you were here,"
that arrived two weeks too late.

But he ran his fingers
over the serrated edges of Gauguin
and Matisse.

He lingered over squares that commanded,
"Place Stamp Here,"

the five lines underneath,

and the naked message running downhill
on the left.

He loved finding them by chance
bookmarked somewhere between the water bill
and Life magazine,
always coveting the subtle perfume
of old news.

sibylline

I can see in the dark on confetti nights,
the eve of the ides,
while the syncopated world
skins the cat,
glows red in the year of refraction.

I hear no evil,
but it signs
behind a small window
on my not-for-captioned soul.

I speak in tongues,
tea leaves, and lifelines,
sketching the unknown with a cattail sparkler,
singeing phosphorescent veins
on the palm of the night.

I touch a fine madness
as it hums beneath the hoods of cars
and flat-bed trucks.
Ticking.
Whirring.
Spark plugs firing.

I taste the smell of liver and onions
frying in a black iron skillet
at 2:00 A.M. on a Sunday morning
with a whiskey chaser
and the elegant finger of ash
from an unfiltered cigarette.

I can read your mind
breathe your waxen air,
fall upon the mushroomed floor,
reach inside the gilded mirror,
and hold your fevered laughter

crystallizing there.

THE SHOW

TEARS APPEAR ON RAINBOW COLORED FACES STAINING
    FLESH
DRYING INTO WHITE CRUST,
THE CLOWNS KNOW IT IS ONLY MAKE BELIEVE
ALONE THEY LAUGH AFTERWARDS
MAKING FOOLS OF US,
BUT LITTLE DO THEY KNOW I WEAR A MASK ALSO
NOT FOR PAY OR AMUSEMENT BUT FOR SAFETY,
FOR I AM AFRAID OF MY EXISTENCE,
MY FEARS OF BEING CALLED UPON TO TESTIFY
THAT I WITNESSED THURSDAYS TURNING INTO
    GOOD FRIDAYS
BOWING DOWN TO PRAY FOR FORGIVENESS
OLD MEN, AGELESS COUNTING ON YOUNG MAIDENS
    TO KEEP COUNT.
CHILDREN SELLING WHITE GOAT POWDER
HOPING TO BECOME MAKERS OF GOLD.
FREAKS INSIDE SHOWS CRYING HARD AT NIGHT
NOT WANTING TO BE LOOKED UPON, ONLY LOVED
BATTERED WOMEN MAKING EXCUSES FOR BRUISES
OLD MEN IN DARK SUITS MAKING POLICY FOR
    UNWED MOTHERS.

IN SPITE OF ALL ODDS

IN SPITE OF ALL ODDS, BEING BORN AT AN UNEVEN
    HOUR, WHEN ALL
CONCESSIONS ARE CLOSED, TRAINS MOVE SWIFTLY
    THROUGH TOWNS,
WHISTLES ARE SILENT, RESPECTING FOLKS THAT ARE
    ASLEEP.

PASSENGERS LIE STILL IN DARK UNINSULATED COACHES,
BREATHING HARD
NOT KNOWING WHERE THEY ARE.

I WAS BORN ON THAT DAY, I CAME ALIVE, I TOOK MY
    FIRST BREATH.
BORN INTO NOTHING, NO ONE APPLAUDED FOR ME.
    FOR HOURS I
NEVER KNEW WHAT GENDER, UNTIL I REACHED DOWN
    AND FELT MY SELF,
WHO WOULD TEACH ME THE DIFFERENCES OF LOVE.
WHO WOULD TEACH ME HOW TO HATE.
WHO WOULD BE THERE FOR ME WITH EXPECTATIONS.
I WAS CONCEIVED FREE ENOUGH, WILL I BE LABELED,
    PUT INTO
BONDAGE, SOLD AT AN AUCTION, WHO HAD ME
    TONIGHT, TONIGHT,
WHO WAS I ATTACHED TO, WHO CUT THE CORD.

ALMIGHTY GOD, DEEP IN YOUR HEART, MAKE ME
    AMAZING, GIVE
ME GRACE, CORRECT THE SEED, YOU HAVE THE POWER
    MY FATHER
YOU ARE THE LANDLORD.

OLD WOMAN

OLD WOMAN, WAITING FOR OLD AGE
TO EQUALIZE OLD THINGS.
HER BLOOD RUNNING NAKED AND FREE,
SHE WHISPERS TO ME LOW DOWN DEEP
STEALING A VOICE, BE BRAVE YOUNG WOMEN.
STAY HONEST STAY TRUE TO YOU.
HAVE A DEFINITE MEANING FOR THINGS YOU
DO, DON'T RELY ON OLD MEMORIES
AND YOUNG FOOLS.

I AM AN OLD WOMAN NOW, DAYS MAKE
NO DIFFERENCE AND NO ONE ASKS HOW I
SPEND MY NIGHTS
I AM AN OLD WOMAN I CAN NO LONGER
MAKE MISTAKES OR EXCUSES I AM HELD
ACCOUNTABLE FOR MY ACTIONS
I CAN NO LONGER BE LATE FOR REHEARSALS
I'VE GOT TO PERFORM MORE THAN THE BEST
OF MY ABILITY, STANDING OVATIONS AND
APPLAUSES HAVE TO COME WITHOUT HESITATION
I AM AN OLD WOMAN LIVING ON MEMORIES
WAITING TO GO UPSTAIRS.

Senryu

The wrist watch lost—
    the sun still rises and sets
        on the mountain peak.

China mountain road—
    trucks estimating number
        of inches to spare.

Heart to Heart

As for the pine tree, said Basho,
Be in accord and learn from it.
Become a pine tree into which
Your heart to enter is full fit.

E'en though the pine tree not somehow
Its aromatic life impart,
Then, poet, 'tis for you to dare
The life-flow of its woody heart.

Flowing Waters

Within the human spirit it would seem
    There is a something that responds
To water in a running wayside stream,
    A something that our life-flow bonds.

The gurgling brook that spills o'er mossy stones
    Has many voices eloquent.
I hear the garbled, playful tones
    Of little waters' merriment.

The river runs a brash and youthful course,
    Goes dancing to the current's surge,
A truant to its far-off, infant source,
    Insouciant with every urge.

But now full-fledged, it tilts at tow'ring rocks.
    It roars outraged, defiantly.
In echoes awesome, canyon walls it mocks.
    Emerging froth-crowned, wild and free.

It later joins a crystal, sister-stream
    En route to their great parent-sea.
Its flow is gentle now, its pulse my own
    And that of stressed humanity.

CONTRADICTION

How could we reason
Robert E. Lee's Treason
Was somehow patriotic

Yet John Brown's decree
All people should be Free
Somehow made him neurotic?

SWING AND SWAY

I always wanted to sing in the Community Gospel Choir,
One hundred voices praising the Lord sets my soul on fire,

Are there Baptist folks in the choir?
Yes, you'll find that there are many,
Pentecostal, and Holiness too,
You'll find that there are a-plenty.

Now among us Methodists you'll find there's just a few,
Episcopalians and Presbyterians only bring one or two,

Methodists, Episcopalians, and Presbyterians,
can sing the songs of Zion sure and true,
But when we have to rock and clap our hands,
it's rather hard to do.

Now the problem starts in the back of the church,
When we march toward the altar lights,
And we have to sing and clap our hands,
While moving from left to right.

The Baptist, Pentecostal, and Holiness
from left to right they sway,
But the Methodists, Episcopalians and Presbyterians,
Are a-going every-whicha-way.

Our singing and harmonizing is blending in just fine,
But our swinging and a-swaying is completely out of line.

95-65-95 Militant

Folding tip his eighteen ninety
5 Booker T. Washington Fingers
into a 1965 Black Power Fist
raising it to a native American how
drawing it back in 1975 to punch
the white man's clock
then lowers it to a 1995 palm
hoping for a Social Security check.

ON GIVING VOICE

I must speak to you
—of Chili's Atacama desert
that most barren of places
where heat is blue
the sun ceaseless
and sound has no echo
yet, Gray gulls leave
their distant coast,
nest and multiply there.

—of Cofa that lovable daughter
whose father coined
her name from coffee,
nor shall the girls Kaleena
and Thail be forgotten.

—of Spring's new leaves
whose chartreuse, mauve
and orange will be washed away
before the sun's hot rays
descend upon us.

—of your words
heated as a desert
unique as a child's name,
colorful as a young leaf
all of which are like footprints
pressed in a carpet of grass.

THE GIRL IN THE FEED-SACK DRESS

She stood in the school room
with the morning sun brushing desks and chairs.
A field of daisies and wild columbine
starched and plainly made
was hers to smooth and wear as if it were a bag of jewels.
Some classmates kept their quiet distance
since the softness of her smile
had no appeal except to me.
The girl in the feed-sack dress and I sat alone.
Years have disappeared like yesterday's wind or snow
touched by sun.
Memories are but a sachet of moments
as we remember or pretend not to remember.
The girl in the feed-sack dress ——
It makes me want to dance or throw stones.

11/22/63

November, 1963—
Big Bill decided he could fly
and climbed up to the top
of the Methodist church steeple just to try.
He sat up there crowing
like some plucked, alien rooster.
but the day was dry and sunny,
so it didn't matter much.

November, 1963—
Noreen just quit her day job
at the diner down on Court Street.
Her feet hurt, and the boss' hands
were everywhere, she says.
Thinks she'll head out west
and see what Hollywood thinks of her,
anyway, it doesn't matter much.

November, 1963—
Garfunkle sings of silence
through a little tinny speaker from Japan.
At an airport down in Dallas,
a high school band is playing "Hail to the Chief"
as a plane comes in to land.
I bought a pack of Camels and got short-changed,
but it didn't matter much.

Showing the Buyer

"You mind that topmost stair just there. It's loose,
Been loose since '58 when me and John and Crazy Bill
Snuck in one night—was old man Radclift lived

Here then; we hated him as boys will
For something I've long since forgot, I guess—
We all snuck in and prised it up and hoped
He'd fall and bust his skinny neck. Just boys.
I bought the place clear back in '85,
But never fixed the step—no more than he.
Would be a shame to take a hammer and
Some nails and with a tap or two wipe out
All of those years of memories, you see.
Not much else left of me and John and Bill.
He was a crazy one; try anything.
John, he died in Nam in '63,
Just a boy he was. I wasn't there.
And Bill ran eighteen wheels—too long one night.
Just slept himself to death behind a wheel.
The crazy thing. I sent some flowers. Can't do
Nothing else at times like that. That step—
You buy the place, you fix it if you want.
I couldn't hardly stand to pound the nails."

The Estate Sale

"You like that? Just take it for the frame.
The picture's old, no good, and yellow edged.
But though the gilt is almost gone, the frame
Is sound. A dollar and it's yours. You want
To know about her? The one who's pictured there?
Whatever for? Just some long dead great aunt
Of mine, I'd guess. About a hundred years ago
I'd say from how she's dressed. An heirloom? That?
The attic's had it all these years; no one has
Cared, or even known that it was there until
This grand, last ridding-out was thrust off on to
Me, who never cared. I'm the last of them.
The rest have all gone off somewhere—or died.
I never tried to keep track—never thought

This cleaning out the old homeplace would fall
To me. You want it for a buck? Just see
Those vacant eyes, like something off somewhere
Has put her out of touch with then-and-there;
That stare, the common mark of all the clan.
Just like old Uncle What's-his-name who died
Here last. That cast of sullen quiet at the lips.
She's one of us, all right. Now don't be tight.
If you think a dollar bill's too much
For such a fine, old frame, just give six bits.
Well, thanks. What's that? Her name? I've got no clue."

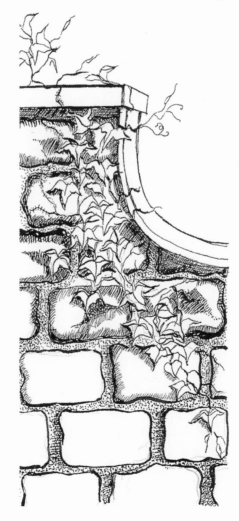

Activist

Reality is always more than real
to simple folks.
It is hard to be fancy
when you're trying to survive.
You can't go back in time
if you never left your place in time
by force or by choice.
Most times you just keep silent,
lying real quiet and still,
like a trapped animal,
until you can no longer stand the pain.
You've gotta holler
even if your yell is your death call.
Some things just can't be left to yourself.
It just ain't right to die alone
without talking to somebody before you go.
Ain't no house haunted
If the ghosts keep quiet.

Appalachia: An Old Man's Dream Deferred

As I ride the mountain curves
That make one mile ten
And my going greets my coming,
I reminisce my past days
In the mountains of Appalachia.
I recall my five-day weeks
Among the diamonds—
That glisten and reflect
The sweat of my brow
And make me proud
Of my aches and pains
And silicosis and black lung

And John L. Lewis and the pension.
I recall my buddies
And slate falls and explosions
And union dues and company doctors
And scrip money and company stores
And friendly coal camp houses
Where smoke spirals from chimneys
And meets the tipple dust
Causing an excess that returns upon us,
my wife and kids and other families,
Causing us to cuss and fuss
and scrub with lye soap
In zinc tubs filled with hydrant water
Boiled in the big tea kettle on the cook stove
That stands near the kitchen cabinet and breakfast set.
I recall the Saturday night balls,
Or fights and brawls
And women and liquor and cards
And fish fries and barbeques
And wiener roasts and excursions
And ball games—
All kinds of Saturday fun
That ends in Sunday School and Church
And occasional revivals
And preachers and deacons
And brothers and sisters
And prayers and collection plates
And rallies and homecomings.
I recall the bare beauty
of stripped mountains
That belch black diamonds
And choke as we crawl inside
To retrieve what is left
Leaving a gully that fills
With leeched water
For children to swim and drown every summer.
I recall the shanties

And houses of bosses
And homes of superintendents
And spring rains, and fall winds
And winter snows and summer sunshines
That bring new faces to the hills every year
And Christmas and Easter
And the Fourth of July
And fishing and hunting seasons
And walks in the mountains
And P.T.A. meetings and lodge meetings
And trips to the county seat
And funerals and birthdays
And other memories that practically
Bring me to tears.
But as I ride the curves of my homeland
I must view my dreams
For she is empty and dried and dismal
And her misery hangs heavy in the air of her discontent
I reach out to touch her but find her vanished—
An old man's dream deferred.

AN APPALACHIAN DILEMMA

I, too, am an Appalachian
For years I have breathed fresh mountain air
    traveled dusty mountain roads
    drunk cool mountain stream water
    and fought the yearly autumn fires
between
    hog killing, game hunting, mule hitching
    soil tilling, harvest gathering, syrup making
    berry picking, home canning, feast tasting
    banjo, guitar and fiddle picking
    quilt making, all kinds of weaving and liquor
    still watching and church revival going times
Yet, to many folks I am not here

My most visible hue makes me invisible.
I move swift and silent through these hills
Nobody sees me and nobody hears me
This is my assurance of acceptance and survival
      so universally understood
        that I am not even a subject heading
        in an index
Still, I, too, am an Appalachian
I dream and I wonder as I wander
      and ask myself
When will Appalachia see me as I see Appalachia
When will she recognize her long lost sons and daughters
      who have toiled on her soils
      laid steel through her mountains
      and crawled into her bowels to retrieve
      her beautiful black diamond overload
      that shakes the chill from all her children
When will she tell my long neglected story
      while accompanying herself on the lute/drum
      instrument that I long ago taught her to
      frail while singing in dronelike rhythms
      in celebration of her beauty
When will Appalachia see me as I see Appalachia
When will she open her arms and take me to her breast
      truly understanding that
I, too, am an Appalachian

GETTING THE MAIL ON MUD LICK BRANCH

Oak branches vein the moon
rolling across the ridge
and through crystallized air I hear
diesel gears groan
a mile away at the crossroads
I walk through an alley
of sycamore limbs
leaning over the stream
and in half light I watch
intricate shadows
soften in water. An ice sheen
hardens on wet rocks.
In a reverie I trudge furrowed mud
to the hollow's mouth
where racked mail boxes,
lined up like trumpets,
announce events
about the world where the hard road runs.

BELLS ON PARCHMENT CREEK

ON THAT FEBRUARY MORNING
DINNER BELLS SURGED AND SWELLED ALONG THE CREEK
CARRYING SHARPLY IN THIN AIR,
SENDING THE WORD SOMETHING
HAD HAPPENED AT THE HANNING FARM.

FOR A MONTH AFTER GIVING BIRTH
THE MOTHER KEPT SWELLING
AND FOLLOWING DEATH HER BODY
WAS PLACED IN THE ICE HOUSE
UNTIL MUD GROOVES DRIED IN SPRING.

WHEN THE FUNERAL FINALLY CAME
FOUR SMALL GIRLS STOOD
AROUND THE BEVELED STONE
NOT ABLE TO READ FINE SCRIPT
NOW WEATHERED INTO BLANK SLATE.

EIGHTY-NINE YEARS LATER
SHE RETELLS THIS STORY
ABOUT A MOTHER SHE HARDLY KNEW,
AND THE BELLS STILL TOLLING.

SABBATICAL ON WINIFREDE HOLLOW

You see them fixing second-hand Fords
parked in the yard
red hoods propped up
under willows.
Now and then they raise
their heads, cock them sideways,
and spit tobacco juice.
On their foreheads you see
creases, deep-cut grooves
like the hollows in these hills.
No one comes to ask them
to ride
buggies into black tunnels,
so they change oil,
swap talk, and wait.

The Executive Director of the Coal Community Y

Someone said he'd come from Panama.
I'm not sure about that, but I know
    what a difference he made
    in the place where I lived as a girl.
Black, straight-combed hair I remember
    bristly jowls, shaven but shadowed,
    and a voice jovial, loud.
Sometimes he stood overlooking the swimming pool.
Sometimes we glimpsed him going into his mysterious
    sleeping quarters near the auditorium stage.
Sometimes he stood in front of the crowd leading songs
    and he sang too in his car taking us children
    to visit another Sunday School.
But I remember him most clearly behind the soda counter
    saying, "There's my little fairy."
I thought of his words sometimes at home
    as I heaped fairy-shaped wings of shampoo suds
    on my bony shoulders in a Saturday tub.
Years later, greeting him briefly,
    grown up, home from school—
    "How chic you look," he said.
    And I was a small girl again—timid, shy,
    but wearing fairy shampoo wings,
    reveling in swims, and chocolate sodas
    served from the damp marble-topped counter
    in the cool dark building
    of the coal community "Y."

Men Sitting at Mahogany Tables

What of the men sitting at mahogany tables?
Do they never see faces of beautiful children?
Not the starving faces, the hopeless dull eyes—
We block our minds, shield our thoughts from
these. But faces with eyes open wide,
trusting, seeing, smiling at times, soft faces
with laughing eyes, beautiful faces
    in countries not ours. Not faces with
red-rimmed eyes like those of the tall lad
who came to our door selling candy,
hiding a coin in his sock, evading questions
about his home, his mother, and the man
who supervised the candy sale, but faces
unlike his, and different from the masked
still face of the boy at the grocery store
who asked for money, then hurried away
    with a man someone said was his father.
But the beautiful faces, clear-eyes, pleasant
faces of children in countries not ours.

These men, sitting at mahogany tables or
standing before microphones—do they never
see the faces of the children they plan
to kill? Soldiers are trained, of course,
taught to obey. (Ezra said some die pro patria,
believing in old men's lies, and Ezra was called
a traitor, of course.) But what of these men
sitting at mahogany tables? Do they never see
the faces of the children they plan to kill—
children with beautiful faces, children
    in countries not ours?

mountains are there even when you cant see them
        the sunshine
brings back the wind & the oak leaves hang tough
        we are all three
getting ready to walk

I think about all those unwhittled free birds lying in wait
        to dry
outside on rocks lifted off the ground for air circulation
& those standing & swaying with shadows   &
        I want to say something
important &   clever about the vine

they grab you give you the itch   trip   &   evade
        your blade & come
back when pushed away thorns stick through your
        rubber boots & you
can pluck with pliers for hours

I have made attempts at halos but end up with wreaths of
        grapevine
which are posted around the house   &   on paths
        in the woods for
hikers to take home

                    / / ∧ \ \
                    (:)
                    [ ]

My.th epilog...

Marginal Figures of Eight

rock of notch to tree
enter th. imagination
unfold the stick child

sail th. boat
see the ball
build a play house

get out th. dominoes
resolve th. arc
get it straight
pluck the crib
take the test
come to pass
& th.ro PO morph
(ic) th. ball

deal with th. tree
cut the figure eight
vita to invita
have th. heart (ic)
follow th. blood line
complete th. task
catch th. fish
tell

enter the halls of time
resolve the tides
to chapter & verse
come to terms
play the figure eight
out fit to trim
to th. muse (ic)
make sense to eternity

(:) >*< (:) >*< (:)

Ix

Letter

If you ask what brings us here,
staring out of our lives

like animals in high grass,
I'd say it was what we had in common

with the other—the hum of a song we
believe in which can't be heard,

the sound of our own
luminous bodies rising just behind the hill,

the dream of a light which won't go out,
and a story we're never finished with.

We talk of things we cannot comprehend
so that you'll know about

the inner and the outer world which are the same.
Someone has to be with us in this,

and if you are, then,
you know us best. And I mean all of us

the deer who leaves his marks behind him
in the snow, the red fox moving through the woods.

The same stream in them is in us too
although we are the chosen ones who speak.

Please tell me what you think cannot be sold
and I will say that's all there is:

the pain in our lives,
...the love we have...

We bring you these small seeds.
Do what you can with them.

What is found in this beleaguered
and beautiful land is what we write of.

Give It Up

The message on the cereal box says
You Must Love And Not Ask For Love In Return.
Throw away the box.
We can't be well. There are millions
of neurons connecting and no one knows
what, or why. So we invent antiviral serums
but the side effect is fatal. Give it up.
The watermelons are stacked in the kitchen
at Big Boy's. The breakfast bins are empty.
It doesn't matter.
We vainly attempt escaping
by acrobatics but it becomes
an exercise in vanity.
The bell rings its inexplicable sound
saying Brigitte Bardot, Howdy Doody,
Tony Bennett. Give them up. They're no longer
in the news. Their names surface like a clear light
from the muck. Margaret Atwood. There's nothing
wrong with her. She's fine
but we'll forget her too.
These words and all words reflect
the nature of the work
to the extent that they're not used. Relax.
Describe Something Without Mentioning It, said Alice Toklas.
Gertrude Stein replied When A Jew Dies, He's Dead.

Then William James told how he was against greatness and
bigness in all forms. Who cares.
There's nothing to save. The magazines
keep collecting their dates
piled in the corner. The recipes aren't cut.
I hope you are all well and warm
but composition is the quilt
over the blood and
the only suspense is in following its trail.
There is a moment when we opened the box. Oh yes, and
the sound came out
where we all began.
Now it becomes a hiss from the lips saying
It's Over.
Human hair in the trenches will make
beans grow tall. But how much
do we have to give for tall beans.
The waitress mistakes my poem for paper and
throws it out with pizza, burgers, fries,
Kleenex, pickle juice.
I love you and expect no love in return.
I've given that up.
The garbage man finds my poem and says he's the
only garbage man who ever found one.
I take it all up again.

THE PROTEST

I was supposed to make a five-minute speech
so I took a tranquilizer
but the speech was canceled,

I was to give another speech but
this too was canceled,

As you can imagine, I stayed

tranquilized my whole life without speaking,

When the fire and blood came up
in thin spouts through
the kitchen floor
I called the manager
but it is never his fault
if we are speechless and in exile,

He said the problem in the floor
comes from being too emotional,

I had another chance to speak once
but the mashed potatoes lay thick
on my tongue and my indignation
sounded less than noble,

All the audience learned that night
is how anger sounds
through mashed potatioes,

"The physical is spiritual"
I said hotly, but
other people's impressions
had already brushed off on me,

By the time the audience left
I was a widow in a nightgown
and I had not told what
I'd come here to say.

You Can't Start the Spiritual Journey
Until You Have a Broken Heart

Take the edge of the past,
not the whole
just the edge,
the way the art teacher
said You Blink Too Much,
the way the English teacher said
Your Father Must Have Written This—
It's Too Good…
This must be why
God started talking to me
in my own voice with
thoughts of
consequence and
ideas I never knew,
in my own voice,
even though I thought
a better one surely
should be found,
and certainly could be found—
It sounded at first
like a fiery sun
and a silk moon
spinning through me,
in tongues
and languages
I finally understood
but fast—so fast—
by the time I got the pen
it was gone.

HER FACE, MY FACE

My wrist has womb memory.
I tuck my left hand just so
Into the hollow under my chin when I sleep:

Mother cells.
Here is the woman that enclosed me,
That introduces me now as eldest daughter.
Her face, my face.

My brothers and sisters we are
A field of pumpkins grown
From seed to consciousness.
But their rhythm is different, circular.

We surround her bed,
Crowd of ten. Her body was our garden.
Memorizing the warmth,
I, the seedling transplanted:

She, wrapped in warm white flannel,
her hand tucked
Into the hollow beneath her chin.

THE ANCIENT ART OF SHAPE SHIFTING

Cars on the hard road.
Speed their way to anywhere else.
Once in a while someone will say.
There's another of those old hollows.
Wonder if anyone ever lived back in there.

Easter flowers clump green, yellow
Everlasting at the old home place,

Where from mountain's mourning mist rises
A once-warm chimney weathered down
To lovely crumbled stones in the drenched grass.
The people who lived there
Tried to take their history with them
But their spirits refused to go;
Mountain homes are power.
Gnarled arms in the old orchard
Still clench skyward.
In the falling-down barn you might hear
A susurration of voices past:
Sonny crouched on the milk stool calling
to peach-fed sister who scatters
Cracked corn, ouching when
Her leg brushes the nettle patch
That thrives no matter how many times it's cut.
Pop's gone somewhere to trade horses
and Mamma's wiping pie dough from
Her fingers, humming, thinking about
What all she has to do this day.

Cars on the hard road.
Shssh! Be still a minute, kids.
I could swear I heard someone
Humming one of them old-timey love songs.

That Girl With Pre-Raphaelite Hair

Flecks of cream
arrange a broken circle
on the pale blue iris of eye.
This is the bedroom
of sorrow and wisdom—
love-flying-outward
their offspring.

Cora Two-Moons

I remember your silent profile
deep as the Earth's core
smoldering
like a spent volcano.

You sit on the front porch swing
Your skin recites an ancient prayer
no shirt-waist dress
can silence.

As you notice me
and turn your head for a better look
your silver hair
glides back through Time.

I don't know what you ask of me
(Smooth skin of shelled beans
slides across my palms)
Please speak to me, Great Grandmother
(Tingle of wild strawberries
melts on my tongue)

Lift me up
lift me up with the breath of your soul
and tell me what you see
When your head turns.
When your silver braid moves.
And the eagle
flies
toward heaven.

LENORE MCCOMAS COBERLY

There Would Come a Day

when gold stretched
from the dry road
to the steady sun,
ragweed poured pollen
eight feet to the ground,
and one child would cry,
"Let's go back to the hill!"

Starting up through
dry crackling broom sage
to the rocky blackberry level,
where rattlers took the sun,
over barbed wire fence
into pasture, they

would follow the cow path
to the mountain creek
where stones shone pink,
up and over to the south slope,

where pawpaws,

soft, dark, and warm on the ground
like manna the Bible told about,
would break in the middle
so children could suck
the first black seed,
sweet melting on their tongues,
with the taste
of some place else.

Take an Old Cherry Table

on a Wednesday afternoon,
crowd the chairs around,
gather a family of friends,
and let the talk begin.
Add some apricots, peanuts, a cake,
mix with premeditated metaphor
and wit to fit the day,
until everything starts to rise,
filling crevasses of lonely rejection
that will never be so deep again,
and the table glows.

Reminds me
of a beach I know

I go out to the driveway, attack
the snow, and am taken aback
by stillness, interrupted only
by a gentle scrape. I barely
feel a shower on my coat and hair
as I shake the pine tree's bough, higher
now, freed from its load of snow.
I hum and throw, take bucket in hand
and go for a gritty load of sand.

DANDELIONS OF APRIL

when I was young in April
    my child's heart pulsed with the green sprouts
      everything could return radiant
dandelions came first after the frost
      timid faces snuggled tight
    ready to burst into yellow giggles
      spokes of butter spun in the breeze
I ate them; they were tart like metal
      their gold stuck between my teeth
I worshipped them in plain white bowls
    on the mantle, my mother called them weeds;
    dandelions smelled like my own fingertips,
      now when I pass the dandelions
    I think how sudden and ugly they age
      grey and sparse like the hair
of the elderly who die often in the spring;
    and the lonely women and men who cannot bear
    the glare of dandelions, who kill themselves
    in peak numbers in April
    still I am child enough
to pick dandelions fresh like churned butter,
    admire their simple tender lives
    in plain white bowls.

NOAH TOTTEN

all his years smoked with the haze of coal dust
    his broken father whose sad harmonica voice
    struck haunted chords in his sleep
a mother who died slowly; her smallboned hands
    wrenching the pain daily from her breast
from childhood he dug into the black wombs of the mines
    his day smelled always of carbide and black water

never enough women's arms to shelter him
from the crash of shaky roofs over his head
never enough whiskey to wash down the acrid taste of coal
he kept in a warped desk drawer the ancient toy pistol
of the blond perfect son;
once he came home young swinging his lunch pail
but the look on his wife's face through the dirty pane
made the pail stop in mid air
one fragile daughter was shattered by rheumatic fever
those who survived made his heart hollow
over the years with their griefs;
but he held his spine Scottish gentry straight
as he had in the terrorized days of union battles
he grew to resemble a rocky cliff
where the sun seldom broke out
an old man who stalked barren fields in winter
looking for the wasted fruits
and i know he did not lie corset stiff
and funeral home painted inside that
alien ruffled bed
because i watched him slip up the far hill
the brown flannel of his hunting shirt
riding the path to the top of the mountain
where he waits for me.

GOLDEN GLOVES
BECKLEY, WEST VIRGINIA

girls in fist tight jeans
with mandolin string voices ringside
their eyes dance with the moist legs
of the elderberry cheeked boy
with blue ribbon eyes
and mustard flower yellow curls
scattered damp across his forehead
his Pentecostal mother, her hair in a grey net,

rubs fear and pride between her palms
his father, in plaid short sleeves,
who stamps and boos
    calling punches in a voice
  sharp edged as a power saw;
a smiling miner in a Big Cat cap
  leans forward to catch blows
the blond boxer staggers and balances
        muhammed from the mountains
    grinding the hard shell prophesies
        of our coal dark years
    under his stubborn muscles tonight.

Saturday Night Jamboree

Ukelele player for the top western bands,
my stage the raised hearth of my parents' front room,
fame was my earliest craving.
No matter what I stayed mute most days in 2ⁿᵈ grade,
I'd be the lead with Flat and Scruggs
in yards of gingham, starched and stiff
as a cupcake liner, spit curls
pasted to my forehead like deformed horns.
Porter Waggoner waited in the sound-proof booth
of my t.v., ready to step out
the way Rock Hudson had that Saturday night
when he limo-ed into Marietta, Ohio,
in the uniform of our local war hero,
the subject of his latest movie.
Too drunk to make his speech from the park's
flag-draped platform, he paraded
with our local pageant winner, waving and smiling
before he kissed our mayor on the lips
and rendered him silent. All more glorious than words.

Cold Light

You ask if I'm homesick
and I think of soup,
gone cold, in need of salt.
Or a blue quilt, faded,
frayed at the seams,
its hem uneven, its threads
beginning to unravel.

Again, you ask if I'm homesick
and I remember the gray doves
who gather each morning at my feeder
by the back window
to croon their lonely notes.

I think of the lights of a distant
house, far back from the highway
at the edge of a snowy field
with no sound but the icy hiss
of my car tires
and my windshield wipers waving goodbye.

Fifth Grade Poetry Class

I squat beside him, and with his gnawed pencil
in my hand, urge, <u>Tell me what your hand looks like</u>.
All morning, while his classmates compared clouds
to cotton, snow to feathers, this boy
so eager he couldn't stay seated, shouted out,
<u>A wet dog smells like liver</u> and <u>Ice burns</u>
<u>like a piece of sun</u>. Even the teacher looked up,
amazed, at this boy who's spent two years
in 5th grade, the kid who can't write,
who needs special help on every assignment.
Now, he draws his hand close, fingers folded under,
then extends them, grinning, as he says,
<u>It's an old woman's wrinkled face, Five men</u>
<u>in a field, Five roads to nowhere</u>. Metaphors spill
so fast the pencil fumbles, words blur,
lines tumble clumsily off the page.
It's like the time I took a horse
outside the riding school's fenced-in arena
and rode off, for the first time, alone.
It was April in the Blue Ridge, and the horse,
released to the open fields, gathered speed
as eagerly as the earth drew strength from the sun.
Behind me, the gray barn, where all winter
I'd trudged the muddy ring, grew smaller,
until it stood like a door that blocked off
another world, leaving me free on the outside,
giddy and breathless, vowing I'd never turn back.

ALL THAT AUGUST KNEW

Though Sol was at his meridian,
The touch-me-nots glistened
With midnight's spangled dew,
Their blooms orange sirens
Singing to thralled hummingbirds—
And though I loved them too,
I swung the scythe across
Each brow, widening my path;
Leaving three flowers or four,
That one man's will on August
Might not erase all
      that August knew.

WINDLESTRAW DAYS

I confess, I long for
      windlestraw days:
Where air is light
Atop the soul, and
Corn pickles in cloth-topped
      churns;
When life is mostly dreaming
Underfoot, making spring in
Improbable ways, and
Stripped Allegheny tops row
With wayward clouds —
O, I long for windlestraw
      days,
Always and always;
Cattails brittle and brown,
And geese on the wing, and
Hounds baying in the hollows,

And winter prowling up my sleeve,
And that haunting death song
    the wind chimes sing—

Benediction

Once more the season
    gains on me;
I sweep the roof
Of what the maple tree
    no longer wants,
Let winter have
May's canopy;
Good riddance
Seems boughs'
    drowsy benediction—

But we who cannot sleep
    half-years away;
Who must stare down
Each January day,
Souls in mortal wrestle
    with despair,
We care
When autumn founders
Into gutters
In brown multitudes,
There being thus
No staying grace
To swaddle wishes in—

Here are the facts of the matter.

What we see and know will live forever in this snapping
light in the eyes, the mouth shaping one question after another,
the voice sounding one question after another, the piracy of
time saying *I can go no further than this. It is unsafe to go
further than this.* Flowing back into the blank hard eye of a
soldier's one job, this last freedom failing into the heart, never
fully knowing how far you can go if called to the task, how
long the darkness is or how far above your head it extends,
how long you might walk before the earth gives way in a watery
lost moment, knowing the soldier's one job is not a complicated
affair: locate the enemy and, having done so, destroy that
enemy by any means available before the same intention is
visited from the opposite direction. It is a game of sorts, a
contest, winners taking nothing in this elaborate boys' contest
taken to the limit of imagination and current possibility. Look
around: the jungle sings. The insects and snakes and hard-
woods breathe, and I can nearly believe they know we are here,
sense our passage and find us ridiculous, transitory, at odds
with existence, objects suitable only for pity. The sky reaches
ground in patches, its weight giving root to the forest floor we
cross, the forest a book we cannot read, legs moving against it,
insect rattle, hollow monkey bone. I could conjure an entire
magic out of this forest floor, braising dead leaves and mud
between the palms, chanting under my breath *monkey bone take
me home, take me home, take me home*

HE COULD WRITE
for Robert

Man, that dude could *write*; slap dashes,
carve clauses and frame phrases glib
as Gettysburg addresses; he could
exclaim for days, disclose, aver,
utter, blurt, confabulate, assert;
subjunctify, testify and expostulate;
hyphenate, punctuate and coordinate,
process prose to make Moses landfill
those meager tablets in shame.
Alphabet rivered from his pen in a rush
relentless as bats unsprung from a cave,
verbs awhirl, diphthongs skittering,
prepositions proliferating shamelessly,
locomotive prose shunting recalcitrant
noun clauses like one-wheeled buckboards,
sentences careening from line to line.
His page became a veritable word-bird cage,
syllables gaggling into paragraphs every shade
and shape of feather, cunning-beaked,
hell-bent for meaning, damn the torpid
drones, full ink ahead!
Yes, that dude could flat gab
in manuscript, tango with lingo,
wordplay his way straight into your heart,
gyrate, pontificate, then, dipping,
rip out the page—FALSE START!—
and begin his word-wooing all over.

HASKELL AND THE WIDDER WOMEN

Folks love in funny dern ways, Ed,
and I'm writin to try and explain
one of the strangest love rectangles
I've ever been flummoxed up in, hopin
you'll read this letter sometime
and not think ill o'yore old grandpa.
Y'see, I'm some acquainted with love,
havin' spent most o' my life with a saint,
and 'fore that, I escorted many a young
filly to barndance and county fair,
stealin my share o' kisses, spoonin
'neath the moon after dancin was done,
our sweaty clothes clingin while we hung
on like paint to a barn, wantin to spark
till dew drenched us and the cock crew.
And I've had my share o' women troubles,
like my first love Bess sinnin on the sly
while I's innocent as a newborn babe,
and, Ed, while your grandma Brownie's
tiny, played-out body was yet warm in her grave,
widder women began plaguin me night and day,
droppin by with rhubarb pie, peach cobbler
and bananer pudding to make a man cry,
and talkin till I thought I'd die 'fore
they'd leave and I could 'suage my nerves
with a snort o' Jack out in the john.

Lucy Kendall had to of been the worst,
That nosey, know-it-all fat floozy
was at my door day after the fun'ral.
"I's so sorry," says she, "when I heard."
Says I, real sly, "But Lucy, I never
knew you cared two licks for Brownie."
Says she, "Oh, yes! So many kids to keer for,
I wondered ya'll had time fer...you know what!"

The brazen, blue-haired jimmy-jawed hussy
grinned her lop-sided dentures at me,
and though I's mad as a scalded dog,
I decided two could play her little game.
"But Lucy, I heared 'twas your vote
barred my wife from the Eastern Star;
and Katie Ellis claimed you never forgave
Brownie Wyatt for sparkin Don Wayne Ross,
that gentle farmboy you courted and lost.
'Course that's all just hearsay; here's fact:
yore daughter Emmy's husband's servin time
fer defraudin the IRS, and yer son Brian's
wife filed fer divorce after catchin him
with more than his hand in the glovebox
of one of his female driver's ed students;
and is it true yore late husband Elias
died without leavin behind enough to make
a down payment on a pot to piss in?"
Lucy's upper lip commenced in twitchin
like a fresh-landed bass twirlin on a strang,
and a little vein in her neck throbbed
like a lid on a boilin-over teapot just
'fore she flapped her wings and flew the coop.
It's a shame and a disgrace when a man
must stoop to rumor to guard his virtue.

HUMANITIES 297:
APPALACHIAN FOLKORE

There's a clogger in class,
cast a glance at fleet feet
as she Appalachian ambles
'cross the screen-door floor,
Fiddle wheedles, wood sings
notes cock-a-doodle float
while she flits, skirts kick,

heels hammer clamber clack.
Hambone, juba-pat,
double-tap toe,
soles slap thunder as
she Charlestons down rows
to stand stiff-fisted,
clomp a rigid Irish jig,
Indian stomp, swan-walk
buck dance slow.
"Your body's a drum," she cried.
So we ham-boned with her,
watched her rabbit-skip back,
toe out, toe in,
click heels and halt,
drag a foot forward,
smooth as just-churned cream,
still ticking time to
the wheezy fiddler's squawl,
then stop like a pulled stump,
roots torn loose at last.

SEASONAL

The maples are aflame and the mountains shout the
    Glory of God,
Bright fountains of goldenrod line the roads beside drifts
    of purple asters.
Over the milkweed hover the butterflies.
Ripe apples hang on the trees like Christmas decorations,
And shy deer venture close to eat them.

OLD AGE IS NOT FOR SISSIES
(A Russian Version)

A family are driving across the steppes in a troika, and
    are pursued by wolves
They throw out the fur lap robes. The wolves tear them
    apart, but follow on.
They throw out the lunch, the leather luggage
They cut the horse out of the harness and abandon it.
    Still the wolves pursue.
Despairing, they throw out the baby.
Still the wolves come on.

FARMINGTON No. 9

We lie here
waiting for the men
with rubber blankets
to take us up
and put us down again.

Remember us
when you fly over mountains
and land in a city at night
and see the thousand things
they've done
with our eyes.

PANIC ON THE LOWER JACKSON

With one step
the pool becomes too deep to wade.
I reel in my line,
weave up the clay bank
through trees and briars.

As I bend under a low limb
a snake slaloms through the weeds.
I leap for the stream, groping
for a root with one hand,
my rod with the other
in the air
on the way down.

Water rushes into my waders:
a diver descending in lead boots.
I yell at Dubee downstream.

If this is where I die
I want someone to know.

Death of a Black Dog

Rows of mobile homes like cemetery markers
    call up the bleakness
    of this dark grief.
This is not the darkness
    of crimson cockscombs,
    Carrie's dyed black hair,
    nor an attic filled with drying herbs.
This is the darkness
    of a shaven beard,
    of a voice in a dream saying
    "You are going to lose your father."

This darkness intrudes like
    a chimney sweep
    when he isn't needed.
Its silence signals
    Appalachian Spring has ended
    and won't be heard again.
This darkness mortars rocks,
    saws lumber, builds roads,
    hits heated yellow spheres
    across a tennis net—
    until exhausted.
This darkness searches out companions
    yet never mentions Shadow.
This darkness sleeps to keep out light
    Emptiness in Indian Cave.

Gift From Joe Gluck In July

You bring to me sweetpeas picked
today from your growing net.
The white of the linen and embroidery
you were wrapped in after you were born.
Burgundy, the shade of painted glass
your father sold in the Auburn store.
Purple of the sashes your sisters wore
when they locked you in a corn crib
for safekeeping and non-interference.
Melon, the color of calico quilt squares;
Speckled maroon of printed feedsacks;
Soft coral of a cameo worn at the neck
of your mother's tucked voile blouse.
Traditional soft pink mixed with modern.
With twining, distinctive pale green
leaves, freshness beyond belief.

13 WAYS OF ERADICATING BLACKBIRDS

I

Reason with them. Speak softly. Hide your stick.

II

Buy them off. Six tons of feed corn, old wheat
and rusty sorghum ought to do the trick.

III

Drop brochures of Capistrano, complete
with winter rates. Tell them they are swallows.

IV

Frighten their children with authentic stuffed owls

V

Stand in a field and threaten. Stomp, bellow
like a nincompoop. Point and shout, Pow! Pow!

VI

Declare a park. Hire then to pick up trash.
When they call in sick, relocate the park.

VII

Dye yourself black. Whirl about wildly, thrash,
flap, chirp, and tweet like a demented lark.

VIII

Set out tanks of discount peanut butter.
Verily, it gloms to the roof of their beaks.

IX

Take a million hostages. Then mutter
about one death a day. Ignore their shrieks.

X

Convert the Super Dome to microwave.
Tell them it's a pie. The dumbbutts can't count.

XI

Build a monstrous runway near their roost. Pave
it with bird brains. Black feather the airport.

XII

Give them to THREE. To TEN. To a THOUSAND.
O.K. Call the Marines. Show the bastards.

XIII

Napalm and flame throw. Douse 'em in lead.
Waste 'em. Rack their dark wings. Gas them real dead.
Laser, defoliate, butt stroke and blast.
Pop out each beady, inscrutable eye.
Pound them to soup! Win! Win! Win! Die! Die! Die!

Mantle's Knees: A Kind of American Prayer

5/22/63 — Yogi cried, "This is it!" But the ball struck the
right field facade just inches from the top. Eyewitness
swore the ball was still rising. A computer projection
calculated the distance at 734 feet.

An all too American drama, played out
In played-out hard-scrabble Okla.—
Cherokee red earth, Hanging Judge Parker
Badlands, bootlegger territory, Knife-
Fight Saturday nights towns. Belle Starr country,
Jesse and Frank's neck of the woods.

Where Mutt, his dad, with his big splayed hands, pumped
it at him right, and Granddad winged it left,
taught him to crush the ball from either side.
The lead mines sucked lean life from such lean men,
Throwbacks tossed up from endless rust and dust.
Towns full of folks hanging on for the dear
Life of those who had legs enough to run
For glory and sign on the dotted line.

All waiting for those scouts from The East—
Wily as Indians, cagey considerers,
Seen-it-beforers. Squint-eyed, toothpick-suckers,
Yarn-tellers in quality boots and real Stetsons,
Scratchin in their rumpled notebooks (Too slow.
No arm. Can't hit curve). Code that said you'll be
A bent-back miner, boy, sooner than soon.
With wife and three kids to bow you down, down.

There he was just tow-headed Mickey, with
Nice teeth, and girls buzzin round and all that
Happy talent in the coil and sinew of him.
And his joking ways they say he got from his mom,
Though what she had to laugh about, God knows.

And then he was legend. He was Mantle.
Baggy pinstripes couldn't hide that swing, those
Bull shoulders. Then he was Whitey, Yogi,
And Bobby. And Elston Howard, Hank Bauer,
Joe Pepitone, Clete Boyer, Rizzuto,
And tormented, fated Roger Maris.

He was Mantle, hobbling the base paths
With crumbling knees. And even later when
He broke our hearts with booze and regrets and
His cheesy restaurants, he was still The Mick.

Yet he was Mickey. You knew it when you saw
That easy country lope, tender on his pins
When he rounded the pads, not like Ruth's
Mincing, Baby-stepping, stiff-legged prance.

Knew it when you looked up and saw the ball
Rising toward you, over the Bronx, over
Broadway and the Town That Never Sleeps.

And it was like you had grown up with him,
Had always called him Mick. And you
Had been there too, one gritty, baked-out, red-sun
August evening when one of his homers rose up
Out of god-forsaken Commerce, Okla.

And all you could do was sit with your hot dog
Halfway to your mouth and whisper, "Jesus,
Jesus, that ball ain't never coming down."

Late Winter Snow: South of Morgantown, WV

The scene is too beautiful, a Rockwell
straight from Country Home. Such moments we take
without judgment, and we join the traffic,

moving with a Sunday's benediction.
The ruddy sun, cooling beyond a swath
of shaggy horizon, stretches fingers
into these old hills, humped like the backs
of great drowsing long gone buffalo.

In this watercolor, snow has sketched log
and trunk and ridgeline, glyphs in black and gray.
Each meadow's a page where deer browse amid
the brush strokes of our musings.

                                       Taillights string
ruby beads across the hills. We follow,
linking up our little glow. Dark holds off
until our driveway. It seems we have been
gone for years. But one look up at the gables,
the pitch of roof, and we know things—though
a bit worse for wear—are as we left them.

                                  We open the car doors
and the air's kindness surprises.
Around us, spring whispers—soon, soon.

STREET DANCE: WEST VIRGINIA

Girl with a patch on her pert rear
bumps a trucker in a REO hat.
Swing stomp hoe-down, chugalug beer.

Two women in their granny gear
allemande left their down-home fat,
right by that patch on her pert rear.

The crowd goes clapping, stand to cheer
whoops at a clogger—"Stamp that rat!"
Swing stomp hoe-down, chugalug beer.

Lean dude with a mutton-chop leer
sure doe-see-does and tries to pat,
girl with a patch on her pert rear.

Fiddle and banjo hone the ear
of a mountaineer aristocrat.
Swing stomp hoe-down, chugalug beer.

Hey, promenade! You city cat!
Ain't she a foxy pioneer,
girl with a patch on her pert rear?
Swing stomp hoe-down, chugalug beer.

The Relief Sale

It was a two hour drive
in a different state
the first time without parents
or a youth group.

Linda wanted to see
straw hats and overalls
listen to jokes in Pennsylvania Dutch.

We'd patched our favorite jeans
with flannel hearts
and french braided our hair.

Five of us in an orange Scout
yelling quilt names
pretending we'd each buy a pie
and eat them altogether Sunday.

We knew how to replace shingles,
fix lawn mowers, change tires.
We baked lentils,
sunned tea in the backyard,
played pool and drank Coke
Saturday nights at Abe's,
summertimes we roasted chilies,
canned and froze till midnights
listening to the Cowboy Junkies
dreaming about Mennonite boys with rhythm.

We were loud and beautiful
braless lifting our tie-dyed T-shirts
to flash men with beards
in Semis, Sedans, Chevys,
like handing out blessings.

Two awkward boys lip-syncing to Meatloaf
followed us twenty miles.

First thing we bought was carrots,
crunching them as we wandered through the quilts.
Janet went looking for strawberry-rhubarb pies.
Brenda bought five quarts of apple butter
remembering her home church
the men starting it at night
the women stirring it thick all day over a fire
in black pots big enough to bathe in.
All afternoon we listened to the auctioneer
drank cider and ate sausage and kraut sandwiches,
and wondered if our hands would ever be thick
and wrinkled, sitting behind a table
of homemade soap, wooden bowls
and rag-weaved blankets,
ready with a thousand stories to choose from
to enthrall anyone.

Heaven and Things

Sometimes I'm afraid to think about God,
sitting in tight pews,
squashed with girls in pretty dresses,
boys in clean blue jeans.
A round suited man paces,
faster, higher his arms rise.
His hands curl in tight fat fists,
"Wide is the path that leads to hell,"
his voice booms on long after his mouth shuts.
He unveils the felt board,
grotesque men, women on their knees,
jaws gaped open, limbs burning.
"But you can be saved, repent of your sins
and Je-Sus will wash you white as snow!"

I want to like Jesus.
He told his grouchy disciples
to let children come to him.
He held them in his lap,
said grown-ups should be more like kids.
But the picture of heaven
has girls in white gloves and frilled skirts
holding their brothers' hands,
mom and dad walking in front
on winding gold streets.
No parks, No baseball diamonds,
No candy stores.

Boredom seems better than burning,
so I keep going to church with Katie
Wednesday nights.
Sometimes we make gingerbread cookies in crosses,
thin haired women with tight grey buns
laugh over us and give mushy kisses.

But mostly Rev. Simmons yells too long,
like he has twenty cups of coffee
and the wrath of God inside him.
He tells us to bring other kids, neighbor kids,
girls we ride the bus with,
boys that shovel our mothers' drives,
in doing so we are leading others to heaven.

I don't want to lead anyone there.
Figure if they're good
and don't know about salvation
maybe God will exempt them,
and they won't have to go anywhere
after they die.
So I'm teaching my younger sister to say
please and thank-you,
telling Billie about the importance
of saying you're sorry.

I wish heaven was like Mrs. Frey's home,
stuffed with children,
filled with the smell of Whoopee Pies,
tall cold glasses of milk,
camp songs with motions,
games of hide-and-seek.

I hope the angels are like
Michael playing jokes with eggs,
and Wanda whispering secrets.

I want God to be like Mrs. Frey
holding you in her aproned lap,
singing till you fall asleep.

God and Farmers

I'm not sure
but I think God likes farmers best,
people that work outside in blue jeans.

I don't get it
why they're so poor
unless God wants them
to have the very best of heaven.

I bet He doesn't watch us much
in offices,
over spreadsheets and lawyer briefs,
He gets bored.

Mom said when the bridge on 92 went out,
the one the horse and buggies use,
the Council proposed a hundred thousand dollar plan
to be completed in six months.
The Old Orders decided to do it themselves,

in a week it was done
for five hundred.

Farmers know how God made the earth.
When something dies, they make something else live.
Their bodies last longer.
They don't need gyms, Spandex, magazine diets.

Farmers get that noontime famished feeling
not the dull rumblings after inside work.
They know where food comes from;
they pray better.

It's easy to forget God in offices.
I can't see God calling someone to be a financial planner.
Even jobs we think of as good
get all screwed up.

Nursing seems noble, working with old people
but sometimes I think
if I just let the residents go outside more,
bring in Golden Labs and chickadees,
stop giving out pills,
God and the old folks would hold hands more.

It's easy to like lobster in the city,
to go to Pittsburgh to see the ballet,
to have nice homes in pretty neighborhoods
to keep the kids safe,
but I don't know that God wants our money
if we're rich.

I think in heaven
God will tell the farmers jokes
the rest of us won't understand.
I think they'll still farm

because they want to
but if a crop goes bad
God will order them pizza and beer.
At noon when the angels harp
and the rest of us sing,
God and the farmers will be playing games
making the corn and wheat sway.

Minor Gods in the Coal Fields

At play on the ridges
they lap the dewdrops from the moss
and weave into fronds the ferns they've plucked, for fans
and the green snakes and the striped
lie across their napes, and the hollows of their throats
very cool, and about their wrists, like bracelets.
They feast on oak galls, the amber of pine and fungi resembling
    tongues
and gulp down bloodroot, its red juice .

and feed the mantis tidbits of wandering wasps and wild bees
and at the outcrop, sprawl on the sandstone rubble
trailing their fingers in the sunken spring, freckled with leaf-fall
to stroke the salamanders' skin
to dip their hickory shells and splash themselves, and bathe.
They watch the ground ivy wilt, the trilliums fade
and never speak, or descend, but to entice the children.

The boys fly when they whisper to their gaping souls
out of the houses, past the slate, the coal car drops, the tipple
to lie in the milkweed pods, wide as wings on the stalks, as silken
    beds.
The asters pale, and pokeberries shrivel
while dreams are being ripened in these thin-boned boys.
Copperheads linger, and dragonflies hang over the pool
where the water drips from the driftmouth of the abandoned
    mine.
Sycamore bark is flaking, the scrub pines droop, mullein dies.
Heat wavers over the weedy mine road. The leaves strangle.

And the minor gods, who had descended from the ridge
and paused at the graveyard on the hill
with its flowered mounds and sockets in the grass
to mince on lichens on the stones

have found them, high in the beechnut tree
picking away the hulls at a little feast
and in bawd summary, hand in hand
surround them in thrall, and in the heat of August
dance and withdraw.

A man on a cloudy day

A man, as it got overcast, was sitting on a kitchen
    chair in front of his trailer and when the rain
    started he started to disappear—
    head, neck, shirt, shoulders and so on

and when a drop fell on the last spot—a bit
    of scrotum on a shred of pants—
    it went *ping* and the sky cleared.

A small lime butterfly juggled by and stopped
    on the chair where he used to be, pressing its
    wings together and spreading them like a lung.

He had sold his acres along the hill and now the strip mines
    are overhead with their caterpillars in the bittersweet
    chocolate and in the afternoon when my grandmother
    went up the hollow to pick a few apples off the ground
    where his house used to be one of the caterpillars
    pushed too close to the edge and she was covered up
    to her ass in mud and broken rock.

She shouted *Where's my children* as my grandfather and I
    pulled her out with a log chain coupled under her arms.

And one of her children who's in Cincinnati and Cleveland
    and Raleigh and Winston Salem with money and Johnny
    Cash in his head didn't hear her—he was on a Greyhound
    bus coming home before his wife and kids could pack
    and get to his efficiency apartment.

When he got home we sat up all night with the dead man in the
trailer, my grandmother slicing cake and cleaning the
mud from between her toes.

Well Somebody on Buffalo Creek

The Buffalo Creek disaster
Logan County, West Virginia
February, 1972

Well somebody on Buffalo Creek from New York City didn't do it
again. This time it was Pittston Coal, a conglomerate of
Brinks Armored Cars and a lot of other crap and everything's
fucked up and a lot of people are dead, including

Robie Waugh   Larry Waugh
Jimmy Waugh   Mike Waugh
Donna Waugh   Donna Lesley Waugh

Robie's my uncle and the rest of them are his kids except for
Donna Lesley. I don't know if the kid had a Daddy or not
but it doesn't matter now does it? I mean they never found
her.

They marked the kiltery houses with a yellow X like Passover only
it already happened. I wonder where they got the paint?
Probably got it from Island Creek Stores. It's still there.

And big numbers on the doors: 34, 37, 42. That's not how many
died. I'm not sure how many did, something over a hundred.
Maybe the numbers are for the houses next in the smouldery
fires, and some people said that Pittston dumped slate over
the creek and later tried to dynamite to let some of the
water out only it didn't work, and some others said that
the slate dump was on fire and blew up, or the water did
it, just an Act of God.

There's a flood-line up in the windows of the Becco Smoke House
and Marie's Beauty Parlor but nobody died drunk or like a
doll's head. It was too early in the morning.

Becco's where fifteen houses backed up behind the railroad trestle,
and they found a lot of bodies, and people said that snakes
came down out of the mountains and dogs peered in the cracks
of the houses, sniffing around.

It was early in the morning and Kat, Robie's wife, got out of bed
with one of the kids because he was sick and gave him an
Alka-Seltzer Plus and went with him across the road two houses.
She was having a cup of coffee with the neighbor woman and
saw the flood when they looked out the kitchen window. That's
how come her and her last one didn't drown.

They sent Robie's body over to Beckley to see if he had black
lung and so the funeral was on Friday instead of Thursday.
He had it, so now Kat's got money coming in.

They're bringing in trailers so the next time there's a flood
the people will already have their coffins with little
windows and doors and a small latch on the front to drag
them to Paradise, California.

SING APPALACHIA

Sing your own song Appalachia.
This is no time for silence. From darkness
I would hear the genesis words again.
Sing a parable of people; and pride
Of a heritage stored within the vein.
I would not have you worship at strange altars,
Nor have you stand, a beggar, at the gate.
They tell me you speak little, in trust;
They are wrong! Your trust was your undoing.
They say you are indifferent to the winds
Of progress; that you are steeped in complacency.
Strange voices sing a ceaseless requiem.

I am the hills. I will sing your song.
I will not let them write your epitaph.
They tell me that you have stubborn pride,
And say I do not see your many faults.
I am not blinded by my love for you.
I dare encounter truth's demanding stare.
I am aware of more than eye can see.
I will defend with honor and with mind.
There is a permanence about my people,
And strength. For hands that tamed a wilderness
Cannot die. I will not let them write your song,
Appalachia. They do not hear the music of your heart.

APPALACHIA

I am Appalachia. In my veins
Runs fierce mountain pride; the hill-fed streams
Of passion; and, stranger, you don't know me!
You've analyzed my every move—you still
Go away shaking your head. I remain

Enigmatic. How can you find rapport with me—
You, who never stood in the bowels of hell,
Never felt a mountain shake and open its jaws
To partake of human sacrifice?
You, who never stood on a high mountain
Watching the sun unwind its spiral rays;
Who never searched the glens for wild flowers,
Never picked mayapples or black walnuts; never ran
Wildly through the woods in pure delight,
Nor dangled your feet in a lazy creek?
You, who never danced to wild sweet notes,
Outpouring of nimble-fingered fiddlers;
Who never just "sat a spell," on a porch,
Chewing and whittling; or hearing in pastime
The deep-throated bay of chasing hounds
And hunters shouting with joy, "He's treed!"
You, who never once carried a coffin
To a family plot high up on a ridge
Because mountain folk know it's best to lie
Where breezes from the hills whisper, "You're home";
You, who never saw from the valley that graves on a hill
Bring easement of pain to those below?
I tell you, stranger, hill folk know
What life is all about; they don't need pills
To tranquilize the sorrow and joy of living.
I am Appalachia: and, stranger,
Though you've studied me, you still don't know.

I WAS A FOOL

Was I a fool
To think these urgent hands
Could fence wild pastures,
Glass in mountains,
Keep out concrete lands?

I was a fool.
I gathered butterflies
And decorated myself
With small defenseless flowers.

I was a fool
Who rose to morning gold,
And shook myself
In complacent green.

I was a fool
Who laid my weary head
Upon extended arms;
I was a fool
Who sighed
But gave herself
To the lords of ruin.

I AM NOT WEANED

I saw a clump of oaks reach up and climb
The mountain's back, then skirt the shouldered hill
To where a winding road cut meadow grass
To separate the land. Soft-breasted earth
Curves gently in its fertile strength and sighs,
Content at the dogwood's feet.

The yawning earth stretches on her bed
As pine and maple strive to take her length.
Here, sapling oaks struggle up the hill
To arch their backs against the heavy air,
Like steeds that thunder in a playful meet,
Then briefly pause to let the road be there.

And I, in this wilderness of green,
Am 'kin to rocks and trees and rills;

As my land strips her limbs, makes bare her breast
To suckle clammering children she can't wean,
I press my thirsting lips on full-veined hills.

POTATO ROAST

While soft the early autumn breeze
Blew from beyond the near-by trees
The moon rose full at eve to paint
With silver gleams and shadows quaint
Weird fantasies of shade and light
Which are forever sheer delight
When children round a bonfire sat
With neither clock nor curfew chime
To still or spoil their friendly chat;
It was potato roasting time.

Potatoes hot in ashes baked
On garden plot fresh dug and raked
When daddy spies his girl and boy
And joins the neighbor clan with joy
In manner almost unobserved
To keep the chatter unreserved
On Wild West life or pirate slain
On fairy tales or nursery rime;
He had become a boy again,
It was potato roasting time.

Age? How do we equate it?

When we see it,
what do we see?

What do we see?
Or does it matter?

Is it always represented
by a shriveled skin
or a bent body
leaning on a cane?

What about the path you took
to fulfill your desires and dreams?
Was it the path of do anything/
everything,
no matter where/
what/
why?

Does care for a person mean anything?
Does care of anything
mean something?—
When your body is leaning
on a cane,
your condition will be noticed.
No matter how or
why
you ended
on a cane.

Morning parking

right at the bench
at Ritter Park,

under the Sentinel that has been
guarding my actions/
absorbing my frustrations/
drying my tears.

I can talk to
him/
her/
it
and it can wave its bushy arms that it heard.

And one never worries about it
telling a soul.

CHINA TOUR

In the pale gray evening sky
the rose colored Peking moon
casts a glow on
the golden willows
dipping into the edge of
the imperial lake.

An American tourist
complains of
the dust.

the journey

i have come through the years,
the eons in Atlantis,
drowning
where we fell from grace
at the sea's breast.

on my soul,
the sin of soldiers
who bear the sword of just war
to the brink of genocide
for God's sake.
on my soul
the blood of children.

i have come through years
flowing into years,
following my footsteps
through silent halls,
through lifetimes
twisted beneath course cloth,
the dark habits
of the unmarriageable daughter,
the pariah,
the monster infant.
trapped in
life after medieval life.

i have come through years
bearing
flaxen-haired children
in the sunshine
of short Nordic lives.

i come through years
to slip beyond my mother's gaze
into a soft Southern night
and join gray forces
marching to death
in West Virginia in 1861.

Then,
i am at ground zero.
and
i fly the Enola Gay
into the dark morning
of the atomic age.

i come through the years
in my journey
burning
with passion
to be One with the Web.
i am
captured
fractured in Light
at the dawn of Grace.

Side of Beef on Third Street

I'm flying through town
Jamming profound thoughts in my pockets
Along with Scottie's sugar packets.
High.
Alone.
And laughing at myself
Past the: Red light,
                 Bank,
                 And YMCA.

Then you yell: Hey honey!
                   Hey Baby!
                   You look good to me.
And I hit ground so fast I fracture.

I'd forgotten you're out there in a jacked up:
                   Chevy,
                   Ford,
                   Van,
                   Pickup.
Making me into a piece of ass.

Clever Magician!
You jerk me from a sunny West Virginia day
To a meat hook.
Hanging.
Waiting for your omnipotent price per pound.

Well buddy,
You may be somebody's:
                   Sugar daddy,
                   Old man,
                   Stud.
But by the time I hit the corner
You're just some butcher who took a cleaver to my day.

greyhound blues

all night i dream we drive
through a city of circles:
concentric cow skull arches,
buzz of gnat traffic.
swollen and catatonic,
i reach for you.

all night I wake to cry
on your empty seat lap.
i dream we settle down
on an avant garde, unlikely avenue.
then we're driving again,
laughing of roads and rimbaud.

the bus rolls by billings.
i climb into a book,
and falling out recall
your shudders making love.
my face melts down
my chest in a choke.

i scream: you have left me!
though it's i who wouldn't stay.

all day montana passes.
my rival. how you love her!
lazy ribbon rivers.
snow-laced bitterroots arching
through warm earth
stretched blonde and tan and very young
beneath a giant canopy.

my vision blurs:
her beauty pales beside this pain.
leaving you is madness,
and i left half mad.

How
(Spelter, West Virginia)

Once, in my aunt's white house
in the room with the hundred figurines
the walls opened.

I remember standing with Aunt
by the Lazy-boy, holding
plastic flowers for the dead,
and where the paneling should have been
the horizon stretched wide.
It was summer. Birds and wasps
in a silver sky. We did not think it strange
that wind came in
and we could see the long backs of the mountains.

If I explain this, if I dig it out from memory,
I would say Uncle was putting in a window
or taking out a window
or something that required
peeling the skin of the house away.
If you need an explanation,
you can take this one,
but what I remember is: The house opened
like the Red Sea
to show us summer, like a jewel,
and mountains, like a shroud.
In all these years I never
once asked how.

At War
(December 1998)

Today, I mixed sauces,
chopped carrots, pierced my hands on holly.
I leaned my heart into the cool weight of plates.

We are at war and do not speak of it.
I smooth the tablecloth, lay down bright shapes.
My numb hands drop ice cubes
into glasses, small bombs
from a flesh-colored sky.

In my mother's kitchen, among poinsettias
and Santa mats, I scoop cream, sprinkle garnish,
run a knife through pastry hearts.
I am a shareholder in death,
part-owner of the deaths of mothers
and agile, coal-eyed boys.
The Perpetual Christmas Music Channel
plays tune after tune—eager
and wordless.

Me, I live on rich color, cinnamon scent,
candles and polished wood;
I breathe the easy laughter of guests,
but my heart is off in dark streets
speaking another language, I cannot understand it.
It sees skies spill fire, it is not
Seasonal, it wails above the cheerful chimes
and weeps among the cheese logs.

CHANGELING CHILD

I was through birthin'.

seven boys
seven girls
no twins
eleven lived
three wee ones sleep
gone before they came
gone before I could nurse them
gone without one angel smile
gone with nothing but their names

I was through with birthin'.

too many inferno summers
spent preserving food
for winter-hungry mouths
midnight needles
stabbed through worn out britches
altered hand-me-downs
while tired eyes
fought tears of doubt

I was through birthin'.

I'd learned arithmetic and doctorin'
fourteen times nine equals hard labor
plus three thousand mornings
sick
seven long years tip-toed by
lullabying my mind
until you jarred me with your kicks

Changeling child.

you witch my days
you wake me nights
the ghosts of fourteen babies
dance in your shadow
mingle with your smile
I was through birthin'
until you came
my changeling child

Young Gods

for Robert Swanson

It is told that
wood and water
shared her with the sun—
They named her
Lorelei—
every woman
smiled. For Lorelei
sang as they
sang, loved, slept,
rose to eat.
Women
lived through her.
Nymph, breathing
naked light,
chose the myth of flesh.

Once as rain took her
in an olive lair of leaves,
nymph caught summer-
sculpted boy, wild
watching her—
Soon he knew more
of the sea, the long shore,
than she had meant to
give to one boy—
call him Valentine.
Soon he seemed to her
nearly man.
Mourning the light
shoulders, eyes and lips,
she made him wings.

$$\begin{array}{c}
A \\
P \\
P \\
L \\
E
\end{array}$$

Bite into it red
or green, there's nothing
like it. Best of fruit, gives you
everything! Flavors what your teeth
are for. Gives brow sweat high coming
after just the right sweetness if it ain't mush.
Good apple is everything. Simple, not lush—
Who could improve on it? The green is cool,
demure. The red surrenders eagerly. Dusky
ones are better, so distrust a shine—
The apple!—I break off to eat!—
What I mean is: here in the solar
system of sweets, Apple
is Earth.

The Conversion

It is revival time
at North Street.
You are twelve.
You wear a white dress,
sleeveless,
pink roses and
green leaves on the bodice
embroidered
by Robert Hall.

You kneel at the altar,
your conversion
underway.
You remember a circus,
a folded paper box
clamped with thin wire.
Inside the carton
you hear/you are
a small cold beast
scratching. Are you evil?
Are you serpent?
You are chameleon,
your eyes frantic.

You have been lost
like a thousand others.
Your eyes,
protruding,
rolling,
independent,
search in all directions.

You are trapped.
It is 1956

and salvation,
at least for chameleon
in a Shriner's hand,
costs dearly.

You are lost
in the too
white dress.
Your eyes
wide open in prayer
find the lovely roses,
hide in green green leaves.

THE FIRE CHIEF

A strong back indeed
she seethed remembering
a wedding toast years ago/
how he thumbed her
like magazines on his lap
and his liquid flame
singed her cheek/
how she'd heard her own mother
smoulder like her rocker
damned to ashes because
it screeched once too often
in the room where the big stove
burnt any offering/
and then the way he'd whisked
the girls with great tin buckets
down to "call on Mr. Coal"
lying in the railroad yard/
and when the Ohio threatened
to run its banks
in shiny black boots
from the window he'd scowl/

she'd watch for the waters to rise
and him out there floating/
but not yet not un
til the girls leave home she'd thought
so she mopped the hall
where his tracks blackened
and knew herself spineless
while he smoked at the fire station
where men in hard blue coats
called him/captain.

Iced Tea Recipe

On a hot West Virginia afternoon,
Take one handful of black tea;
Throw it into a blue crock;
(Blue rim worn off from sharpening the butcher knife);
Fill crock with boiling water;
Pour in sugar;
Mix and stir;
Breathe the steamy sweetness.

Send the children down the railroad track
To borrow ice
From Maxine.
Remind them to run straight back.
Never mind balancing on the rails
Or that running over the ties
Makes the little one dizzy.

Pour cooled tea
Over precious ice,
Listen to ice crackle.
Drink.

THE SEASON

As the days deepen
the names come back.
One of them holds a drink
in the party light
and is telling a story. You
can still see the capillaries
in the shine of his face.
And windows, seldom opened,
ice up in the corners, trees,
without warning
release their brief cascades.
When the days are glacial,
sweaters are shaken out,
refolded and put on the shelves
and meetings in the kitchen
become small serenities
like drinking green tea
and watching the hush
of fallen snow.
This is it, we say.
This is it.

Defeat

"Well what can be done about it?" demanded a young
woman whose peevish face belonged to her mother. Spots
sometimes seep into walls for no reason, leaving a stain no
one can remove, no one can explain. Only time, they say.
Outside, her small boy throws a ball against the garage door
and shouts as if there were others beside him, some of whom
he catches off base. It will be years before he looks up from
his desk near the supervisor's glassed-in office and wonders

if it could have been the sound of pantyhose on crossing legs
that momentarily distracted him from his handful of careful
audits. So it may be that nothing can be done, that chance
alone — a pattern perhaps, or design whose configurations
we cannot make out — takes the neighbor's animal beneath
the branches of a dead tree where the tick awaits release
from years of somnolence. Even now, in the park across
town, a man newly married but still young enough and said
to have speed takes to the mound again knowing little or
nothing of his need for defeat.

NOT NOW

It's not always easy
to know what needs to be done.
The brass on the lamp
begins to tarnish
leaving a stain
like a birthmark
that cannot be removed.
Or the refrigerator breaks down
the day before the inescapable celebration.
In the quiet of his well-lighted study
a writer of little reputation
may draw another line
through the title
of his unfinished book.
And who can ignore
the game that decides
the championship,
says an affable friend
taking off his coat
and inhaling the smell
of a fish stew
that simmers
like so many things
we know nothing about.

DARWIN'S WIFE

Quiet settles over the neighborhood
where a man out walking
wonders why his wife
keeps putting her hands on the arm of the deacon.
At noon, a woman with bad teeth
whose loud voice suddenly
embarrasses a stranger,
flirts with three men
waiting for a bus in the town square.
That evening, in candlelight,
a seated woman who has not eaten
the small tomatoes in her salad
confides to the man on her left
her grandmother called them
"love apples." Of course,
it's no surprise
when Darwin suggested
the human eye evolved
"by slight but in each case
useful deviations,"
Emma wrote in the margin.
"A great assumption / E.D."
But it's not impossible, the man avers,
nearing his home. It could well be
that small changes
enable us to see.

At Four

You took my two brothers to the Cincinnati Zoo
And left me behind. You took Mom and the Plymouth
And left me an outer space gun for a parting gift,
As if I lost on some television game show.

You said I was too young. So the gun hummed and zoomed
And glowed in the dark where I cried every morning I shot
The baby sitter knowing at night while I slept you were far
Away with my family. I dreamed of lions and bears and

When you came back with photos
I snuck into the closet at night
Firing my glow gun and with each burst
Of light I tore them up one at a time.

I then knew I had bars
One day I would break.

Putting a Patent on Hope
Part I

I am given the room with barred windows.
Here I construct my limbs in a fold in the crevices
Of a corner. Here in the tripod clover of thought,
Crumpled under pillows of flesh, I soften my jagged world.

I can make my own bed now, but instead sleep in this place
Not very worn by the wear of light. In this dusty room
Spiders weave lifeless spokes coming first to feed.
I drop my head, bend my chin and watch a spider

Letting go: drinking and grazing the fine vintage air
With his sprawling legs, he streams downward

Until there is this quiet invisible
SNAP

The carpet catches
The fall.

Part 2

Perhaps suicide is to the poet
As life is to the elderly.
When one can't improve upon it
When one can no longer be effective

It is time to let go.
I heard somewhere that plants have this
Enzyme or something that they can release
When they are no longer content with their

Environment and this *thing* in them is let go
And it's like some kind of natural euthanasia
But there is nothing natural about
This gun.

It is man made cold metal
Napping on a trembling tongue.

Last Night

We whistled, played piano, put on
Classical, Country & Western, and Rock n' Roll.
You were on the flute later as I danced naked
On the Indian rug.

We tried but your brand new
Canary would not sing.
Tonight you call me to tell me
The percolator finally brought

Notes to her throat and your
Canary has become a cantor
Over coffee. As I type this in my old house
The bat living in the wall next to the chimney

Begins to chirp. I am serenaded by his fright
Between the dead clicks of these keys.

Earth Time

Summer greens
turn to mountains of
Cinnamon
from the touch of hoary frost
ancient eglantine and ebony fruit
now lie parched and withered
on knotty limbs
the season's toil
bowing to the gathering
hands of men
ice creeping down
my window
warm grandmother's quilt.

New Year's Eve, 2000

I had wanted to forget for now
the turning of the human year,
and seeing south-driving blizzards
of snowflakes I almost succeeded,
reconstructing the planet's tilt
and the cold air like a glacier
moving whitely down from the tundra,

dimming, obscuring the stripped trees
conquering the street lights
until finally rows of houses vanished,
lights flickered and instantly ceased,
and I was in the glacier's tomb
with cold seeping in and breath
making crystal rime on windows and eyes,

where I observed an age of ice,
and for the last hundred years
the only sounds were small cracks and
creakings of ice or thunderous
cataclysms as cubic miles of snow
fell from palisaded cliffs
to float as islands in the hoary sea,

where the inside of my scoured mind
glowed a nacreous light, like
opalescent vaults of pearl
ringing with coronas and halos
of sun and moon, sheeting, writhing
with city lights, like oil shimmer
irridescing on frigid walls,

until the whole century just past
dominated the room we had made
with mountains and valleys of snow,

with weight of white catastrophe,
with mocking light of sun and moon,
and one cringing arctic hare,
dark eyes paling with panic known,

which mewled, not in escaping the fox,
not in finding a lichen morsel,
not in some symbolic plea of pain,
not surprise at such doom, not
lamenting the extinction of one,
not adding to the full chorus
of the century of megadeath,

but which squealed dying, naïve and
ignorant, the planet's gas chamber
snuffing out least and best in one breath,
while, faintly, through the walls of ice
I heard the celebrating firecrackers
pop and explode like rapid thoughts,
and remembered the millennium had come.

FROSTBITTEN MEMORIES

This is a night where water clinks—
Ten below and a black crystal sky.
If I held up a finger to test the air
It would probably flip off quickly
Like a loose, old piano ivory
Landing with an edgewise plink.

I thought I had escaped the cold,
That nine hundred miles south was far
Enough down the latitudes to forget—
Even the white-throats wintered here.
But memory must be frostbitten too,
And Lake Superior must stay in the veins.

I remember the dazzling winter day
I helped push a stalled Volkswagen
Up a stubborn hill in Champion, Michigan—
Twenty-two below and breathing through a scarf.
Yet, after five minutes ponderous icicles
Were stabbing the small caves of my lungs.

I remember the giant spears of ice
On the granite shores of Munising,
The crusted ice of the Presque Isle piers,
And the snowy owl on a house in Marquette,
An ice statue of the whole season
Swiveling a hoary head to stare at me.

Then there was the morning at Negaunee,
Seventeen below where two of my fingers
Became marble white with frostbite,
My eyes warm with Bohemian waxwings,
Or the Barrows Goldeneyes at Dead River
For whom I almost lost a toe or two.

And so, southerly, I stand
Again in cold pleasure, warm pain,
Recalling fondly and fatefully,
Smiling, frowning, safe and sorry.
I hold my finger up anew and smile.
It tingles a white dirge, singing to me.

DEPENDING ON TREES

Walking along the levels of this life,
I sense the perpendicular beauty

Of trees, defining the earth and sky and me,
Standing forth as maps to gain directions by:

Exquisite lines, curves, whorls, and traceries,
All separate shading, shape, and weight,

Trunks, limbs, twigs, and last slight wands
Building ladders for incoherent eyes,

Asserting graceful forms and angles
Against space or other clear vacuities.

I see the dark necessities of trunks
To hold those green complexities aloft,

Columns or woody stalagmites rising
To oppose the weight of stony earth.

I scale the airy height of branches
Finding the ways wind gnarls and twists them,

Calculating the adjustments of line
Each supple twig makes to shade and sun.

I measure the canopy's webbery
Thinking how lives articulate from it.

Bright tanager gleaning the shaking leaves,
Brilliant cardinal whistling on a perch,

Cicadas finding a nook for shrilling,
Leaf hoppers sticking on like leafy stubs,

And mind implicating the tree in thought,
All depending from this home of patterns,

A dependable form in every kind of weather,
Even in the sham death of empty winter.

Trees persist, dark, solid, and complete,
Where time is quick and creatures nimble,

Where animals scurry on the forest floor,
And people promenade by without a glance,

Where memory flits and thoughts go whirling,
Where moon and sea run changing courses.

When I am pondered to perplexment,
Dispended beyond the gravity of my desires,

I can see where patterning has triumphed,
Where the canopy slowly fills the waiting air,

There I can place my fragile hand on a trunk,
There I can rest my mortal mind along a branch.

GREEN LACE

For Maggie Anderson

Did you ever see
        green lace
        hanging
                from
tree branches?
        I did.
        The weeping willows
            overnight
                had
            crocheted
yards and yards.
        Yesterday it was a tree
            of green chains.
        After night the Master
        crocheted all second
            and third rows—
        Double and triple
            crochet
        into beautiful green
            leaf loops.
This morning it was out
        for display
            but
        not for sale—
Just for looking and wondering.

My Treasure Chest

Dedicated to Louise McNeill

Sixty-nine years ago, Louise,
   my college friend,
      inspired me to discover
        my own unopened Treasure Chest.

Nine Greek Muses,
   who presided over literature
   and the arts,
      had guarded it for me.

When I opened it to the light,
   uncut gem stones changed to
      faceted WORDS,
        tools for creating poems.

Words like crystal beads of beauty
   strung together in rosary fashion
      displayed on a clear background
        for others to read and enjoy.

My Treasure Chest is never empty—
   the more it is used
   the more it is filled.

A SUMMER RIVER

A summer river where the game bass leap,
A stream that mirrors trees and hills and sky,
A river with a song the heart can keep
Forever as the years go gliding by;
This is a thing of beauty unsurpassed,
This is a work of art which God has made,
A memory to stay...a dream to last...
A picture of dame nature on parade.

I like each rocky crag within this land,
Ridge-rooted pines which rise to kiss the sky;
Sure every hill-bred soul will understand
And revel in the scenes which bless the eye.
I like each hill and dale, each quiet cove
And laughing little creeks which ramble down
To join the river by a neat green grove...
As happy as an old-time circus clown.

Yes, there are summer scenes beyond compare
Within these West Virginia hills we love
And all have outdoor beauty rich and rare
And mountain skies of blue which bend above.
So when I yearn for peace of heart and mind,
For carefree days, for happiness sublime
I know that they are easy things to find
Along a summer river any time.

Copper Wire

A man walks out each morning on the wide sheet
of sand that shimmers into water to see if anyone
to see if she is bringing in the mail is part of the mail,
walks down the long rope of road to the highway,
the row of mailboxes, the names painted on tin,
walks out, he is walking out to carry home
the circulars, the bills for copper wire
and shells, the *Mojave Monthly*, a row of names
he hasn't heard aloud in years, he hasn't heard
his name in years, looks first as he would
in his shoes, scrapes out the scorpion, puts his hand
in the mailbox, a tin coffee can, his name.

And then back, walks back. The work, the umbrella
glued to a stuffed raccoon standing on a giant spool,
wire running from legs and ears and tail to mirrors
scattered in the desert, mirrors wedged between rocks and clods
of dirt, a chair beside the spool, a switch hooked
to the raccoon's throat. He sits, thumb on toggle
answering each voice with a flick, sends a current
to seven mirrors in the sand, which hold the fight as it passes
into water, the liquid surface of shadow, on/off,
on/off, he's waiting for her to hear him, how she said
to wait, he's waiting. And so a lizard feels a footstep,
the snake's long stomach sliding close. A lizard
just pretends to look away until the time is right and
it runs, it runs without its tail if you step on its tail
you can keep the tail, it runs, it knows. "You'll know,"
she said. He is certain he will know. She is not the concertina
of ribs he found bleached and ruined near the Stone of Visits.
She was taken away and she will return. She will.

Driving east from Barstow I'm driving east, the radio
a storm of sand and then it's him, speaking his history

as frequency, the blown history of a man in his trailer.
He takes me out yes here I am on the wide water of sand,
the many ways of water, he places my hand on the raccoon's back,
I run my hand along its stiff spine and he speaks into a can
strung to the coon's teeth. He says, "I hear you,
do you hear me? I hear you, do you hear me?"
He hands me the can and I hear well I hear
the sea as I would in a shell, the many ways of water.
I hold the can high to the desert wind, to the dust scraped
from the heavy sand, I let the desert answer the sea.
And as the wind rises it becomes a moan in the can.
And when I turn it just a little, the moan becomes a whistle.
We are calling her home.

Photo

Jessica holds her canteen purse
like a last drink of water, the strap wrapped
around her wrist, her other hand in his.
Their first date falls on the last day
of summer, and he's exactly old enough
to be leaving soon for good,
his scalp shining through
his new haircut, his shoes
spit-polished for practice.
The Fun Zone is free
unless they want to play or ride
the Hurricane, lean out above
the sea and scream
as the old roller coaster strains
to hold the rails, as the car fills
with white chips of paint,
the wood struts shaking and shivering,
the burnish flaking off
at the end of another season.
In six years it will all be over,

the Fun Zone closed forever, the Hurricane
a pile of rotting two-by-fours slowly
softening to dust and salt,
a souvenir or two for the sad
and nostalgic who think it quaint
to keep a piece of wood,
maybe use it as a mantel
or carve a clock into the grain.
But Jessica wants a different
sort of keepsake. She pulls
the curtain closed, his face
next to hers in the little booth,
holds her cheek hard against his,
holds him still until the red light blinks
and the flash explodes and for a second
then light is all they are, the booth filled
with floating diamonds,
orange and yellow spots that aren't perceptible
in the strip of photographs
that drops from a slit in the wall.
But there they are, three times for a quarter;
Jessica and a boy she'll remember
like a ride on a rollercoaster, his haircut
new and too short, their faces fused
at the cheeks for as long as it takes
to stop time on the last day
of summer, 1967.
She keeps two of the snapshots, one
for her scrapbook, the other "just because."
The puts the third in his wallet.
"I'll look at it lots." he says
as they get in line again to ride the Hurricane.
She wants to scream, to feel
the wind pull her hair from its ribbons.
He just wants to kiss her in the air
above the sea as they take
the blind turn at the top,

where the whole world is there to see
if anyone's looking
though who would, the fast drop
just ahead and beyond that
the end of the ride: a platform
where they'll climb from the little car,
where someone else
will take their place
for as long as it takes
to get through the line again, since what
they've decided to do
with the two dollars they have left
is ride.

Mother to Daughter

Each regret, like a sweater
or scarf, finds its nail in the wind.
Just as light puddles in the stalled moments
of an evening stroll, when she remembers how easily
her mother swept the petals off the table,
crushed them in her palm, pulled her blouse
away from her chest, sprinkled the dried rose
between her breasts.
                And now she helps her
find her place in a book, her bent glasses
in the butter dish, the inexplicable framed photograph
beneath a sofa cushion. She had hoped, always hoped
to hear this: the thank yous, the soft
endearments.
                But how could she know
her mother's lapse into tenderness
could hurt so bad? And now she's trying to tell me
but she can't, just can't, her fingers talking,
sewing the air with the last few sentences
she can't say.

I won't help her
hate herself; I'm here to open a window.
To hold her inside as everything she's known
rushes out into the garden
to take its place beside her mother,
who's on her knees in the earth, digging up
the bulbs she planted yesterday.

THEM

*Whatever your hand finds to do, do it with your might; for
there is no work or thought or knowledge or wisdom in
Sheol, to which you are going.*
— Ecclesiastes 9:10

The rain is hurled in gusts,
whipped across the lot,
the cold salt
in the wound of their breathing.
Husband and wife forty years,
more bad times than good
and little to show
but their thin-skinned trailer
on its half acre of steep ground,
photographs on shelves below counters,
colored lights in windows
once lit for Christmas.
The coop of chickens is rocked
by the storm's battering.
They wade toward it, one shadow,
over frozen mud, dimming light.
it must be ritual or habit,
pain deep in the why of it all
that carries them forward.

* * * * * *

Reasons? I don't know
any can be found.
There are simply
things that are done,
repeated, necessarily. They
repeat a pattern

of a labor
that maintains a living.

Now is the time
to feed the chickens.
The shed is glazed
with ice in the morning,
twenty degrees colder
since yesterday.
Even more difficult
on such a day to understand
what is there
beyond what is
enough to keep them going.
Their arms linked
helping each other
over the slippery path.
There is that,
each other's arms
in the hard times.
There is that
knowing how
to find each other
without looking,
knowing that where
they are going,
they are going
together.

* * * * * *

But where now, this day?
Familiar places.

They return
from henhouse to table,
its chrome and linoleum

cracked and dulled and
piled with cereal boxes and mail,
egg cartons and tools and dishes and
coffee that burns at, but not through,
their cold-stiffened limbs.
They sit quietly a moment, touch
at memories with
only the barest of words, familiar
talismans of shared identity.
And the going on of the day itself,
the most of it, requires
not even this, only gestures
independent of memory,
no language, only endurance,
persistence:
no charity, no welfare, no creed, no church

As for where they are going, why,
they are going to town for groceries,
they are going to the henhouse for eggs,
they are going to sleep in the same bed.
They are going to all the familiar places
and someday beyond,
and going each, without looking, to the other.

THERE WILL BE DANCING

A fiddle tune bearing, rough-shod,
    the memory of the village:
sunlight on stucco,
leaf-plastered paths in autumn,
spectral sheep
    in moonlight and bracken,
the lilt of the market tongue,
    grandmotherly,
        and ancient beyond telling.

A fiddle tune bearing, sweet as fruit,
    a memory of timelessness:
candles on narrow sills
    marching each night through Advent,
a bowl of rose petals, peach
    and orange and crimson,
garlic and lamb simmering
    in a black pan,
kisses long enough for tasting.

All have returned, just here.
Listen. They come round again.
There will be dancing, too.

OXFORD

It was not the age, nor the beauty
of the worn stone and iron,
the medieval lancets and
crenelated towers and walls.
I am not so taken, either, with an age
graced, yes, but blindered, as well, by symbols:
the pelicans and monsters, unicorns
and witherless ponies. Distantly
I admire the craftsmanship, can even
translate it to, but not start it from,
the heart. I distrust the space
between art and act, between
symbol and need.
But I did trust somehow the little boxes,
the little pans hung from windows
in which stood the pink-faced geraniums,
the purple and white petunias,
the glossy-leathered begonias and fuchsias—
these, and a clean lawn
with ancient trees: an oak

crutched and saved,
opening upon red cows
afloat in the blue distance.
And other colors, too,
banks and borders of lettuce and chard
green flowering among the bright
lights of cosmos and dahlias,
dusty millers a gray mist
for red-chalk and cream nicotiana
to spear up out of, pennants
for a Near Sawrey world
of squirrels and rabbits and
these, also, saved, allowed,
kept by someone
who beyond reverence for the dead, beyond
reverence for the abstract, reveres
the particular living, and beyond reverence
gets the pasturing done, the
cattle and sheep in, the plants
watered, the world loved.

CHECKING THE SPRING
for Steve Paull

Up from the house, west, a few hundred feet,
where the ridge hat of poplar, maple,
sweet gum and red haw fills with a dry wind,
we force a clutch of bramble,
wildrose and blackberry,
and through them slip
down the hard bank
of pale grasses
to the green stones
and stand
by the thin, sure sound
of water, still there, August,
and running.

CLARK HILL

The force of a dozen unrelenting springs
fractures the skin of this blue shale.
The cliff face weeps: rain, wind and ice
smooth and crumble it. Change
is in the sharp gravel
below this mud-stone's sheer bank,
change, too, where driving above us
a harness of cloud pulls
green sheets onto a gray-plated sky.
Bird-black flags scatter overhead.
Straight pines open their arms to them.
Resolute is this love the world gives.

Vandals

Sly, silent Indian on the homeward trail,
Slipping through dark forest from the
    Old Dominion's Alps,
With a pack of
Deer skins, bear skins,
Eagle feathers, blankets, and paleface scalps.

Fat, sleek capitalist on his special train,
Gliding back to Wall Street from the West Virginia hills,
With his grasp on
Coal mines, oil wells,
Gas lines, lumber camps, and thousand-dollar bills.

Vacuous journalist on a ten-day tour,
Flying back to press rooms from The Little Mountain State
With stories of
Outbreaks, moonshine,
Lawlessness, feuds, and highland hate.

Wheat Fields

Somber skeletons of oaks
Fret the steel November sky,
And sycamores lift dead bones
Where the stream is running by.

But beyond in fresh green brilliance
Midst the husks of dying maize,
Winter wheat fields lie growing,
Radiance of autumn days.

Life in death, death in life—
So the eternal cycle goes;
Always living, always dying;
Always somewhere a sower sows.

Touching the Stars

You long for Vega and the Lyre,
Reaching, you almost touch the stars.
You would possess the sacred fire
Of starry worlds though space debars
The pulsing warmth of human clasp.
While stardust flames your fingertips,
The old world from your frail feet slips,
And stars are almost in your grasp.

RIGHT UP TO NOW

Uncle Joe, my father's neighbor,
Was a man of common labor,
And he didn't know a camel from a cow,
But on any common topic
He could be quite philosophic,
But everything he praised
Was "up to now."

No matter if 'twas people
Or a graceful tall church steeple
A hymn, a horse, a house, or just a sow,
Or the pigs a-growing fatter,
Or delicious buckwheat batter,
His comment was always
"That's right up to now"

If he heard a fairy-diddle
Or the playing of a fiddle,
Or the whistle of a tug hitched to a scow,
He'd say, "Boys, just listen to it,
And, in case you never knew it,
That is music that I call
Right up to now."

Now old Joe is laid to slumber
In a box of chestnut lumber
And no marble on his grave would he allow.
But he has had his "druthers."
To be well thought of by others
And I'm sure old Joe is right—
Right up to now.

OUR SEPARATE DAYS

Age had worn her body frail
arthritis twisted her hands,
claw shaped her fingers.
But her mind was sharp at eighty-one—
her tongue, too, at times,
for wisdom saw through pretext.
Her sound common sense
held no wake for humor,
she kept space enough for both.

I wanted to be young with her
or have her young with me.

Her time was stingy with leisure,
chores chased the seasons.
With lye-water fingers,
knuckles washboard raw
she hung clothes year-round:
draped dish towels on brushes just budding—
or harassed
by jobs the summer season added,
she folded wasps, unheeded, into bedclothes—
snatched wooden pins from aprons and overalls
when autumn rains sprang sudden—
or pried from lines
ice-brittle long johns and frozen flannels
then rehung them in the kitchen to thaw.

Self-sealing Mason jars marked the season
by her putting in, or taking out.

My time was automated,
leaving room for talk and tea.
Onto a yellow pad, I wrung out words

rinsed in clean water,
shook them free of wrinkles
and fastened them one by one upon the line,
then took them in,
rearranged them,
and hung them out again
mixed and measured for meter and rhyme.
I held them up to sunlight,
searched for streaks or stains
before I offered them to her
like freshly pressed linens still warm from the iron.

Six decades marched in the band around her finger,
mine was new.

Standing in the doorway,
she opened her arms wide in greeting
and I,
surprised by the absence of strength
in her return embrace,
nearly felled us both.
She teetered,
swayed backwards within the circle of my arms,
pulling me with her.
Alarm sprang to her eyes
and passed to me.
My arm tightened against her back.
With one quick step forward,
I steadied us both
and set us right again.

Our times overlapped,
edges caught together under a single wooden pin;

washed in separate loads,
dried in the sunlight of mixed seasons,
we are gathered in at different hours.

ZERO POINT ENERGY

Another faded photograph, another empty glass,
another turning season—
I can smell Fall in the thick air
and witness once more the changing angle
of the sun's trajectory
and the unfathomable will of the universe
silently working away.
In the grand scheme of things,
little is left undone,
and the grandest unanswerable question is
not how it came about, it's how it continues?

I think of strawberries, of soil after rain,
the buzzing whirl in a circle; of
June Bugs with their legs tied to a string,
and of the barefoot soft grass
exceeding the tops of child dirty toes.
Looking heavenward inside and out
at the trick play of clouds
sliding and shifting
into the blinding bright glare; of
seemingly eternal Summer skies.

I touch the velvet soft brim of
a well-worn fedora, and
it contains an unlocked mystery
in the sweat-stained crown,
a mosaic of images and sensations, akin
to a moth circling around and tickled by a flame,
and I have catalogued and built upon
the simple innocent splendor of discovery since.

In many ways my life has changed,
the endless sensations and observations
have not as yet abandoned me,
they remain as old familiar friends,
companions on this journey.

Vespers

Let me be
the spirit that fills
your wineglass, the chalice
 raised to your lips.

Let me be the staff
to guide your misdirections,
the solemn prayer, the host
 placed on your tongue.

Let me be the tabernacle of your joy,
the font to catch your sorrows.
Let me be there, and ready
 when you cross my path.

Early Menopause

Under discussion: The possibility
of adoption, of adopting *me*,

as if she needs another habit
to add to an empty midnight

full of emptied wine bottles
huddling by the porch rail

like ex-husbands
bellied up to a bar, or

another cigarette petal
to add to the chrysanthemum

forming in the ashtray.
At forty she is thinking

motherhood might reanimate
her period of potential,

her youth spent nurturing
dolls, revive her future:

a heat-induced mirage
glimmering in the distance.

Before David Died

My leaves have drifted from me. All.
But one thing clings still. I'll bear it
on me. To remind me of.
— James Joyce

For the longest time
only one gold leaf
remained, tenaciously

clutching its bare limb.
The rest had turned,
lost their grip. Yet

sometimes there are those
who try never to let go.
You must admire it:

such strength, resolve.
Regardless, the crows came,
black as open graves,

raucous and mocking,
settling among the limbs
like afterthoughts

watching us whisper
beneath our frosted breaths
while we rake together

what's left of October.

The ghosts of dogs

don't glow or yowl in the dark.
Like shadows, they stand back
and gape at the moon
remembering the color of bone.

I've seen them roaming the alley
behind the house like aging homosexuals
in search of some remnant
of the contact they once pursued.

The ghosts of dogs don't laugh or whine.
Their tongues never leave their mouths,
and those black eyes don't blink anymore.
One comes to the back fence on cool nights,

as if it wants to be reminded of human touch.
It looks through me like mist, like the wire
and boards it could walk through
to my hand, but never does.

If I stare long, it grows hollow
in the widening night, its fur fading
into wood grain and grass.
Then the star in each eye goes out.

New night for Lazarus

The moon walked up bright-faced as a host.
I had never noticed that near-smile before.
I felt invited to a night party.
Cypress trees caroused above the olive grove.
Stones shone like silver bracelets
saved for a wedding feast.

The city was busy just being. Everything
shimmered. Even leaves fanned and hallelujahed.
What did not know me was eager to be introduced.
All knew I had been saved from dirt and sand,
which hold back and cling together
like the bad memories of youth.
Wherever I walked, being came up
and offered its hand. I couldn't go
indoors. Beauty held on to me like whores.
Where was the sadness I had known?
Everything old was blown off
like rotting clothes. When
I sweated up the mountain,
heaven sang out in the cold moisture
on my skin. I waited in the high,
sweet night for the sun to come
over the hill, like Jesus
running with a basket of wine.

My dog's tongue

had tasted only one human word.
I don't believe he liked it
when I'd stand sleepy-eyed
at the back door of our youths,
demanding, "Out? You want out?"

Before he was two, he could accordion
his neck and squeeze the sound, "Awwt"
from his throat. Sometimes when I'd ignored
him too long or made him perform the trick
twice, he'd shake and his neck bones would pop.

Outside, he'd roll his frankfurter body
in the grass and howl, as if apologizing
to all his kind for having breeched
the human world. Then he'd look up at me,

still guilty; I was the missionary
that could not be forced from the village.

The afternoon I first noticed his tongue,
it lulled out the side of his mouth,
sunshine pinking and glistening its wet surface—
a handshake to the world.
We sat facing each other,
both our tongues obeying their worlds.
His mainly dodged teeth and poured water.
Mine lived in a dark flow of words or
dreamt in a bone coffin of being eaten,
someday, in a rubble field, by starving dogs.

for Jessie Lendennie

How sound gets into dream

Though it's the counting of the clock
against the living room wall,
it begins like thin whispers of snow
teasing the cheek of the land.

It builds like all the lies ever told
and all the other ones a mind contains.
Then in an hour or two, a train across
the river cries. It's the first one

rising over numb hills toward
the slow memory of sleep.
So when the wind begins tuning
the violins in the trees,

their elbows knocking on back windows,
we are unborn again in the audience of houses.
Among the soft organs and sheets, we sleep
with the sounds that know dream is silent.

The possibility of magic

In a few years,
when I've perfected
myself so
no one needs me,
and the witchcraft
of the world is worn
out in me, like a liver
or a lung, I'll go
to Prince Edward Island.

On the north shore,
there's a shale and
plaster cabin. The wallpaper
curls like toothless lips
in and out of a crack
in one wall.

Far out the ocean wears
tired lace about its neck.
With ruffled wrists,
it plays the shell game
all day on the sand.

Each high tide tongues
the rocks and tickles
the crack. A fine spray
whispers through the wall
like the breath of
an excited conspirator.

I can sit all night
my feet almost in the fire,
can smoke whatever has

dried on the roof,
encourage the brown spider
under the mantel,
watch red maple leaves practice
card tricks in the doorway,
and wait while darkness
pronounces its abracadabra,
and the moon rises
from the tips of trees.

ANCESTRY

Sometimes I hear them call
   my name at night.
Why do they make me wear these
   chains
And stake me to this land,
Land stained with their sweat
   and blood
And rich with their bones
This faceless choir that's chanting
   now from mountaintops
An ageless aria
   that penetrates the rock
And writes through hollows
Where streams rush like their
   ancient bloodlines.
Soon I will be baptized in these
   streams,
      in their blood
So as to carry on the lineage
   in their strong tradition
under their watchful eyes.

(untitled)

When mothers grow old
They don't lose their hair
   like their husbands.
They lose their minds.
Their children have carried
   them away
Bit by bit
   over the years
Leaving their mothers sitting

Fondling apron strings,
Stirring cold cups of
    coffee or
Staring expressionless into
    dark kitchens
Waiting for time to pass
Watching the clock,
    the hands crawling
        across the face like
            snails.
The teakettle hisses a warning
As the snails crawl out another
    hour.

Dark-haired Boy

I carve moon-white slices of cheese
with a dull knife.
The planked table sturdy,
the bread basket empty,
the afternoon has collapsed
under the weight of heat and humidity
with a soft thud like a fat man falling
on wooden stairs.
I feel you.
Actually I feel the warmth from your body
standing behind me,
auras swirling like particles in a sneeze.
The stainless steel knife resists the hard cheese
doesn't want to continue.
I bear down.
I know summer is nearly over.
I can feel the greens fading from the leaves.
I know when I pass you the knife
you will slice fast and be gone.

Mr. and Mrs. Death

Mr. Death is redneck-charming.
His wife is what my grandmother
would call, "mousey."
Together they ride around in
a blue chevy pick-up
with a sweating six-pack of Old
Milwaukee between them.
They know all the backroads.
They smoke Winston filters.

Mrs. Death looks like the checker at the
Food Fair.
She always feels a little chill
so she wears a blue button-up sweater.
She doesn't smile much because
she has crooked teeth.
She's a good cook
and keeps a clean house.

In the evening when they go out to visit
she always waits in the truck
and plays the radio low,
smoking cigarettes and sipping on her beer.
She taps the ash from her Winston
out the side vent window
and wipes the condensation
from her bottle with a finger.
She has beautiful hands.
People have told her
she has the hands of a piano player.

Mr. Death looks like your mechanic.
He carries a wallet with a silver chain
running from his hip pocket
to a belt loop.

He looks younger than Mrs. Death.
He has good teeth and knows it,
so he smiles a lot.
He's never met a stranger.
He has the most beautiful eyes,
a blue you could swim in.
When he's talking to you
he touches you a lot.
He wants everybody to like him.

SONG FOR AN ACCIDENTAL TRAVELER

I will wait for you
on a moonlit night
in the piney woods of Alabama.

I will meet you
on the Waterloo Bridge;
I will greet your train
at the Gare St. Lazare.

I'll be the lady
in the see-through dress
across the room in a Key West bar,
eyeing you as you knock back
the night's third beer.

I will glide down the stairs
of one of your mansions,
my velvet rippling
like desire,
offering you
bed & breakfast
within reach
of my outstretched hand.

DISINHERITED

It's like
that old-time cavalry scene
where to a background
of drums & bugles
your stars are torn off,
your epaulets ripped

& thrown
in the dust.

It's like
the last lifeboat off the *Titanic*
the sea is dark,
there's no hope of rescue,
the sharks are circling,
the band's
playing hymns.

It's like
being invisible,
since you have
no name
& no face.
You are off the map.
You are out of the loop.
You have been erased.

You were never there
in the family photos.
Their gardens never knew
your feet.

They don't speak of your
empty chair
at the reunions
when the tribe gathers.
Their drums do not beat
for you now.

Joe Stalin himself
when he purged his foes
could not have done
a better job.

HOW TO SPROUT A POEM

First place
About six
Tablespoons of words
In a gallon jar

Cover the words
With liquid ideas
And let soak overnight

The following morning
Pour off the old ideas
And rinse
The words with fresh thoughts
Tilt the jar upside down
In a corner
And let it drain

Continue rinsing daily
Until a poem forms

Last, place the poem
In the sunlight
So it can take on
The color of life.

HOMETOWN BOY

Now the women all like him
The men call him Chicago Joe
He's got a strange way-out laugh
That makes him a friend wherever he goes
Well, he's not from the windy city Chicago
As any fool can see

He's a knockdown drag-um out lover
I believe from Tennessee
Hometown boy, go back from where you came
Because I haven't seen my baby
Since you got off that train
Now when he comes to a set
He always comes alone
And if he knows anything about etiquette
He leaves it at home
Well, he haven't got fine clothes
Or a long Cadillac car
And when it comes to talking
His vocabulary don't extend too far
But he can make a city woman want him
Until she cries, "please don't"
That's when he lets out a country holler
"Baby, any way you want!"
Hometown boy, go back from where you came
Because I haven't seen my baby
Since you got off that train
Well, he says he "ain't got much schooling"
And that he was born to be poor
But he knows just enough about everything
To get him in any door
He uses old-time psychology
That makes old and young agree
And the way he takes life easy
Brings out the jealousy in me
Hometown boy, go back from where you came
Because I haven't seen my baby
Since you got off that train.

The High Country
Remembers Her Heritage

My people was music.
Their lives were poems told in the old language
of earth and season,
rain and sun,
field and sweat,
stream and blood.

My people was music.
They come to this country
in fiddle cases throwed on the tide.
They burst on the shore
and notes was their babies
and they spread over the land,
moving up the valleys and the hollows
with the piping of the wind,
moving up the rivers and the runs
with the rhythm of the spawn
the pulse of blood on membrane
beating.
coming home to live
coming home to die
coming home to live
coming home...

My people was music.
They throwed down roots
and growed up families and stayed.
Stand with your heart in the earth
and your hand in the sky
and hear 'em in the hum of the planets,
in the songs of the stars
that carry the cadence of time.
Hear your granddaddy in the high fiddle string,

your rogue uncle in the banjo ring.
your button-shoe aunt in the corner guitar
keeping time keeping time keeping time.
Hear 'em in there
     cause that's where they is.

My people was music.
They didn't have no politics nor economics.
They didn't write no newspapers nor history books.
That's not how their legacy is kept.
Their lives are the poems of my soul,
and the songs of my breath.

My people was music.
And if you want to know,
you got to be able to hear.

Voyager
(Petroglyphs at Salt Rock)

With all the technology and skill they could muster,
they left here on the rock
birds, and turtles, and deer.
And a map of the river valley.
And a picture of me.
They sent it hurtling through time to proclaim.
     "This is who we are
     and where we live
     and what we have."

Skipping past the last planet's influence,
the spinning craft flashed into the free universe.
It contains recordings of our music and our mathematics,
expressions of our poetry and science,
a map of our solar system,
and a picture of me.
Built and launched

with all the technology and skill we could muster
it screams to the scintillant stars.
    "This is who we are
    and where we live
    and what we have."

"I am here," this poem says.
I sent it to tell you of this time,
of this arrogant yet beautiful species of beings.
We are capable of great grace, and great terror.
in touch with timeless wonder,
but holding this planet hostage to our social whims
while we slowly realize our relationship with the whole;
our brotherhood with each other,
with every shining part
from the bird on the rock
to the laser-dance of the spaceship,
each thing born
of the blinding bright crack of the void.
Each thing carried
in the common heart of each one.
Each thing reminding us.
    "This is who we are
    and where we live
    and what we have."

It is not hard to see myself someday
trying to translate this,
contemplating the me who wrote it,
wondering in subdued awe,
    "What was he thinking?
    Where did he come from
    and where did he go?"

The Campfires of the Hunters
(The economics of controlled harvesting)

At night
the deer move out off the ridge to graze.
One of the older does
raises her graying head to gaze
with silently accepting eyes
far down the mountain at the blaze
of the campfires of the hunters.
Tomorrow they will kill her for food.

They will need the meat.
The winter will be long and cold
and the high cost of fuel for heat
will cut into the food budget.

The doe does not own the land on which she is killed.
The hunters do not own the land on which they kill her.
The State owns the land.

The State regulates the hunters
and they've purchased licenses to avoid fines.
When they've finished their hunt,
they'll return to their homes,
and their jobs in the mines.
They mine the coal from under the land.

They do not own the coal they mine.
The Coal Company does not own the coal they mine.
The Bank owns the coal.
The State sells the mineral rights
of the land to the Bank.
The Bank leases the mining rights
of the coal to the Coal Company.
The Coal Company mines the coal

and sells it to The Power Company.
The Power Company burns the coal
and produces fuel to run the mines
and to heat the homes of the miners.
The Bank owns a controlling interest
in The Power Company.

The fuel bills will be so high
because The Power Company
was granted a rate increase
by The State,
which sells the rights to The Bank,
which leases their interest to The Coal Company,
which sells the coal to The Power Company,
which is controlled by The Bank
and regulated by The State.
The Power Company sells power
to The State, to The Bank, to The Coal Company,
and to the miners.

At morning
the miners come yawning from the shaft,
dark, minstrel faces
with eyes
that have seen
the hunters' fires.

JEOPARDY

Jim floats above the trailer floor.
As he passes I lift
his shirt and blow in his belly:
It's awkward but he looks so fierce
I want to break the ice.
He doesn't laugh but he is certainly
startled and for the first time
I have his attention. Looking down
he says testily, "Your paycheck's at *Big Boy's*.
Why don't you get it?"
Stupid with his last six-pack,
I'm wondering why *Big Boy* has my paycheck
as he floats to the couch and is folded
into sitting position beside my sister
like Death's plaything.
He died two days short of a pension,
has two daughters in college.
The windows need fixing and the porch sags.
There hasn't been any tap water in years
The mange has cornered the dog in its hide.
"We're the same," Jim says—
and in some ways it was true. We both mumbled
when we spoke and I was never good at repairs;
but I can talk to the living now if they're not family.
"Sure you can," he snorts.
The cats haven't so much as hissed
and Julie hasn't even sighed—
She sucks the poison from a molar and watches TV.
Still, I know she's thinking of him. How could she not—
him there, with his hand wrist deep in her brain?
And the answer to the double jeopardy
is *'What are the Appalachians?'*—
and I've had enough and I rise
and she says, "So soon?" In the yard

I study the grand finale: tied and staked
tomatoes, rows of ripening
corn, peppers rocketing from stems.
The tall sunflowers are praying.
Somewhere a cardinal sings—*cheer-no cheer-no*.
"Don't go," she says to the back of my head.

SHADOW PLAY

The dark stain
in the slag parking lot
is my brother's shadow
catching a ball
in front of Wheeling-Pittsburgh Steel
thirty years ago. He is gone
but the ore bridge still straddles
the landscape and sinter plant stacks
still churn relentless ochre.
Each year the carnival comes back too.
Often I see my father
going in and out of the mill,
though he retired thirty years ago,
though I know he's at home in a wheelchair,
a human shell emptied even of words.
And yesterday I saw my mother
jogging along Route 67.
She was in the crook of the horseshoe
bend, running ahead of me. Beyond the curve
a field of dead hemlock, ragweed,
and dormant trees waited cheerlessly
to take her in, because she is past such effort.
Maybe it was the flowered shirt,
maybe it was the shock of untended hair—
it was some man I did not know.
I saw a childhood friend
blowing up a blue balloon at a restaurant.

Strangers attended him like parents.
I saw Vicki in the parking lot,
ploughing up beauty with a comb
but when she pulled the hair from her face
she was someone else again.
The museum guide speaks in my sister's voice.
I follow her past
the island nativities of Gauguin,
VanGogh's furrowed hills,
the fading lilies of Monet
and countless portraits—my own dead
playing hide and seek among the living.

The Gift

Yesterday you came with flowers;
with crimson roses,
still unopened,
clenched in both your fists.
All day long I watched them
falling in love with me.
Watched them shyly bare,
one petal at a time,
their private parts,
their golden seeds
in a heedless rapture.
In the mindless dance
of a devotee.

Now they're exhausted. Nearly dead,
each marked for the final journey
by a map of wrinkles
and dark with bruises it does not understand.
Some have collapsed into small fists of pain.
Some chose the suicidal leap
and lie in broken curls
on the cold morning floor.
Not one survived the shock.
Such sudden opening.

And here you come again,
hands full of fresh cut victims,
eyes dim behind a life of bruises
you do not understand.
Closed like a bud,
a fighter's fist.
I do not want these flowers you bring
or their revelations.

I know the private face of death
and do not need the roses' blood,
the thorns' remembrance.

Manhattan Street Scene: November

The flower vendor,
a gnarled pine bent above
a passion of summer petals,
dreams of Viet Nam.
He chafes worn hands above their blaze
until the thin white scars across the palms
soften, begin to glow.
His torn muffler twitches,
writhes in the hungry wind.
Overhead a canvas awning
cracks like red and green firecrackers
on a New Year's dragon,
like distant gunfire waking
the small hours of the night.

In the Garden

Snakes grow here now.
It's not uncommon to see them sewn
between the beans and kale:
rising above the rhubarb leaves,
their coiled hoods spread,
their tongues alive.

The side fence writhes in copperheads
and honeysuckle vines.
They slither against the metal links
and drop:

slide across the lawn so silently
that no worm turns.
They climb the giant oak and mass
in a writhing crown:
my eyes turn stoney as they weave
their grisley Maypole dance.

Translucent garters shimmer from the eaves,
boil in the drains.
They've licked the gold nasturtiums down,
their albino stems lie flat
in a lace of sucked out veins:
heavenly blue vipers climb the house
and flicker at the screens,
and boas in the apple orchard
swallow down the sky.

They're moving in.
Their gaudy tongues flame through my shell
and fry the yolk.
I've eaten the forbidden fruit
and stare transfixed at death.
It had the taste of wormwood,
my mouth is puckered and my hands
but now I've seen the enemy.
And now I know which snakes are poisonous.

untitled

In the room of my childhood
Where, through summer screens,
I sat watching the blue-green haze
Trace images of places
Wished into existence,
I now sit letting each breath of my father
Break against my ear
Dreading the one
That will never come.

TWENTY-SIX STEPS

Many days he would stand
on the porch above the river
bank and comment on the

length of time the roots
of the locust had held it
cantilevered over the water.

He watched it year after year
through the change of seasons,
during the rise and retreat of floods

while the melt of snow and ice
eroded the earth around it, and the
wind whipped its leaves and branches.

He talked about that tree all the time;
the fence posts it would make, the
number of board feet it held, when it

would fall, the amount of heat it would
give off. Locust burns hot, you know,
he would say. He went into town one

morning and when he returned it had
fallen, its branches in the river with
the current pulling it down stream.

He got his saw, waded into the river
to cut the tree into pieces. All that day
and the next each time he went up the

twenty-six steps from the river to his

cabin with a chunk of locust under
each arm, and each time he went

back down the twenty-six steps to get
more, he thought of the tree and how
he had wanted to be there when it fell.

MOVIN' ON

I've put the farm up for sale
he said
in a whisper

    it was good, but now it's time to be movin' on

I've walked these hills a thousand
times.
    I can do it in my sleep
    I can do it blindfolded
    I can walk it with no moon
    and not stumble
    once.

I know each rock and tree
    where to find the best fox grapes,
    blackberries, early transparents,
    elderberries, hickory nuts

remember when we made maple syrup
from the Five Sisters trees
by the barn spring

I can follow the deer trails
    show you where they hop the fence
    to the old Ramsey place or
    cross over into Coontz's field

I've got a special spot to watch for them
    as they come up
    through the meadow
    to get apples on
    Maude's Mountain

I wonder if I should take down
the deer skulls I nailed to the barn
    it don't seem right somehow
    they belong here

    But for me it's time to be movin' on.

I've seen bear scat behind the barn and on the Sumac Flats
seen all kinds of signs but only one old boy
    with his eyes shining
    in my lantern beam
    and him rockin' from side to side
        now that was something to see
        the old Jersey
        and the goats was nervous
        that night let me tell you

I don't know how many times
I've sat up there
at the Amphitheater
planned where to build my house
    how it would lie to catch the early sun
    where to build the road
    put in the garden
    Wondering if we could get a well drilled up that high
    never managed to get enough saved
    but it was a good dream

    Now, it's time to be movin' on.

This old farm was a good place to raise kids

swimming in Sugar Creek
later down at Big Rock with
Mountain Laurel blossoms drifting
    in the water

remember when the girls got
all them ribbons from the cemetery
dump and played pageant down in the
bottom

how the refugees from El Salvador
helped build the big barn

or when we caught the chimney on fire

or the flood of '85 when we rowed in the low meadow

how we would put up hay the old
fashioned way in stacks
the boys would ride the rake
and lift it when it was full

or the kids takin' turns sitting on the disc
while I worked the garden

    But now it's time to be movin' on.

This place is full of ghosts
    there was a story about a neighbor dying
    after he fell from the loft onto a pitchfork
    I never saw his ghost but some swear they did
        Queenie is buried here
        ugliest cow in West Virginia
        crooked horns and sway back
        patient with two dreamin' city kids
        learnin' to milk

we thought she was beautiful

coat of butterscotch
big brown eyes
giving us sweet high butter-fat milk
    butter, whipped cream,
    cottage cheese, yogurt
the dogs, Babe and Muffett
the cats, Mrs. Hubert and Satook That Damn Siamese
have their markers too

don't it seem crowded

    yep, lots of memories
    tied up with a lifetime
    of living on a place

    but now it's time to be movin' on.

The Moon Over Morgantown

After spring rain
the night sky hovered
round the glow of windows
and I fell to thinking
what if what if what if—
memory and metaphysics,
a passing phase
of middle age,
and yet, and yet...

Seeing the moon I saw
more than the moon,
I saw the history
of the moon,
and in my memory
were the moons of desire
on back hollow spring roads
when nothing mattered but
the wonder of the risk.

O the fabulous histories
of fleeting things remain,
each once and ever instant
effervescent like the faces
you'll remember years hence
when the hills are mythic
fictions of the night sky—
a moon will rise in memory
over Morgantown,

and you'll be thinking
what if what if what if...

Extra Munction

Parting the gray haze of drought-bitten
northern West Virginia
Timkovich floats down the Interestate ramp
into the time zone
of pick-up trucks and model citizens who
drink hard and die early,

and on through the remains of downtown to
the sleepy light
where the black hearse limo stands
for sale
opposite the canary-colored courthouse.
He taps his wristwatch

and stares past the aftergrim and scarred
brick of the building
being razed (these vacancies grow each
year wilder);
in the rear-view mirror also grows the wild
rumple of years.

The noon hymn blares from the old church
on the corner—
steeple loudspeakers now instead of bells!
Records will show
that this was the hour of the disappearance of memory

(witnessed by Buck Harnish, main driver for
Murphy's Septic Service
who was stopped in back and swears he was
sober at the time),
and in the last flicker of recognition
the new world

looked older than the old, and nothing

looked like itself.
He saw a bicycle man he once knew was
a motorcycle man,
the first drinking establishment of youth
had suffered reform,

and the hollows of lost love all had
new names.
When the hymn ended the loudspeakers hissed
and snapped
and the sun glared on the roof of
the hotdog stand.

The Race of the Century

Sky-blue Desoto's sprung spring
bent centrifugal at eighty
down the long curve
before the straight stretch
at Ice's Run.
Butch on Slob's tail
trying to pass.
The rusted coupe Plymouth
not giving an inch,
all the way down the hill
to the bridge, to the bridge
of belief—Butch on one side
tangled green drapery
of summer on the other,
the whole carload masterfully
awake to blazing hubcaps,
oblivious to the ageless
slow motion of hills.

It was the bridge, the bridge
drove Butch into the chicory,
and there rascaly chance

put their collective conscience
in a roll—over and over
from the gravel to the grass.
In the rearview mirror
Slob saw the yard dogs
barking at someone
crooked in a tree.
It was only a quick glance
as he rounded the far curve,
but the memory of it will
carry into the next century.

The Squab Woman

white head out the window

top floor
in sunlight

above the fruit market

she
feeds them
dried bread
for an hour
after breakfast

invites them
into her kitchen

speaks to them
My pretties
My pretties
Come to see an old woman.

Tryst of Elements

The river sleeps tonight
its rippled surface laps and smooths
and sparkles in the light
of passing moonbeams breaking through
the restless clouds on high
pushing and shoving each other
trying to claim the sky.

And the rains descended...

The river is awake this morning
angry, hungry, and mean,
biting away the root bank,
sucking the muddy stream.
Roaring, clamoring, churning the rocks,
it widens the span of its bed,
'til the sun drops behind the mountain,
painting the river red.

And the darkness descended...

The sky watches tonight
chuckling with stars overhead.
While the river lashes and rumples
the sheets of its troubled bed.
The cloudless night and moonbeams
light the river's wild berth,
still pushing, shoving, devouring,
trying to claim the Earth.

Riding the Shaving Horse

Did you ever ride on a shaving horse
with a rope bridle tied just so?
Did you tickle his ribs with a willow switch
when he reared back and wouldn't go?
Well, the shaving horse with its smooth-worn seat
could easily turn real for me.
I'd climb on his back, brandish my whip,
and gallop o'er mountain and sea.

Now, when Daddy used the shaving horse,
great white curls of wood
fell beneath the drawknife's blade
while the horse so patiently stood.
But, the minute I climbed on his weathered back
he'd turn into a wild gray steed,
and the crack of my whip or childish commands
were the only sounds he would heed.

The last time I saw my shaving horse,
he'd fallen in knee-deep grass.
Put out to pasture in his final days
like a race horse whose glory is past.
I almost let the teardrops start,
but then, quickly brushed them away.
Old memories brought a smile, instead,
a fitting end to the shaving horse day.

Rejection (in a singles bar)

Perhaps it was
the way I asked you.
A little too smooth,
wanting your nod
a little too much.
Perhaps you sensed
my need,
and decided to pass.
Later that night,
I wondered
how anyone this lonely
could ever connect,
as long as the game
is played from strength.
I could tell,
you could smell
my honesty,
as you coyly
smiled,
and lied
about your friend you had to visit.
The phone never rings when I need to hear
another voice.
My way out
becomes this poem,
and I spend
my blues
in pen and ink,
which only feeds
on the mood,
and spirals
down.
You caught me off guard
yesterday,

as you tested the waters
with your flirt.
I never was good at the game;
always slow to see it coming
in time
to respond quickly.
My answer fell
in the corner—
unnoticed.
You had already
moved on.
As I write this down
I begin to see
I had lost the game
by the second
eye contact.
Nobody wants to see
your feelings
anymore,
there just isn't enough
time to bother;
just play,
and move on;
scattering the evenings
down the highway,
one tank of gas
after another.

Cabin fever

The ten o'clock walls
collapse around me
with the entering
of the Wilderness
thought.
High mountain

clear air so pure
it burns the lungs.
Green as far as a
thought can travel.
The future
outside wavers
as the clock strikes
reality,
and I pause
for a moment by the stream,
to watch the
trout disappear
into the carpet.

Hunger

Next to his shack, my neighbor hangs
a six-point buck by the hind legs.
It dangles from an apple bough
In this white papery air between us.
I tell him I used to trap
Muskrat, mink, and coon—coon when
All the kids were randy for Crockett hats
And ringtails brought as much money as mink.

Behind his flensing knife,
The beige hide gives way to red meat,
His muddy yard to my father's garage:
A muskrat hangs from a beam, nearly naked,
Its fur pulled inside out
Like a bloody glove on my hand,
Newspaper spread at my feet.
I'm fast; I never make holes in a pelt.

He smiles at me like an old buddy
But a blade is between us, a carcass, and
Something else. Rifles bark in the hills
And he smiles a demented smile as I quicken
Like a dog, stiffen.
At the back of my mind, a cold garage.
A wild season begins and blood-flowers,
One at a time, then clusters,
As if by magic,
Bloom through the newspaper print.

Back Roads by Night

A need for it grows—not the white-knuckle stuff
With second-gear rubber, racing for a case of beer,

Dusting some kidface with a hot Chevy. I mean:
That first time I soloed in my father's car
I drove for hours, slowly, through state forest—
A gullet of darkness ribbed out with trees.

A deer sprang from my lights, its tail bouncing
Waving like a handkerchief off in the dark.
Wherever I've lived I've driven at night: beach-
Roads in Maine, waves burning white; one-lane
Bridges, the ridges and hollows of West Virginia.
I've got a letter to mail, I'll say. And slip out.

Glide on back roads where I'll meet no other cars.
Roll by darkened houses, safe as graves, and think
I'm the only one in the whole county awake. Then
Eyes ignite green in my lights. A white tail waves.
One night, in France, in the Alps, a wild boar,
A *sanglier*, stood on the road, all tusk and bristle.

I stopped. White peaks gathered behind him.
He stood there carved by my lights, a mad
And necessary thought, then ran from the road.
I watched him in a small silver field, turn,
Run at the dogs, break through a thicket. Finally
I drove on with those white tusks flashing.

Sometimes, for fun, I'll let a radio preacher yell,
Tell me how easy salvation is, how to "get saved."
It's as simple as the past tense. You only touch
The dial...mail in the tithe to Brother Sid.
Tonight what I need is that boar, the magic
Of *sanglier*, a word full of blood; but even

As he breaks thickets in the mind, I see
The pork-butcher, *bon bourgeois*, string him up,
Hang him from an ancient hook in front of his shop.

He turns slowly in the wind and into a small box
Of sawdust under his snout drip the last drops
Of that wild blood, gone, already absorbed.

Nights

Next door, he climbs under
A jacked-up Chevy with a droplight.

His girl rags off
The silver tools before passing them under.

Tire-scream and glasspack-rumble.
The concerto in my room goes weak.

But when they quit
It's a black quiet.

I lie down and my mind gets up
In its sleep.

At my kitchen table
He leans over a blank page—

Cut hands and cracked nails
Rimmed with slim moons of dirt.

He is mocking
Up a list of my loves:

The click of well-seated valves,
A good rock beat for the drags,
A girl beside me,
The beautiful poor white girl
Who will litter me kids,
Adjust the light, shadows for make-up.

TOMATO STAKES

Old man Huffman split these, twenty years
ago, one Summers County autumn, his breath
condensing for a scarf, the Greenbrier
smoothing over its jade, cutting between
bank willows into the trough of winter.
The year Huffman's heart insisted
he sit down, my father bought them all
with a promise, swearing neither would
ever want for tomatoes again.

A country bargain kept: every August,
green tomatoes fried in sugared corn meal,
like oysters shot through with chlorophyll.
Sunday morning biscuits heaped with mayonnaise
and red slabs. Each summer ending in tomato
generosities: canned whole, or juiced, or
simmered into spaghetti sauce; still fresh,
mulch-stained, snuggled into shoeboxes in
the nomadic bed of a pickup truck, Ball jars
to warm me through another bachelor winter.

Sun-bright on pine, evocations of wood-
smoke, this autumn, regular as the receding
of sap, and all over Appalachia the same
hillside hands gather in the tomato stakes.
These saviors are withered to the root, tied
to sacrificial posts with baling twine,
faces to the earth, leaning limp along
the Appian way, all their chartreuse psalms
drained off by some spider of late frost.
Like lovers parting, they will stand for a while
from habit, all support gone, then sink
without excuse into sweet diffusions of mulch.

Our pocket knives shear the twine, we shoulder-
shake and heave up stakes, the mud falls back.

Amidst amber intricacy beneath the pine,
leaning together about the trunk, flying
buttresses of locust, an antique arsenal
of spears. Impervious, they will withstand winter,
the pine-sough and Pleiades about them,

while our bodies unknit whispering, another winter
hardens our veins. Crystals of uncertain
entropy, snow will skirl about them mimicking
May, as they dream of spring, soft
penetrations. As they remember the roots
from which they were split, the whole
axed from their flanks, noble even in shards,
hoarfrost whitening the rough grain of dawn.

DILLY BEANS

for Amy

On the last dog day, frantic
last-minute phone calls in search
of dillweed. Violently red co-op
cayenne pepper. The smell of hot
vinegar, the imported generosity of garlic.

I return from a walk to find them
already canned, the Blue Lakes
I helped plant and pick: green
columns in brine, sunken cities,
crunchy fingerbones I will snap
delightedly between my teeth

on those lucky winter evenings
I am home and my sister chooses
to dole them out. This August
afternoon we sit about the kitchen
smiling, lifting gin and tonics
to abundance, to Ball jar autonomy,
waiting for the seals to pop.

DIGGING POTATOES

Toxic odors of Jimson weed.
Ragweed's gold-dust, pokeweed's garnets,
foxtail dew. Amidst all this useless
richness, we seek out the final
hills. Fogs of the equinox fumble
over pastures, spiral over ponds,
settle like eerie birds in the walnut
boughs already bare. We have come
for the last gifts of the dying.

Look for shriveled limbs. Then fork
beneath those consumptive splays, lift
and shake. What parts poisonous,
what parts edible—for that knowledge,
the past paid, for these safe harvests.
Gold buried does not bud, corpses
do not sprout, tendrils breaking
from fingertips and crawling towards
the light. Only potatoes. And memory.

Today we are archaeologists,
psychoanalysts, digging the dark lobes
for something lost long ago to force
our blood-fires through the snow.
Irish ancestors shove through my shoulders,
curse the tuber caught on a tine, the bushel
handle cutting its load into the palm.
Against heart's famine there is
no proof. Against the belly's,

potato cakes and dumplings, colcannon
and chowder. We hum, exhumations over,
one hunger we can hoard against,
hefting baskets to the basement.
Now we need a little less.

BOYS' DREAMS

I

Melting spring snows
rushed
out of the mountains,
flooding the creek,
carrying
mounds of entangled debris
at racing speed
past my window
to the West Fork,
Ohio,
Mississippi,
emptying into the Gulf of Mexico.

As a boy,
I watched the creek
rise
to the "Y" on the apple tree.
White apple blossoms
drifted to the
muddy flood's edge,
strayed
into the current
to be carried to distant places.
One child's night
I dreamed of
gliding
out of the ghetto mountains
on apple blossoms.

II

I was twelve
when we built a rowboat.
Captain Midnight (still in prison)
supervised the construction.

Celebrating the launching
we stole
corn and tomatoes
And grapes
from the arbor
roofing
the terraced steps of the gardens.
Then "clipped" a case of pop
from a Coca-Cola truck,
then "hit" the stores for candy.
We spread out at the door.
They couldn't watch all of us.
Captain Midnight got caught
trying to stuff a head of lettuce
                under his tee shirt.

We waited for him at the
creek bank under the bridge.
We were roasting corn
when he
sauntered silently,
like darkness, to the fireside.
We launched the boat.

Our fire shadows
danced
across the creek bank to the
sinking boat in the current.
Boys' shadows
                riding dream currents.

THE GARDENS

Beyond the edge
of a muddy bank
at the creek's bend
the ghetto stretched up the mountain.

Handsome
rows
of shimmering corn,
lush tomatoes,
and patches of fresh green lettuce,
fringed the creek,
then
led up the hill
to bootleggers' hideaways.

Dotting
the vegetable gardens
were mysterious ponds,
where frogs croaked
and darting tadpoles turned their
glistening bellies to the sun.
Coal miners and bootleggers
dipped water out of the ponds
to feed
eager mountain vegetables
terracing
past their
neat and tidy homes to the
chaos of ghetto streets.

Then gave
vegetables to
miners, whores, wineheads and bootleggers.
Vegetables
filling

season's tables.
And when the coal mines
killed a miner,
sometimes whores,
not pension funds,
fed his family,
 and thus the spiraling ghetto
  parceled out its morsels.

THE 'NUMBERS RUNNER'

She's a middle-aged grandmother
in a flowered housedress
twiddling bra-less, stockingless,
up and down hills
in flopping house slippers.

She carries news of murders,
babies, and mining accidents
from kitchen to kitchen
through the mountain ghetto.

She jokes coquettishly,
her eyes
shifting
between merriment and cunning
while tallying the policy slips
and counting the grief
  stained coins.

Circa 1935

Women don't wear housedresses anymore.
Soft, with pockets and
Bias seam tape at the neck.

In brown photographs they stand
Beside the hollyhocks
Their stockings a little wrinkled
At the knee.

They move the wicker chairs
Over the thready axminster.
Plump the faded cretonne
Cushions. The radio
Turned to Helen Trent.

They walk to the Cash and Carry
With long, flat purses.
Finger the grapes, wistfully.
Buy a box of Chipso
And a loaf of day old bread.

At night
They put on long white nightgowns
Made in the Philippines.
Cry into
Percale pillowcases
Edged in crochet lace,
Thin as a spider's web.

The Burying Ground

The briar has bound their bones.
Stones, like bones
Mark the spaces where their seed
Waits and waits
Their bone seeds
Signed with the Lamb.
Waiting for the flowering
So split the stones
And send their alleluias
Ringing round the hills.

Sale Today at the Harper Place

The old house
Is gray as a milkweed pod.
Spilling sparrows
From the lightning rods.
Under the trees,
A bed and cupboard
Are too big
For today.
Children
Turn their faces
In the spotted mirrors.
The table
Has a foot like lion's paw
Hidden in the grass.
Portraits from another time
Look out across the fields.
The old barn
Rides like a galleon
Through the rusty
Sea of sedge.

Clock

If you remember to wind it
the mantel clock runs for seven days,
its brass hands twined with curlicues
circling a painted face.
Twice an hour the iron gong
softly bites the iron bell
even if the lights go out
or she calls to say

she won't be home,
as the west wind rattles
her bedroom door.
Beyond the ticking you imagine
a mouse in the walls,
a small plane sputtering over the ridge,
and the phone that rings to say
she will be here soon.

Near a winter's dawn
when there are no other sounds
and the worst you can dream
hasn't happened
steady ticking brings on
one of the shortest days.
Around and around
the hands will chase it into darkness.

Travelers

One ridge over, they leveled a mountaintop
and crisscrossed it with runways. Evenings
the lights of planes aim
at this porch, then veer north for landing.

Small planes in the night wake me
because there are no scheduled flights.
I lie there and wonder
if the pilot knows how to activate

the approach lights, if there's
enough fuel. The 7 a.m. flight,
my alarm clock,
unless fog from two rivers silences

the engines. Then I think of someone
in another city waiting for
someone caught in fog.
And sometimes I think of my father,

that old photograph of him with three others,
jacket hooked over the shoulder by his thumb,
leaning on the wings
of a biplane. In fedora hats, grinning,

they resemble gangsters. He traveled
for a living and we stayed up until he came
home, watching the window
for headlights to turn off the highway.

TWILIGHT

The glaring sun has dipped into the west,
The pale moon glows beside the evening star;
A sunlit cloud hangs like a crimson bar,
Suspended in the heavens. On the crest
Of one lone peak that towers above the rest
The day still lingers. Faintly, from afar,
There sounds the night bird's cry. The soothing jar
Of distant thunder lulls the soul to rest.

Sweet twilight hour, when drowsy Nature sings
Her crooning notes, from gardens, fields and trees,
Where countless insects trill their evening lay!
The owl and bat flit by on noiseless wings;
The whippoorwill chants his song; the evening breeze
Softens the passions of the feverish day.

Wild Bill's Garage

deer horns, squirrel tails, and the skulls
of trout, catfish, bass, and bluegill
nailed to the door with their teeth intact
tails navigating closely behind, as if caught
on a spawning run of the Tygart River,
adorn the entrance, admonishing visitors…
that perhaps inside neither heads nor tails
is being made of anything

the gravel and dirt floor is littered ankle deep
with aluminum flip tops and cigarette butts,
crushed beer cans lie in serpent mounds ready
to be bagged for recycling Saturdays when
alcohol and smoke money will be duly earned,
"They make kidney machines out of the aluminum,"
says Wild Bill—no work is without a purpose

the workbenches are cluttered with nails, bolts,
screws, wrenches, crimpers, pliers, drills, and saws
a cache of caulking guns lines the walls
like a mujahedin stronghold; in the corner
a piece of spouting serves as a latrine trench
sluicing the amino acids outside onto the peonies,
a stained framed picture of a bearded Jesus
is propped against the window, facing inward
Sacred Heart aglow, two forefingers raised towards heaven
solemn witness to the fruits of labor therein

a Lucille Ball era radio drones the daily
funeral notices and the Trading Post,
while the milling workers speak to each other
in scurrilous tongues, getting in each other's way
performing their piddling tasks, wooden
cut-out knickknacks made to order:

gaily painted whirligig ducks, chickens, and bumblebees,
climbing Christmas tree bears, birdhouses, lawn jockeys,
the portly gardening woman, bent over
shooting calico moons at passersby
from suburban poop scoop lawns

all work and no play makes for a long day
at Wild Bill's garage, where "Work!"
as Maynard G. Kreb's feigned, the G stands for Walter,
brings an allergic reaction and a headache is had in a heartbeat,
where the work ethic's not strong and the job ethic's done gone,
where getting your thirty years in, means being retired until forty
where looking for a real job, means finding one
where they can take tomorrow off......paid

Millhunk

twenty-four people were injured
in the steel mill explosion yesterday,
made front pages of the papers
eyeless readers would peer beyond the headlines

BethlemenU.S.RepublicAnnaconda
industrial iron icon serpents
with bowels of buildings
five city blocks long
"takes a half hour to walk
to the canteen boss, donnit?"

inside the pickle house
steel coils are stretched
and streak through acid tanks
which in the 127° sour heat
emit fumes that gnaw
tiny holes in your shirt
while your safety glasses

keep sliding down your sweaty nose,
"peel dose eyes on dis catwalk boy,
or we'll be fishin' for yo bones."

palomino rats with acid burned backs
scurry under tanks and up pant legs
on their hurried march to wage
war with brown bag lunches,
"keep dat sack up high boy, or you
might find a tail stickin' outta
dat sandwich wonna dese days,
har, har, har."

overhead crane, train, towmotor, truck noises
echo down the half inch plate line
"gotta keep dat motha hummin'
gotta keep dat motha oiled
gotta keep dat motha runnin'
cuz I'm a-workin' a double
playin' the daily too
gotta get dat tonnage
gotta get dat jack
gotta get dat ringer
breakin' my back
look out everybody
look outta my way
cuz I have made it to Friday
and Friday is my day
cuz dis is de day
the eagle flies high
and oh Lord,
so do I."

BARBARA MCCULLOUGH

Voyeur

Outside, the colors of light report, "laundry!"
against wrought iron.

Inside Musee d'Orsay I study sculpture, the sum
of profile, eggshell of the eye, as Picasso

leans green orchards across your wooly shoulder,
a reminder of light, its weight. No longer

dying from too much choice, Manet's *Luncheon
on the Grass* fills negative space, includes,

excludes. How public is this place? Such
freedom to and freedom from. Such heavy

light that I no longer discern flesh from bone.

The Child's Song

The song hangs in coal smoke over rows of houses on
    pink streets,
        fairytale pink made of burned mine waste
        that smells like sulphur, burning.
A small boy playing
in the ashes from coal stoves,
pushing his toy dump truck along
a gray-black path to the pink road,
    singing:
            "He has a truck, and
            he's gotta work,
            he's gotta work..."
The mother says,
        "He can't talk plain,
        but he sings clear."

Traveling Song

Inside darkness of rainy night
moving through myself,
flowing with my blood,
traveling as the native going back,
        lost-looking for home,
I follow as the rain soaks away the hills,
sinking into the ground,
merging into the hidden arteries
        of earth.

Miners, low-roof bent in Appalachia,
        in Wales,
we have always lived in the mist,
known hill country fog and brief,
        sudden sunshine.

I have seen my ancestors in
the mad, fierce fury of a young convict,
            damned northward to
            the last rendezvous,
paced the throbbing, surging current of rage,
            that drove him,
know our common heritage,
his name and mine, the same.

Mountain-island people,
twice kin to loneliness,
accursed by a long, dark fury
            that smoulders down,
the sins of the fathers erupting to signals
no longer understood
            in the sons.

Yet my people sang a wild, sweet music,
            sing it still,
a song that dies into him who follows his own veins,
who tastes the sea salt in his blood,
            and knows mountains.

GEORGIA LEE MCELHANEY

Snow Bird

Bandit. Late evening, in the bush beyond the back door
you were spotted long before I head your song. Plump, black-
tailed, white-spotted, robin-headed, size of a blue
jay, bird not to be found in a bird book. Months later

your country counterpart perching on a mailbox
where we stared each other down, I added to the life-list:
"Bird, uncharted. Belly down: white. Tail: black
with white. Masked. A black hood. Backyard and

country birding: I unflinching, it flinched, took to the wooded
cloister of a working pine. Not waxwing, nor kingbird,
nor flycatcher; flycatcher-winged. Hooded." Hooded. Today's
snow brings unsure company to an untried feeder: sparrow

and chickadee crow, then scatter. The cat, tail twitching, inches up
to the window, a clear-cut case of cabin fever, hunkering. In the bush
beyond the back door the white-chested bird sings, its breast as white
as this snow that falls four inches in an hour. I scatter seed

in the snow, and thawing, the birds attend the flow of sunflower seed,
of corn, of pre-packaged bird feed. Slow. Sentinel, the white-
chested bird preens, reads meaning in the dead leaves, translates
claw print's hieroglyph, transcribes messages left

by a starveling's wing. A writing bird, perhaps? Poet bird? It sings
a spring song, warbles a tune turned marble. Trills. Thaws itself
above the snow against a black tree limb beneath gunmetal skies. Shy
or sly? Well, sentient. Patrols. Does guard duty. Belies its harsh

beauty. And *now* the bird book springs its name: loggerhead.
Shrike. Hawk-hungry, it feeds on mice, on voles, on insects, on
small birds. Which explains the blood on the snow beyond my door.
Bandit. Butcherbird. Hawk-winged thief. Horus-headed hunter,

hoverer, bowed-beak. All that sharp white contrives to hide
a beauty that kills, spills kin blood, in snow's own Auschwitz,
in winter's concentration. And all the small birds attend a random
hunger-strike, ritual; abandon snow. Bandit. Butcherbird. Heir

to the House of Krupp, clean mugger, thornbird. What wild
will impels, what old wound fills, festers, thrives, lives, what rage
haggles, what old wind's thrust impales the artful hunter? Hours
later, reporting for evening patrol, the bird still struts from tree

to tree. Preens. Below, sparrow torn to shreds reddens a resting rose—
bush, unrelenting. All's hushed, still. Then some afterthought requires
that the old sun hang at twilight, harrowing the sky, until
like an eye gone bad it bleeds, impaled skillfully on the barbed wire

of night, its stain spreading in the snow. Now night and the bird
stalk. Down-warmed I slip unharmed into unarmed sleep swept clean
by angel-wings. Near fields where unwary birds flock just beyond
the shock of claws, where small winds cry, you and I roost among hawks.

Under the Volcano

> *Did you never go to the church*
> *for the bereaved here....where is*
> *the Virgin for those who have nobody*
> *with?*
>   — Malcolm Lowry, <u>Under the Volcano</u>

Mount St. Helens' trees
are thrust to toothpicks; souvenir trash is
ash in a doggy bag, along with stand-pine
saran wrapped, picked-over

by the tourist trade. Tricks of the trade
include volcanic ash and stone, the future cast
in the shake and rattle of burned deer bone.

East from here, Golgotha stands
a land distant. Bones tossed
reveal a cross, a skull now
toothless, "The Virgin for those

who have nobody with" grins,
ruthless. Nobody with walks
alone, among the bones, among the stones,

into three p.m. where the ultimate sky dies.
Untreed, a small bird cries
as the dark creeps, unending.
Bending, the bones go down

into doggy bags. Tee shirts commend,
commemorate Calvary. "The Virgin for those
who have nobody with"
rises red-eyed wise into the chill of dawn,
queen to pawn to king checked. Still,
like Hiroshima, like an ashen ghost,
nobody with stalks a long white space,

a wholeness of holiness, a hello halo. Hell's
angelic Good Humor Man wheels his cart
among the host of unchartered pilgrims, his bell

pealing an afternoon angelus. West from here
Mount St. Helens stands, a sleight of hand
magician above the souvenir shops, raveling
plots behind the sani-pots. Nobody with

hawks veronicas.

Coal Miners Off Duty

They sit at candy-striped tables
in Wendy's Old Fashioned Hamburgers,
small blue eyes lined
with mascara badges
cold cream could wipe off.
Great huge men
they crawl
through little
black
holes
so they can take their wives and kids
to Wendy's Old Fashioned Hamburgers.
They sigh.
Stiff butts creaking
against the hard red chairs,
they rub their small, mascaraed eyes
and yearn for the uniform dark
of hoot-owl shift.

LABOR

Echoing
in my gut,
The John Deere loader squeaks and rumbles
like a baby
wanting birth,

Tossing earth aside
like a blanket on a hot night,
Leaving
its mathematical tread marks,
crossed lines
in the dirt.

What are you leveling?
What are you creating?
Your hand,
thick, browned and sure,
strokes the throttle
and the heavy yellow
metal parts respond
with the groans of a lover:
    digging,
    lifting,
    turning,
    letting go.

You know the ground
You know what we are made of;
You know.

SOMEONE LIVED THROUGH THAT FAMINE

Someone chewed grass & pushed away scum
To drink green pond water

Someone cracked open
The oysters & mussels & clams
Under the barren salt-licked sand

Someone crawled over stone fences
Through acres bogs cairns
Sheep bones & dog pellets
Gray fur of wolf in white teeth

Someone lay down each night
To peer through a cracked roof
And stare at Job's thumb print
Glowing in the hoof and jawbone
Of a pure April midnight sky

THE FUNERAL OF DEATH

Was magnificent
Pyramid Door-Prizes

Souvenir parchment maps of Atlantis
Charles Darwin just kept boogeying
Chanting in French "Kiss my Spit."

Entire languages
Devouring each other
Without a sound   Emitting ribbons
Of perfume with the scent of the Platonic Rose

Everything upside-down   Hating gravity
A very large kindergarten class   Erasing
An infinite series of numbers from the board &
A thin wounded man A lamb tucked under one arm
Whispers "Give everything away This is not a stickup."

THE DAWN

Walking along the Truro Beach
Cape Cod at dawn   I discover

A complete porcelain doll   White
Black hair Dark eyes Red lips   Flawless

To pick this up on Fifth Avenue
I would shell out two hundred dollars

The dress The shoes The bonnet   Gone
But stamped on the back the words

Michael Bledsoe   Doll Maker   1820
Charleston South Carolina

Where have you been? You missed it all
The destruction of America

& all the rich peace after our wars
The civil one   The first   The second

& the next &   the next   The next
You are the first glass messenger

I have met from the Other World
You say nothing but express a sense

Of infinite grace   I pick you up
To take you home Knowing

You were safer at sea   In the land
Of algae eel & shark

Safer there than on land   Where last week
The neighborhood children slammed

BB after BB into the body
Of Jefferson   The blue & white

Neighborhood cat   Who hung from a bare
Apple tree against a drop of orange sun

THE SHADOW BENEATH MY CORPSE IS ALWAYS

In training   He loves pretending he is
A layer of skin   Peeled from Death's moon burnt

Shoulders   Tonight he is resting under
Me   As I write these words
As I lie here on this bank

I tell him   Beware   I am
Breeding a Herd of Fireflies   I am
Weaving a net to skim the starlight
Off the surface of any river

His silence becomes a species of laughter
He thinks the only noise here is
The scraping of my pencil   He does not know
That I am sharpening the tips of each syllable
To impale him   Him & his little brother Fear

LLEWELLYN MCKERNAN

CHURN

my mother whispers, pouring the rich milk in.
Swish-swash, the stone crock whispers back:
    spellbound by this witch with a strip of skunk-
white hair among the black. She tongues the flame
    of a song—it bristles, porcupine-sharp, splintered
like the Old Rugged Cross. I sit at her feet, I press
    my cheek against cold blue stone, flesh shivers to
a blush, heightened by the shrill noble voice of my

mother, her spindle-thin hand, the pressure of her
palm (it teaches me all I know about the deathless
    grip of love, making everything behave as it ought).
How it stings, caresses, clings to the dasher! How it
    squeezes and shakes the pole (at whose end is nailed
a wood cross). Up and down it jiggles and dances. Chock-
    a-block it sings and my mother sings as inside the belly
of the crock a churning hum bursts its white wave upon

a stone surf, and cursing the final seamless dark, draws back
and swells again, pounding like a heart trying to drive out
    everything but its love of God—a merciless, muscle-bound
moan singing to the bone the arm of the churner, my mother,
    that fury! Sweatbeads freshen her face, her stalwart elbows
crack, but she keeps on churning, for the swift current she
    broods over pitches and rolls inside the dark, rocks white
and riding up and out of it pinpricks gold as the hands of a Swiss
    watch twist and turn, burn to tiny sun-colored balls, then

to bright chips and blocks, shaped like nothing but theselves
alone, swirling in foam: icons of froth. I breathe in this cloud
    of work, I grow as my own heart learns to be small, anointing
my mother's kitchen, where the icebox and stove, the sink and
    walls bolt everything down—all but the curious trees that peer

in the window, the salt and pepper of a storm-tossed sky, and
    the lips of my mother telling me no lies as her arm, clenched in
the constant motion of love, grows what will melt and make
    rich whole loaves of bread, blessing our tongues, our bodies.

THE GIRL IN THE BLACK LEATHER RAINCOAT STANDS AT HER FATHER'S GRAVESIDE

If my father's in heaven, he's butchering.
They've given him the go-ahead to slaughter
    every animal. He's an expert, especially
at skinning a squirrel, poking out the eye
    of a rabbit. Those naked squirrels, bulging
like a cock. Those white rabbits, one eye
    round and blue as the sky, the other
a slit with blood pouring through it.

They let my father walk around in white
pajama shorts just as he did in the house,
    splay-toed, flat-footed, quiet as a hat or
deerslayer. In those sleepless hours before
    the dawn when I lay in bed, sweating out
adolescent fevers, he would make his soundless
    flight from room to room, checking the locks
on all the doors and windows. Once I found him

    bending over me, his eyes red, poker-hot, and
over his forehead fell the beaver cap he wore
    when he was dreaming. My breathing stopped.
Who was I in his dream? His daughter? One of
    his stuffed animals? As he bent lower, I saw
the hair in his nostrils and smelled on his breath
    fruit-flavored brandy. He lit a match and held
it under my eye, singeing my lashes.

    Sometimes at dawn I would find him dusting

the glass eye of the deerhead mounted above
    the mantle, or smashing to powder the sweet
porcelain of one more animal because, in
    holding it up to the light, he'd found a small
blemish. (That menagerie on the coffee table,
    where the lion lay down with the lamb, the
tiger with the monkey, dwindled each day

    it was left in his safekeeping.) Later he would
sweep every inch of the hardwood floors, all the
    rooms spotless but for the dirt under the rugs.
He never turned them over. He never took me
    to church either. Sometimes when I was out and
had to call home, he let the phone ring 20 times
    before he answered. In his tiny tin voice he
would say, "Hello, who is this? What do you want?"

    Gradually he took to stealing bits and pieces
of my clothing. The black leather raincoat,
    trimmed in white stitching. The green felt hat,
with a pheasant feather sticking up in back; the
    suede pumps, the alligator bag. I never saw him
wear them, but I never got any of them back but
    the raincoat. It vanished one Sunday, only to
reappear a week later on the sofa, without a single
    mark on it. He'd propped it up so it looked like
somebody I couldn't see was sitting in it.

    He taught me to imitate the sound of every bird
but the sparrow. Lying in his bed nine months, big
    with death, he wanted to hear the longest song, so
I sang them, one after the other, from the bray of a
    peacock to the small still voice of the phoenix.
Propped on feather pillows, he would fall asleep,
    nodding his head as if he were saying "yes"
constantly, his body slipping down into a hollow of
    sheets. On the wall opposite, the picture of a

lamb locked in the arms of Jesus stared out at me
    as I changed the bedclothes that grew larger and
heavier as my father shrank and grew weak. In
    them his body swam like an old coin under water.

    I only sang because he asked me to, my song
forked like the veins tattooing my body, frivolous,
    free, blue just under the skin, and carrying
buckets of blood from one organ to another, my
    tall legs taking my father to the threshold of a
door so small and narrow only someone whose
    body has been delivered by death can enter.

    If the soul is a wild animal, who can love it?
"Love it, love it, love it," echoes the sparrow.

SWIMMING IN GREENBO

        My daughter slips like a vow
through blue water, rides a white
        lion that slides through her fingers,

    talks learnedly of touching
her hand to the bottom. She points
    to leaves with the hearts of

        trees stamped on them, ducks
with angelic brown feathers, bits of
        shiny debris. "Watch out for glass,"

    I cry as she moves away from me:
her hair a red patch, her body gingham.
    Her toys float with her: the doll

        with one eye that says "yes mam"
like a stuck record; the ferris wheel of
        her limbs turning over and over;

and her own bright dive, which
tumbles her like Alice down into black
    depths, out of which she rises,

        herself the Wonderland, with hands
that make a church and steeple, opening
        the door so here's all the people—

    The toy that beats all the others
to pieces being the one she never
    got from her father because he

        wouldn't buy it for her, his only
gift his death served up like rare
        meat on a platter.

    The water sings, drawing her
to me. Gently she floats on the
    surface, turns over on her

        shadow, her glistening body
a certain cloud God spins into
        waking and sleeping.

Visiting My Gravesite:
Talbott Churchyard, West Virginia

Maybe because I was married and felt secure and dead
at once, I listened to my father's urgings about "the future"

and bought this double plot on the hillside with a view
of the bare white church, tall old elms, and the creek below.

I plan now to use both plots, luxuriantly spreading out
in the middle of a big double bed. — But no,

finally, my burial has nothing to do with my marriage, this lying
    here
in these same bones will be as real as anything I can imagine

for who I'll be then, as real as anything undergone, going back
and forth to "the world" out there, and here to this one spot

on earth I really know. Once I came in fast and low
in a little plane and when I looked down at the church.

the trees I've felt with my hands, the neighbors' houses
and the family farm, and I saw how tiny what I loved or knew
    was,

it was like my children going on with their plans and griefs
at a distance and nothing I could do about it. But I wanted

to reach down and pat it, while letting it know
I wouldn't interfere for the world, the world being

everything this isn't, this unknown buried in the known.

Deep Mining

Think of this: that under the earth
there are black rooms your very body

can move through. Just as you always
dreamed, you enter the open mouth

and slide between the glistening walls,
the arteries of coal in the larger body.

I knock it loose with the heavy hammer.
I load it up and send it out

while you walk up there on the crust,
in the daylight, and listen to the coal-cars

bearing down with their burden.
You're going to burn this fuel

and when you come in from your chores,
rub your hands in the soft red glow

and stand in your steaming clothes
with your back to it, while it soaks

into frozen buttocks and thighs.
You're going to do that for me

while I slog in the icy water
behind the straining cars.

Until the swing-shift comes around.
Now, I am the one in front of the fire.

Someone has stoked the cooking stove
and set brown loaves on the warming pan.

Someone has laid out my softer clothes,
and turned back the quilt.

Listen: there is a vein that runs
through the earth from top to bottom

and all of us are in it.
One of us is always burning.

Sunday Morning, 1950

Bleach in the foot-bathtub.
The curling iron, the crimped, singed hair.
The small red marks my mother makes
across her lips.

Dust in the road, and on the sumac.
The tight, white sandals on my feet.

In the clean sun before the doors,
the flounces and flowered prints,
the naked hands. We bring
what we can—some coins,
our faces.

The narrow benches we don't fit.
The wasps at the blue hexagons.

And now the rounding of the unbearable
vowels of the organ, the O
of release. We bring
some strain, and lay it down
among the vowels and the gladioli.

The paper fans. The preacher paces,
our eyes are drawn to the window,
The elms with their easy hands.

Outside, the shaven hilly graves we own.
Durrett, Durrett, Durrett. The babies there
that are not me. Beside me,
Mrs. G. sings like a chicken
flung in a pan on Sunday morning.

...This hymnal I hold in my hands.
This high bare room, this strict accounting.
This rising up.

VIRIDIAN DAYS

I was an ordinary woman, and so
I appeared eccentric, collecting gee-gaws
of porcelain and cobalt blue, mincing
deer-meat for the cat. I was unhooked

from matrimony, and so I rose up
like a hot-air balloon, and drifted
down eventually into the countryside,
not shevelled New England nor the

grandeur of the West, but disheveled
West Virginia, where the hills are flung
around like old green handkerchiefs
and the Chessie rumbles along, shaking

the smooth clean skin of the river.
If I wanted to glue magazine pictures
to an entire wall, or walk around nude,
I did so, having no standard to maintain

and no small children to be humiliated
by my defection. I spent years puttering
around in a green bathrobe, smelling of
coffee, perfume, sweat, incense, and

female effluvia. Why not. That was
my motto. I collected books like some
women collect green stamps, but I read
them all, down to the finest print,

the solid cubes of footnotes. Since no one
was there, nobody stopped me. Raspberry vines
slashed at the Toyota's sides as I came in.
Flocks of starlings, grosbeaks, mourning doves

lifted the air around the house. Fragments
of turkey bones the dog chewed on, a swarm
of ladybugs made into a red enameled necklace,
hulls of black sunflower seeds piled

on the porchboards. Locust, hickory, sweet gum
trees. Absolute silence stricken by crow calls.
Copper pans, eight strands of seed beads,
dolphin earrings. I climbed over the fence

at the edge of the woods, back and forth
over it several times a day, gathering ferns,
then digging in the parsley—shaggy, pungent, green.

Fodder

So I was the Scavenger-Child, whuffling
in filthy attics, scrounging for
broken-backed editions of Edgar Allan Poe
covered with pigeon-droppings, accumulating
old yellowed books from abandoned schoolhouses

buried in the woods, smelling of piss
and mire and all abuzz with giant wasps
building a nest in the pump organ.
These were my fabulous loves, my secret
foods. These were my handholds

into shaky light, my emergence from
the pit, and loving the furniture of
the pit, my dedication to the darkness
and the shadows of fireflies' bodies
found between the smelly pages, the vile

effluvium of bookworms' paths trekking
with intention through one after the other,
out one cover into the next, eating
their way through shelf after shelf,
Byron, *Sheep Shearing in America*.

Kiss Me Deadly to *Paradise Lost*, and
Lo! The Bird. Why should a hungry worm
care what it ate? It was all paper
and words, all black magic marks
in an unmarked world, all height and

depth and beautiful fodder, a method
of moving the eyes until they brimmed
with startlement, the swollen pupils
reading themselves to death, and up
beside it, and into it.

TWILIGHT IN WEST VIRGINIA: SIX O'CLOCK MINE REPORT

*Bergoo Mine No. 3 will work: Bergoo Mine
No. 3 will work tomorrow. Consol. No. 2
will not work. Consol. No. 2 will not
work tomorrow.*

Green soaks into the dark trees.
The hills go clumped and heavy
over the foxfire veins
at Clinchfield, One-Go, Greenbrier.

At Hardtack and Amity the grit
abrades the skin. The air is thick
above the black leaves, the open mouth
of the shaft. A man with a burning

carbide lamp on his forehead
swings a pick in a narrow corridor
beneath the earth. His eyes flare
white like a horse's, his teeth glint.

From his sleeves of coal, fingers
with black half-moons: he leans
into the tipple, over the coke oven
staining the air red, over the glow

from the rows of fiery eyes at Swago.
Above Slipjohn a six-ton lumbers down
the grade, its windows curtained with soot.
No one is driving.

The roads get lost in the clotted hills,
in the Blue Spruce maze, the red cough,
the Allegheny marl, the sulphur ooze.

The hill-cuts drain; the roads get lost
and drop at the edge of the strip job.
The fires in the mines do not stop burning.

THAT GREEN FUSE

For Naomi Suconick Myrvaagnes, violinist,
Because the proper response to poetry is
Not criticism
But poetry.

How can we control our lives,
We whined over the phone between Boston and West Virginia.
Then you read me your poem which you said was optimistic
And had a constructive point to make
About the tomato seed in the peat pot
Who made it on the first try
Without homework or formal education
And produced fruit
From each slender wrist.

BISON TRACE

O Great Allusive
the road that lies along the long curve west
drives the deep shadows of the grasslands
once in New Mexico
driving from Clayton to Springer
under the first stars
heart in my mouth
I watched two silent coyotes
melt into the dark
of the Sangre de Cristos

I have not forgotten
the great unwinding of the wind
the bone white moon

under the buffalo shape
of the mountains
the gleam of water in the gorge

Always beside me now
they run
long gone their fiery and snuffy shapes
thunder and swirl, their steep cries
still   as I drive
there and there
the dark curves sweep
the sharp sky opens
I smell the rain
and taste the sweet
the wild
original

FOSSIL FUEL

Mostly I wake up because I am crowded
by little hairs
by gases underground
by the necessity to be polite
even in sleep
by a song over and over
because I am too hot
and would rather lie flat
and the pillows are rocks under my head
because I have not written anything
because a friend maneuvered me
     into washing the dishes
     and it's his house
because you will wake up and ask why I am awake
and not want to know

but I will be burning to tell
I can't digest anything properly
the desire to please
is stark as death
oh yes/I said to the vet
I'll wait/excuse this delicate
dying animal yes
    she who had waited two days lost in the long grass
tea?
for the undertaker
    the flowers of my mother's china broke and wept
you were a prospector?
I play these tidbits to the hilt
how interesting! imagine!

O empathy impedes
and pleasing bleeds
and here in the night I lie
steamy and dangerous, and press of my crushed ferns
making charcoal
I will burn slowly in this bed I have made have made
for a long time.

THE LONG TRAVELER

All that I am
Except the combination
Was here on earth when tyrannous Rex ruled over
All my calcium, carbon, potash, et cetera,
But not my particulars;
Not my conglomeration.

Still I was here—met myself
Coming, and will meet again,
For I am a long traveler,
A long hunter of one chance circumstance—
Have traveled here from the big bang—
Or, say, my NaCl is pacific.
A wild gene from County Clare,
I have wandered the broome hills of Scotland—
A particle blown on the windy steppes.
I am white milk from a black cow's udder,
Snow crystal—photon of sunlight—
Corn blade, lime rock, lonesome water,
I am very old;
Old mud is in me—swamp black,
The dinosaur tracks in that mud;
I am old Virginia clay,
Connecticut wetland,
A pink moccasin flower that one summer in the Berkshires.
I was here—all of me—
From The Beginning.

The conglomerate breaks—
Hard bone blows to fern spore.
My lips back to the red seed, the rose hip . . . .
I am very old.
And will be older still
When I wander the plasma fog,

Return, recombining, return and return once more, my
sediment drifting, always returning in brooks,
I can hope—
Falling in silver cataracts through April woodlands,
Seeking to become a Self.

FALDANG

Cider in the rain barrel, corn in the popper,
Shoats in the mast woods, mash in the hopper,
Taffy on the window sill, rosin on the bow,
Grab your partners, Boys, dance the "Do Si Do"!

Logs in the fireplace, pone in the baker,
Taters in their jacket coats, salt in the shaker,
Kick the rhythm with your heel, catch it on your toe,
Grab your partners, Boys, dance the "Hoe Down Hoe"!

Pick and shovel in the loft, boss man under kivver,
Dish pan in the chicken yard, boat gone down the river.
Rags stuffed in the broken pane, wind a-howlin' low,
Grab your partners, Boys, "How you oughta know"!

"Old Dan Tucker," "Old Zip Coon,"
"Old Ninety Seven," any old tune!
Pat-a-foot, Granny! Break down, Ma!
Hug-em-tight, Annie! Step high, Pa!

Cider in the rain barrel, corn in the popper,
Shoats in the mast woods, mash in the hopper,
Taffy on the window sill, rosin on the bow,
Grab your partners, dance the "Do Si Do"!

MOUNTAIN CORN SONG

Oak leaves are big as a gray squirrel's ear,
And the dogwood bloom is white,
While down in the crick the bull frogs boom
For a "Jug O' Rum" all night.
Out in the fields while the dawn is still
Four bright grains to each sandy hill
With, *"One for the beetle and one for the bee*
One for the devil and one for me."

A drouth wind gasps and the clouds move on
So the red clay fields bake dry,
But pea vines throttle the green young blades,
And the grass stands boot top high.
This is the time for scraping the hoe
Around each plant in the hard-packed row,
"One stalk for the smut and one for the weed,
One for the borer and one for need."

A drizzle sinks in the stubble field
And the wigwam shocks are brown,
While under the thorny, brush-pile fence
The leaves are bedded down,
So this is the season to kneel in muck
And strip each ear from its withered shuck,
With *"One for dodger and one to feed,*
One for likker and one for seed."

MARTHA MacELMAIN

Since Josh was in the Northwest woods with Clark
And Granny Saunders watched another bed,
She was alone with birth, then with her dead
Until an admonition from the dark
Strengthened her courage. Well, the ground was rough

And had been frozen hard since early fall,
This hemlock tree was closely branched and tall,
The hole between its roots was wide enough
But needed deepening…Yes, a trough of bark,
Lined with the silk of Grandma Renick's shawl,
Dirt and some willow buds…well, that was all:
Her man was in the Northwest woods with Clark,
When he came back they'd have the preacher sent.
She passed along the timber, crossed the sands
To Gauley River, dipped her swollen hands,
Dried them on wisps of blowing air and went
Along the footpath, up the jagged shore.

While passing by her woodpile roofed with snow,
She thought by now her hearth-fire guttered low,
And kneeling just outside the cabin door,
Gathered some bark strips edged with frozen clay
And bundled them into her apron sack.
Then quavering a psalm, went in the shack
To poke the embers up and wait for day.

Hill Daughter

Land of my fathers and blood, oh my fathers, whatever
Is left of your grudge in the rock, of your hate in the stone;
I have brought you at last what you sternly required that I
    bring you,
And have brought it alone.

I, who from the womb must be drawn, though the first
    born, a daughter,
And could never stand straight with the rifle, nor lean with
    the plow;
Here is ease for the curse, here is cause for the breaking of
    silence.
You can answer me now.

It has taken me long to return, and you died without
   knowing,
But down where the veins of the rock and the aspen tree
   run—
Land of my fathers and blood, oh my fathers, whatever
Is left of your hearts in the dust,
I have brought you a son.

Poet

I am trajectory and flight—
The archer, arrow, and the bow—
The swift parabola of light—
And I the rising and the flow,
The falling feather of the cock,
The point, propulsion, and the flood
Of blackbirds twanging from the nock,
And I the target and the blood.

Corner Tree

This is the place it starts—
Beyond the Allegheny, where the primordial river parts the hill.
Here, from this old stump, the lines visible and invisible go
   westward,
The survey lines of a continent—

The old surveyors squinted into the sun's eye in the evening,
The old land lookers with their chains and tripods
   measuring west in the long summers.
The old maps eaten on the edges by silverfish and fire.
But their lines still there among the hobble bushes,
Straight lines where the ferns wander,
Straight over the tangles of grape, of scarlet woodbine.

And this old stump by the river, the tree that *was*.
The tree that was the beginning.
The great oak, pole oak.
Corner tree of the west.
Point of points.
The leafy father.
And all the other corner trees out of his straight lineage,
The unseen plumb bobs hanging from his first branches,
The mark-stones planted from his hard seed.

For two hundred years he stood here holding it all steady
    with his great bole:
Holding the borders of states, the blocks of townships,
Straightening the black furrow,
Stretching the barbed wire fences across Nebraska—
The sun's eye always moving toward the sea.

Rock-rooted on the bank of this Virginia river,
Drawing the river into his veins,
Leafing in the green Aprils,
Shedding in the fall winds,
But never budging—
Squaring up the old law suits,
Straightening the streets of cities,
The paddock bars,
The golden windrows;
Hanging the harps of bridges.
And still clutched fast to his ledges,
Girded the steel rails,
Braced the gatepost,
Marked the cornerstone with a purple lilac,
And tamed with his long parallelograms the wild acres,
The wild-running stallions,

The wilder dream.

WHO IS MY NEIGHBOR?

The temperature plummets.
Time moves slowly in comparison.
Predicted wind-chill factor
Influences weekend plans
Or lack of same.

After brief shopping sprees
To stock up on staples
And junk food
In unequal proportions,
Motorists hurry home,
Seeking security and warmth.

What is the time? After five!
Yes! Now, I may turn right on red,
And soon I will veer to the right
And take the steeply graded street
Home, my respite from this frigidity.

His thumb points toward the road I do not take.
I shrug my shoulders and perfect my "I'm sorry" gaze.
I activate my right-turn signal
To make sure he knows and understands
He will remain in the cold,
Not because of who he is,
But because of where I am going.

All the while, we know full well,
Both of us possess this insight.
He would be left standing
Regardless of my route, the cold, or his attire,
Not because of who he is,
Or even who he isn't.

In either case, I know him not.
But because of the time in which we live,
When priests, Levites, and Samaritans
Pass the strangers by.

The Nazarene Carpenter

One day in a dusty Nazarene shop,
Joseph chose a rough piece of wood,
Seeing potential with a practiced eye
As only a master craftsman could.
Jesus, obeying His father's command,
Nailed, according to Joseph's plan—
A finished work for His father's house...
A door where all could enter in.

One day in a dusty Jerusalem hill,
God chose a rough piece of wood,
Seeing potential with a practiced eye,
As only a Master Craftsman could.
Jesus, obeying His Father's command,
Was nailed, according to God's plan—
A finished work for His Father's house...
A door where mankind could enter in...

APRIL'S MOON

She was quite old, and he made conversation
in words of that uncertain, partial tongue
one speaks to both the very old and young
on duty visits among vast relation.
He said, "Who ever thought April was pleasant?
The weather still is cold." She smiled, "Too soon
to judge, until the month gets its own moon;
the old March moon holds over at the present."

Her calendar agreed. Thought told him there
was ageless truth beneath her quaint old saying,
for many stormy Aprils turn to fair
in their own time, despite all tears and praying.

How futile, then, to fret or importune
the atmosphere till April gets its moon.

Haiku

Early morning fog
the color of skimmed milk
looks like loneliness.

On the Eighth Day

God, in a playful mood,
Piled up West Virginia,
Then patted her down again.
Pile, pinch, press, punch,
On a hunch he left her
That way.
And it was good.

On the Hard Drive

There is no escape key for my brain,
no Ctrl/Alt/Delete.
Only memory is stored there,
programmed for nightly jungle treks.

Like an elephant
plodding down rutted trails,
I come across bleached bones,
fragile and familiar.

Cradling fallen carcasses,
I trumpet my despair.

THE VISIT

I bring you flowers
dutifully arranged and
left on the window sill
—out of the way.
We talk about your doctors,
the nurses' faults, of life,
of pain, of death.
I wash your infant-soft,
age-wrinkled shell
Remembering strength
Remembering joy
Remembering—
I see my future in your
palsied, blue-veined hands.
You ramble with old stories,
people whom you loved I never knew.

We hug, you cry, I slyly watch the clock.
We take long walks down the short hall,
you grasping at my arm.
Returning to your room I put you back,
dutifully rearrange your gown, your tubes
and wonder as I leave how flowers
feel left on the window sill
—out of the way.

TWO CINQUAINS

A lark
Will climb the sky
To race the waning light,
And sing triumphantly above
The dark.

I know
My soul has wings
To shun the cloud and seek
The rainbow shining through the mist
Below.

Marigolds

for Bessie Ostrowski

After harvest and before a killing frost,
she snapped their brilliant heads
like royal executions,
preserving them
till dried, bundles brittle as straw,
miniature shocks of gold

that she spun between calloused
hands till crumbled, freckling
her patched apron, the seeds
collected, and stored in a jar,
suspended in the canopic gloom
of a coal bin, its use extinct
as the bits of anthracite
glittering in the dust.

Each spring she exhumed the remains
of previous flowering, presenting
the jar to tilled black earth
like a gift the Magi might offer
to the mother of a god,
its worth untold,

this seminal resowing,
her ritual, cycling
like the water she hauled
to her husband's land,
how it flowed,
persevered,
like grain surviving in spite
of darkness, deprivation,
and the death of the self
she had learned
to live without.

Ivy

Fearing a head-on collision,
Baci rode in the back seat
next to me, uncomfortable
ground for grandmother
and grandchild to share.

She never spoke.
Instead, she directed
her son-in-law's movements,
tugging his sleeve, nudging with her shoe,
refusing to translate Polish he should know.

"Koniec!" she once shouted,
gripping Dad's shoulder.
He braked, his eyes stuck
to the rearview mirror,
me, scrambled on the car floor.

The Fairlane skidded
onto the berm of Route 65
where cigarette butts,
beer bottles, re-treads,
and abandoned cars collected.

Purse in hand, Baci opened
the door to an angry horn,
a near miss, a dust storm.
I watched her brace pearls
against a floral blouse

and gather a dress hem,
cotton stockings rolled to her ankles.
She trampled roadside weeds
to where something green caught
the glint of a rusting sun.

She returned triumphant, "A pinch,"
a clump of black soil cradled
in an embroidered hanky,
ivy leaves the color of spring
reaching out like infant hands.

Arriving home, she hurried
to the sparse backyard slope, knelt,
broke ground, and planted roots,
"for you to water after sundown."

After her death, I witnessed
the expanse, the growth,
the close-knit tangle of hands,
perennial, clinging to earth,
holding one to another.

the new river

Carrying the raft
to murky water's edge,
we take our places, me in front,
you, my son, safe in back,
next to the guide,
whose tanned arms muscle
and carve white water.

My paddle pointed forward,
I turn to you.
You surrender
your paddle to the floor and hold
fast the raft, hands white-knuckled,
danger yielded to, despite life
jacket or a father's smile.

The first rapids snarl,

battering the raft,
we, its irrelevant contents,
tossed about inside.
In the relentless rush,
I forget you.
We ram a boulder. I descend.
Foam swallows me.
I disappear,

a part of the river,
apart from you, hidden
in amniotic darkness until
forced out into calm waters.
There, I look for you.
From the raft your eyes
capture me.

In silent pools, we swim.
Above us, the gorge-rimmed sky
mirrors the river.
Our bodies bob in dark waters,
the immeasurable depth below us.
As the current takes me,
you reach, certain
our hands will join
in time.

On the raft, down river, you grow
bold. Confronting the final
rapids, you grab the paddle,
breaking water. The river
has not forgotten you.
The white hands
of your mother
hold you,
suspend you
above earth,
below sky.

Pissing in the Woods

Need that crouches behind a screen
of young hemlock
that pulse
heavy
as monthly blood in the belly.

I perch
boots apart
settling heavily
into last fall's duff
but release will not
come
old shames
old fears
air on buttocks and the intimate grass.

Lean into a young tree
friend and prop
recognize
black cherry from glossy bark
that rambling weed as
New England aster
poison oak
(of course)
and beginning its climb
convolvulus.

My stream does not arc
a proud horse's neck
of intentionality
nor fall straight.
Schooled muscles
refuse
clench
relax

the spray veers
runs down my leg
twisting a path
to earth
wetting leaves
and soil
fragrance on its way
to ammonia.

I leave a marker
like the doe
by the pond
that pauses
urinates
moves on
restless
for the buck that follows
tastes her need.

ABOVE DUNKARD MILL RUN

Every farmhouse rides
at anchor in a phosphorescent
harbor of sodium
vapor light; every cargoed
barn waits
for the tide-turn.

Our roofline is long, square
as an ark, and we rise
prow-high against the swells,
sailing into dark fields
on this late warm wind, smoke
driving back from our chimney,
    North,
    North, baying

like geese
high and invisible, white
reaching toward the white
that holds off—
building like a typhoon
over open ocean.

Deep inside, we
feel the lift
and settle, the creak
of timbers, wind-
bent, borne up
as though righteous.

HOW WE LIVE

Bay leaf and pepper, mushrooms,
garlic, sometimes juniper berries,
vinegar and onion: I have my own
familiarity with the doe
you shot in our third field;
my hands trim
the yellow rinds of fat, wake
the spark lying quiet
in this dense red grove.
Sometimes,
despite your scrupulousness,
I find a fine brown hair,
zoned with the colors
of concealment like fur from the cat's
back or the way my hair turns white.

Some people cannot abide wild
meat, the resinous aroma,
the color
like knife-openings

in the palms of their hands,
blood loamy as old
wine and thick, unmingled with water.
To eat and live:
like breathing in and out,
and acknowledged or not
there is always
some spiral toward coldness.

Still, those of us who eat
have a duty to know—hunker down
and smell fresh droppings gleaming
like berries on the path,
hear the snort
of the lead doe warning into white
flight a band of yearlings,
in uncut fields
to walk our way into the beds of deer,
rounded as the stopping-place
of boulders, where a moraine
knuckles under inexorable glacier.

CHRISTINE LAMB PARKER

Four Year Old's First Test

You do a graceless swan dive
off the couch
when the new woman appears
to test you for kindergarten.
After you have shown her
your hockey trophy, your sister's photograph,
she begins
with authority:
"How are a pencil and crayon similar?"
You say, "They are both skinny."
She checks the box marked wrong.
"Fill in the blank - red, white, and..."
"Green." Wrong again.
"Where does ham come from?"
You think and think,
then say, "God."
Wrong.
"What would someone who is brave do?"
You answer quickly,
"Walk through rose bushes."

Older Brother

I always believed you
when you said
you were going to come in
and kill me with an ice pick
while I was sleeping.

My heart
beat too loudly
at every approaching
sound.

I lay there
on that rejected studio couch,
my bed,
whittled within an inch
of overload,
waiting for sleep...

*

Under the quilt,
adrift...
seals on the linoleum floor,
not cute like at the zoo,
but slithery, sharp,
clamoring over one another.
I pressed myself against
the angle of wall and mattress
hoping for anonymity
from the flash of their eyes.

Eagles in my closet,
a flamingo on one leg
in our parent's bedroom.

*

But the glitter
of that pick—I could
see it,
feel
the smooth bulb of the
wooden handle...

*

Always tired
when I woke up,

I had to take inventory
of my parts,
prepare for sitting in the bathroom.
Once I heard your calm voice
outside the door,
heard water spilling from a bucket,
as you asked, "This time, do you think it's gasoline?
Do you want me to light the match?"

The Community of Women

Each quilt is a thumb print.
They progressed from Shoo Fly and Ohio Star
to Drunkard's Path and Grandmother's Flower Garden.
Geometric shapes pieced together
stitch after stitch, conversations flourished
alleviating numb fingers, the needle's sudden prick—
startling as a firework's burst.

New leaves budded, then colored .
in Fulton County
as Harriet Dishong, with her sister Mary's help
stitched for fifteen years on her quilt.
The final optical effect of 22, 640
familiar triangles and squares
must have startled even her eyes.
Countless abandoned dresses cut
to snippets, threaded into new life.
On the moon-white border
she appliqued hearts and clocks, flowers and urns.
Birds and crosses, grapes and cherries,
butterflies, a pair of scissors all
scrolled the edge. Amid that turmoil
she boldly stitched her name in red,
then, "finished March 20, 1890."

Gathered over the wedding quilt
the Phoebes, the Blanches, the Libbies,
Elizas and Hannahs rolled and stuffed.
It was their engineering feat—
compasses, rulers, calculations,
Log Cabins arranged with a red patch
chimney in the center. The worst
quilters were flattered into fixing lunch.
Their imprecision banished from that communal
field of muslin, of brilliant color
in favor of Boston beans, quince jam, rhubarb pie.

Wind Blown Square, Dove in the Window,
Cross and Crown, Milky Way, Broken Dishes—
names more inventive than those
of their offspring: Sarah, Lucy,
Herbert, John.
They waited
to pick up their needles,
their thimbles, their thread.

We gather weekly, the Barbaras, the Cathys,
Elaines, Sandys,
an arm's length
from the dissecting planes and duties
of our lives, so altered
from our counterpoints a century before.
Our baskets explode—
with endless spools of color,
fat quarters layered like earth strata
Wait to be combined. We analyze
possibilities, murmur assent.

We purchase fabric from Amish women
an hour's drive away. Blouses, still
buttonless, fasten with straight pins,
they acquiesce to light bulbs

so we can distinguish prints, then go home
to their oil lamps.

The valleys between us unroll,
bolts and bolts of green.

stones

The stones were here then.
The stones were here
before the bones found underneath them.
The stones have been here
a very long time.

The stones were here
when Neanderthal man
grasped fire from the sky.
When red skirted red skinned man
shot arrows into leaping tigers,
the stones had been here
a very long time.

I stood on the stones one afternoon.
As drop after drop of rain
ran down my face and fell,
I saw markings left on the stones
showing tribal brothers the way to go home.
I bent down,
arranged a few in the direction
of my cousin's farm on the next ridge line.

The stones will tell.

street-lit jesus
on jackson street

Half a block from
our parked and
rusting Fords
we
are

lying against curbstones
looking straight
at street lights.
We see
a guy on a tree
just nailed there,
stuck to boards
on the outside
of this wood building
at the end
of the street.

The guy is sort of
smiling,
He's laughing,
maybe
at you
at me
maybe the doper
down the alley
maybe
everybody we know
or might meet,
or maybe
he's just afraid
he might fall.

We sit here
making a tally
sipping beer
guessing at
that smile.

You know
we've come
so far
and gone nowhere

really.
Drank lots
of wine,
smoked for peace.
Spouted from
psychedelic sockets.

We've lived so
damn long
and fine,
and yet
hardly lived
at all.

We've spent too
much time thinkin'
about rockets
and free fall;
we've hardly lived,
hardly lived
at all.

I call
that karma.

The guy on
the tree
is still smiling.
He can see (maybe)
The guy is made
of stone
yet seems to move
down the street
from us
toward the old
pay telephone.
I wonder why?

Do the poems
we have move?
If so —
then why?

What do we
think we
are finding
at last?

The streetlight
after several minutes,
is blinding.

The homeless guy
on lee street
clutches his cup,
the snow on
the grate
is piling up
fast.

retribution

The second floors of brick houses
in the city are ovens of retribution
for lying cool in country wood houses
with breezes off the hill. An institution
almost it seems; heat up in waves
of torrid discontent—payment
for exploring new found forests and caves—
& standing in streams fishing for rainbow trout
In some universe it is, no doubt,
creating fusion.

Augury

Drifting out of the night like a pale green piece
of the August moon,
a luna moth crashes our party,
fastens itself to the wall;
and all at once, the yellow glow
on the porch comes from a bare bulb
mounted beside the screen door;
the night presses in around us;
we can smell the dirt, the pungent weeds,
the crowded trees on the surrounding hillsides;
have moved toward us secretly
like the treacherous woods
that brought down MacBeth.
And all of us are suddenly separate,
though we continue to sing and talk
as we had just a moment before.
Big as a child's hand widespread, this emissary
must be a warning—
we are not the wall,
nor the woods around us;
we're not the wine we're drinking.
This ghost of a leaf, thin as paper,
is a note pinned to the door.

Mixed with the Piping

Mixed with the piping
of birds this morning
some insect rattles, five or six wooden beads,
strung together
and shaken again and again:
more August than April.

But the window fogged up high
makes it Spring and cool again;
and the tree outside is veiled with lace
that is and isn't,
will and won't,
gives and takes
like a young girl,
like beauty defined in an almanac.

Sequoyah

Until *he* lived, if they read at all,
they read the white man's books.
Only a half-breed—standing on the edge
of his mother's world—could see
what would be lost.

Son of a Cherokee woman,
he studied books he couldn't read—
stories in a tongue he couldn't speak.
His father's words
lay like twigs in the forest.

He copied the silent signs
and gave them Cherokee sounds.

For his people, he put the wind on paper
and asked the sea to spell its name.
In his black marks, he asked all colors to burn.
He begged favors of the worm and locust—
made promises to the sun.
The signs he took from his father's people
he patiently filled with bird song, with rainfall,
and lumbering bear.

At last, Sequoyah gave this gift to his mother:
an alphabet
in which the spirits dwell.

Crazy Quilt

If I had my way,
we'd all sleep together in a
rickety, four-poster bed:
eight beagles, two tabbies, grandma,
three tots,
my old man, and the hen.
We'd squirm, squeak, and giggle—
snores and sighs rising like balloons

under a silvery roof of tin
under a tent of silvery rain
under a silver-dollar moon—

we'd snuggle
safe as spoons
and dream together

while the clock
chomps the night
like a bone.

JAYNE ANNE PHILLIPS

SNOWCLOUD

Walker in a tunnel of sleep, she passes up and down
the road. It's the Winters woman say the old ladies, twisting
their rings. The one whose eyes my mother won't let me see.
Any woman with hair that red has nerves like a bowstring say
the men, and their wives stand arched at windows when she
walks for hours in the fields. Her clothes are fuzzy and
stained. Some noons she rolls in the meadow, mashing grass
like a horse.

In thunderstorms that burn old trees we see her running to
the creek. Lightning flashes the valley white. She stands
by the water ringing a bell and shouting Oh. Oh.

Riding my bicycle down the hill beside her house I want to
fly. She is in the field picking armloads of ragweed. My
feet lift off the pedals. I lean forward, weightless. The
bicycle moves up and down, I slide into air. When I wake up
she bends over me, face and hands yellow with pollen. Hair
flaming above her face, she obscures the sun. The road is
empty. Blood is a syrup on my cheeks. She stands gazing down
and releases her ragged gold.

SHAPING

We stand in the kitchen making crescent rolls. She shapes
pale dough
        into twisted moons. I color them yellow
                with my buttered brush, its bristles
dig tiny patterns
        in the smooth white. "I felt nothing
                but relief the day my father died." My mother's
                voice is broken. "He was much older than mother,

lost his money and his mind slowly. When my friends
stayed with me   he used to stride into the room
pull the sheets off us and tell them to
get dressed, he didn't want
strangers in his house at night. In high school
I bought myself a chinchilla coat. One night
he put it on and went out to the barn to spread fertilizer. I
remember standing by the window
watching him carry buckets of manure from cowyard to garden, the
shoulder seams already splitting
silk lining
the color of honeycomb.'Leave him alone,'
mother said, 'He doesn't know
what he's done.' Then one autumn we were
burning trash up on the hill. He
picked up a pitchfork of blazing leaves
and chased mother around the fire. After that
we had to have him put away.
The morning they came and got him
he turned at the door and said calmly, 'Gracie,
aren't you coming with me?'
A couple of weeks later a guard knocked him down
and he died." The cookie sheet of crinkled moon is full. She
picks it up and bends
to the oven. As she
opens the door its
heat falls into the room like
a pealing of bells.

CHEERS

The sewing woman lived across the tracks, down
past Arey's Feed Store. Row of skinny houses on a
mud alley. Her rooms smelled of salted grease and
old newspaper. Behind the ironing board she was thin,
scooping up papers that shuffled open in her hands.

Her eyebrows were arched sharp and painted on.

She made cheerleading suits for ten-year-olds.
Threading the machine she clicked her red nails on the
needle and pulled my shirt over my head. In the other
room the kids watched Queen For A Day. She bent over me.
I saw each eyelash painted black and hard and separate.
Honey, she said, Turn around this way. And on the wall
there was a postcard of orange trees in Florida. A
man in a straw hat reached up with his hand all curled.
Beautiful Bounty said the card in wavy red letters.

I got part of it made up she said, fitting the
red vest. You girls are bout the same size as mine. All
you girls are bout the same. She pursed her red lips
and pinched the cloth together. Tell me somethin Honey.
How'd I manage all these kids an no man. On television
there was loud applause for the queen whose roses were
sharp and real. Her machine buzzed like an animal beside
the round clock. She frowned as she pressed the button
with her foot, then furled the red cloth out and pulled
me to her. Her pointed white face was smudged around
the eyes. I watched the pale strand of scalp in her hair.
There, she said.

When I left she tucked the money in her sweater. She
had pins between her teeth and lipstick gone grainy in the
cracks of her mouth. I had a red swing skirt and a bumpy
A on my chest. Lord, she said. You do look pretty.

Reunion

We carry covered dishes down the hill to the lawn,
shady from trees my grandfather planted.
Once I toddled among the tall adults,
ran laughing over the grass
with my cousins,
or stood joking, soda in hand
amid a cluster of teenagers,

but now I have somehow joined
the aunt generation,
so I tempt children and grandmas
with sliced tomatoes and baked beans,
just a little piece of cold watermelon,
a tad of lemonade,
as if I were born to it.

Wadding up the soggy plates afterwards,
wielding plastic wrap and foil with assurance,
we aunts catch up on lives and reminisce
with our aunts and mothers,
now ranking commanders
of the clean-up crew,
and with those former generals,
our lawnchair-anchored grannies.
The men wander down to the river
to swap bass stories and drink beer,
and the baby, asleep on a ratty blue blanket,
nurses a phantom nipple
while leaf shadows play on his face.

I scan for my daughter
as the cousins run shrieking up the hill.
"Let's roll down," one says,
and my daughter flops lengthwise onto the warm grass.

She throws her arms over her head
and suddenly,
still standing by the picnic table
I too am thudding
    over and down
        bits of twig crunching under me
            sky spinning by
                smell of damp earth
                sun in my eyes
                    grass brushing my face
                    whirling downhill
                        lying still.

I stand up, grinning,
brushing leaves out of my hair,
as my daughter stands up, grinning,
brushing leaves out of her hair,

and then I snap back to myself
transfixed,
holding a large black trash bag.
I look to my mother.
Absorbed
in fanning imaginary gnats
away from the baby's eyes,
she does not see me.

She never told me there were times
she rolled down a hill with me.

DAVID B. PRATHER

Ignominious

I remember the dogs of childhood
comforting my sleep through every phase
of the moon. Like the dog soldiers
who would spear their bright sashes
to the battleground and fight even
the Devil, whose domain is the grass,
always underfoot. The sedentary earth
is the only place I know, as though
I am counting coup with every step.
And I think of everyone's shame,
how at school we never spoke
of ancestry, all the teachers afraid
that we were half-breeds aware
of the lives we had lost. Blackfoot,
Cherokee, Crow and Sioux. Blood
traveling so far to reach us,
we couldn't even guess, such longings
that take our bodies river after river,
silt and sediment to the sea,
the infinity of voices. I still know
the screams of the hellish birds
of night, the terrifying war party
trilling their fists across their mouths.
We all have ways in which we must
prove our courage. Mine is quiet
as Tuberculosis, Smallpox, Influenza,
any number of pandemics entering
the flesh unassuming as words
that go deep into the body to track
our fears and our lives to the ending point.
Facing the people we were, with
the notion that everything has the capacity
for change, like a world
that doesn't exist. But this is another

measure of bravery, finding the enemy
that lives in the folded layers
of our own skin and lungs and heart,
the enemy that calls us by our secret names
when we are alone, the animals are quiet,
and anything can be used as a weapon.

Remission

Some of the worry is illness,
the tiny mating clouds of gnats, the startled
and choppy flight of locusts, the ragged
white moths too grounded with the season to fly.
Gypsy crickets react to each step
like reservoir water to skipping stones.
Afraid not so much in the loss of this life
as the nearness of another. A definite weakness
splits the air, rips through sure as a crow,
the noisy, certain birds of autumn. Forcing
the predilection to haste, the need
to get things done, to take in everything,
even the wash hanging two days dry
on the line. But, it will wait, simmering
like the compound leaves of black walnuts
dropping slow and yellow and one at a time
throughout September. The rocky ground good
for nothing but tearing open fermented hulls,
while gray squirrels chisel the dark shells
all day to find the sour and wrinkled flesh.
Buttons on shirts press at the chest
to remind the body of small, round cysts
that congregate under the skin. Some days
it is all that can be done to keep from counting
them over and over, expecting more,
and hoping for less. There is nothing
so quiet as the earth, the field plowed

by gluttonous moles, destroying the roots
of jimson weed and ribbon grass to find
grubs and earthworms and anything desperate
to change in its own body, come free from the soil
and rise. Some of the worry is shared,
the nervous silversided minnows, the directionless
cicada song disappearing into hill after hazy blue hill.
A pebble in the shoe will coerce the legs to stop,
the hands to do what they must to continue.
Because some of the worry stays
and aches wherever it finds a place to rest,
a place to winter, waiting the long months
to emerge again as though reborn.

Genesis in the Uncut Field

I would name the world
        starting with needlegrass,
        chufa, three-awn, a spiky
        and painful beginning, which creates
        persistence, like a saint
        of weeds and anything undesirable,
        seeds that twist themselves
        into the toughest layers of soil,
        where the millet of survival is found.
It is as though I am
        the first human to discover
        the properties of common rye
        wild rice, barley and wheat,
        as though I had picked up a rock
        and called it a grinding stone,
        and everything just fell
        into place, and how alone it feels,
        this knowledge,
        this handful after handful of grain.
Something simple, perhaps,

will save us all, bluegrass,
    sweet grass, June grass, sour grass,
    something we crush by stepping
    past our concrete walks
    and tile floors, something we can praise
    for its stubborness,
    for its decision to grow
    in the cracks of the constructed world,
    and live with us,
    despite our faults.
And those that wouldn't
    willingly come near
    I call rope grass,
    swamp grass and blue-eyed grass,
    the winding and suffering
    and minute spots of color
    that warn most of us away,
    while others quietly approach
    to find a cure, an answer,
    a comfort, a serum
    to lessen their affliction.
But, not, I should start over,
    let my animal brain suggest
    names from its prehistoric position
    at the base of the skull,
    whisper spider grass,
    cricket grass, horsetail,
    letting whatever body found there
    make its claim with web
    and song and touch,
    letting fallacy become reality,
    knot weed, sticker bush,
    cottongrass, bluestem, grama.
Or let the fears of childhood
    call out witch grass,
    spirit grass, wizard grass,
    but we know they wouldn't last long;

there would be lightning and wind,
darkness and a grievous night of rain;
there would be change.
I will lie in the grass
like my father, appreciative,
and bend the sweet reeds
of the hillside with my weight;
you will find me watching
the endless parade of clouds,
speaking words you have never heard,
until now, and maybe
you will lie beside me,
adding inflections to everything I say.

These Winter Evenings

In Buffalo the snow flies horizontally on the wind,
clumping on windows in dense polka-dots.
The lake effect is hard to take seriously,
all that silver light, all those dots. Here, in Ohio,

the winter blows in without much sense of humor,
but ever since I hung a bird feeder from the eaves
I've had wild cats on my porch. I feed them, too, now
but they are as wary of humans as the chickadees,

racing for cover when I open my door. Through the blinds
I glimpse them: gray and white, sable, calico, shaggy and sleek,
they are arranged like ornaments beside the balustrade,
on the railing, waiting. These frigid evenings

they're bolder than ever, one cat or several cats, yowling
at my door, and from the living room sofa
I can hear the thump of them, jumping off a rocker,
off a ledge, each sound saying you are not alone,

saying this world is subtle and complex.
Sometimes winter goes on and on like this,
nights when the wind is so shrill
it seems the outside world cannot be kept

from inside the house, or, times when,
seeking warmth, maybe in front of a fire
perhaps on a velour sofa, wrapped around
with a woolen throw, I long for the stillness

of prayer—how quiet things become, how warm
to stay motionless in dim light and drift off.
There is a portion in the Hebrew service
called the *Amidah* when all heads are bowed

in private supplication, a congregate stillness,
the articulation of silence. There's a certainty
that all thought goes somewhere, that the meditations
of the heart know, without question, where to go.

But here the wind chill is below zero, tomorrow
may be cold again, and for the rest of this week
there may be no sun, nor any certainty at all
beyond the slow disappearance of bird seed

and the sudden startling retreat of cats
as I open my door, and the wind, which blows
through the eaves endlessly, as if it is not yet able
to find respite from itself.

Amesville Flood, 1996

There has been a town surged under.
On this road beside the river, on
This river that wouldn't stop
Rising—houses stood gaping, giving over
Here and there in this town. It's all
Headed west, I think, like
Something you can't catch,
Like the already gone sun,
When the land goes dark
Before the density of air against it,
When gray clouds are brighter
Than the flat black cutouts
Of house or hill, and too many grays
Drab this darkness. How
Gray this brightness we call sky,
Or black this blackness
We call water. Here and there
In this town, it's all
Gone. The fences, some houses.

Silver Trumpet, Satin Cap

The last time I saw a silver trumpet
it was pressed to the lips of a tall
black man, maybe the tallest man
I had ever seen, he was all
legs and sound, his cap tipped
back and his eyes shut
tight, but this is not a poem about
a man or music, or how
a note can bend and sway
through aperture and mouth,
this is about the way
words can bend and swell, leave
somewhere and almost turn
to music, like the unheard
sound behind the gloss of word,
behind image or thought—it
can be anything: a silver
trumpet, a satin cap—the
note can only linger
so long, the sound can only be
the thing for such a little bit
of time, and then it's out of time,
then it's tapped out, and then it
stays lost for so long.

emergency

kerosene lamps waited
on top of home-made cupboard,
and one on the bureau near her bed.
wicks coiled wet in almost white fluid
inside glass bases.
thin chimneys were cleaned each summer week
for most electric storms put out the power.
when permitted, i loved standing on the front porch
close by the door, hand on screen pull,
ready to dart inside when wide sheets of rain
would break over rails and sweep
winged maple seeds from the floor.
inside, dragged by the hand,
humid stuffiness plumped like the fat strawtick
on grandma's bed—and her hand-wringing fears:
touch no iron, put that cat down, stay away
from all windows!   so i
couldn't watch the beautiful lightning
and my cat was chased out of the room;
but the sweating dimness brightened anyway
and my old teddy bear was almost as good
as the cat—and i held grandma tight
and patted the hair bun above her neck
when she cried.

fatherwood

deepest shade covers
curving mountain approach road
as swallows swerve and dip,
crop-filling before night's rest.
no hawk rides updrafts,
where are you?

whitepine giants
filled fieldspace now rotated
with scientific care
for corn, beans, wheat, alfalfa,
and slow cows—all fruits
of rich mother soils.
darkness covers
cardinal male's reddest mating feathers
near where he flew into the side of my car,
mate-chasing,
did love's changes and chance
drop you from some cosmic fender,
stunned and dying?
heavy bees search porchbox flowers'
twilight colors, muted in creeping darkness.
eagle soared over from river
yesterday. father, gone without being known,
unremembered, visioned only.

now I wait, watching the woods
for this night's owl coasting silently
from old barn,
down across cut field, looking for mice.
did you flee south with the monarchs
not to return
to milkweed i carefully left uncut
by the line fence?
like full moon rising—
you are always almost here;
for this vigil has no ending,
and tomorrow hawks will soar again
above fatherwood.

STEEL MILL ORNITHOLOGY

As far as we know here
no crane normally wades
among reeds in shallow water.
As far as we know
there are just four species:
bridge, gantry, jib, and mobile,
all most commonly safety yellow,
all intelligent creatures,
able to dip, swivel, pivot, and glide,
while hoisting several times
their own considerable weight.
One subspecies of the mobile,
smaller and more agile,
is popularly called a cherrypicker.
Most cranes are extremely responsive
to humans.
As far as we know
there is no such thing
as a whooping crane.

IN A NUTSHELL

Had you wanted apples
the mill would not be here.
This would still be orchard.

THE POSSIBILITY OF TURNING TO SALT

It was impossible to sleep there
not a level spot in one hundred and fifty acres
except the kitchen table wobbling so violently

we were afraid it might bolt for the woods
which is what we did when we went there
isn't it? No electricity no gas no phone
no international papers for a while no world
and no news of its absence. By sunday morning
I was convinced some tick had bored into my skull
and was gorging itself. My whole brain ached
from the damage which of course was irreversible
and terminal. I was terrified
already though at what we'd said on saturday
that moss in those woods was thick as carpet
and tanagers there were merely sparrows
who had flown through metallic paint
and now I'm afraid the next time the world ends
it will kill me remembering what the world was like
the sudden overdose of all that peace and quiet
the withdrawal headache the looking back.

IN EXTREMIS

Coming here, I saw land billowing
as if a corner might flap up
and reveal massive gears perhaps
but there were cattle for ballast
and stitching disguised as fencing.
This is a place where light crashes
through spruce needles just outside
my window or crackles in cat fur.
Time seems to roll both ways at once
here. I saw a robin extract a worm
from one of its young then fly
backward to the ground where
it fed the worm to the earth
while the ice in my drink melted.
The language is familiar and deceptive.
A man said *chair* and the perfect chair

tumbled slowly through the air.
When I admired a woman breathing mauve
her breath faded to azure.
The odd music I heard this evening
was asphalt. The stone wall chants
a work song. I have chosen my epitaph.

IN REM VERSUM

One drink and I wanted to swing
from the hardwood Casablanca fan
but Amos could not find the switch
so jingled some quarters and played
Sinatra on the dusty juke box
flashing chartreuse and violet.
Kimo snapped his fingers and laughed.
Lenore asked him to please leave
his clothes on this time which he did
until the song of celebration
got the best of him. Our steward
came in as plastic palms shimmied.
Another drink and I forgot time
forgot Marxist implications
of what the press says we have done.
I knew I would go home and sleep.
I was okay when I went in
and asked my wife and her sad friend
to take a bubble bath with me.
Both women laughed when I snapped
my fingers and did my little dance.

IN LOCO CITATO

Deer still on the island venture
onto the slag perimeter road

to feed on corn thrown down
by the payloader operator.
The deer are not cunning.
This is simply the way it is
between them. I understand
this is not an experiment.

The spotlight of a tug
shoving barges upstream
sweeps the river
catches for an instant
a few deer on the island feeding
one or two of them looking up.
The light veers from bank to bank
but always returns to the herd
as if whoever is at the light
doubts the deer exist.
The boat moves one way.
The river flows the other.
The deer continue feeding.
This is simply the way it is.

The operator knows deer
linger on the island.
He drops corn for them
or apples or whatever he has.
He sees the yellow deck-lights
of tugs on the river. At night
he loads conveyors with coke.
Although he works alone
building the huge coke piles
he is not lonely. He sees
the beam sweeping back and forth
across the river. He sees it stop.
Deer still on the island venture
onto the slag perimeter road
to feed on ears of corn. Sometimes

truck drivers from the mainland plant
cross the bridge to the island
hoping to see a few deer.

A truck crosses the bridge
moves along the idle battery
past the quencher that never really worked
past the empty and quiet payloader
past the inclined conveyors.
The truck stops long enough
for a passenger to get out.
I have to bleed the propane
from a defective cylinder.
I walk over to the river.
A tire floats downstream.
The river is high and muddy.
I wonder how fresh the deer tracks are
have barely enough time to look up
and see five or six deer stumbling
through the brush. Later
with propane still leaking
I find corncobs on the slag road.

The Little House Where They Brought Me Home

Today it looks bombed,
More like a drawer really,
Exploding with old clothes.

The cheap, brown siding which spells
"poor" in Appalachia is still here,
glittering like dirty teeth.

The recently stripped windows are eyes
Ripped from their sockets,
As if to say: *"Leave no witnesses!"*

And the pump, here is the pump
Where water spilled
Its cold diamonds over my hands.

The crows that fly overhead
Are the black clothes of the prowler
Who stole into the house then took
The bride's gold watch from the bureau,
In a room where she slept.

Somewhere it is still ticking
With the cruel astonishment
Of her bitter heart.

Over there is where the sleepwalker
Slipped off her wedding band,
And tossed it behind the broom
In a pile of swept dirt.

In the next room is where the groom
Lay unconscious, his naked forearm
Like a bandage over his eyes, leaving

The mouth uncovered, as if he is praying
For the godless or cursing out the dead.

Here is where the little boy sobbed in his bed
When the drunk wrecked the Christmas tree.
Here is where the baby lay in her crib, and thought hard,
As light shoved its way through the drab curtains.

In a short time, this house
Will be no more than a boxcar flying
Out of the hills of the imagination.

Today no one can remember waking up in the place,
And there is nothing left to fear.

THROUGH WHICH THINGS ARE WATCHED HARSHLY

There's a wind I recall.
Winter opened its mouth and the breath came.
Gradually, white covered the overgrown places
of those planted like slabs
in the field. Houses stayed.
Bodies walked through them
warming their rooms. Their light
became the amber glow of a urine specimen
through which things are watched harshly,
as if they might pass out of sight,
like the dead; we like to say
they are sleeping and how they
do not know they are cold and blanketed,
which leaves things clean and undisturbed.
Snow has a way of erasing winter's damage.
This wind I recall.
It must have been the moaning of my father
when the lead casing of his brain would start to glow,

lighting his eyes to the lurid colors of tiny
gas flames. And there he would sit, red hand
a greasy rag on his brow. In times like these,
we would lie on our beds stiff as slats,
wait for the blue coffin of daylight
to slide away from the window,
praying for blackness to fall
so he would be tricked into sleeping
and we could just forget. But,
my father would lift the paper bag
to his lips, take in the warm swallows,
leave his liver to smoldering,
like a campfire someone left
to stammer in the woods.
The wind, it rattles things.
I believe it is my father turning over, mumbling,
rapping his knuckles against the rafters,
knocking his knees against the eaves. The dead,
they are so pitiful. They want to stand up
and limp away on their stilts. They want
to strum some ruckus on their collarbones.
This cannot be so. Snow has a way
of erasing their faces, just like
my father's, boxed in metal,
a far cry from here.

HERE

Tonight the world is knocked unconscious
Like a bum in the alley.

We tilt with the planet barely,
Our brains lunar flowers
Turning on their stems.

Nothing lives here except the dead
Who lie on their hammocks
Waiting to be let in.

Let the rest of us be thoughts
That move in the mind
Of God like swans,

Where the heart is confounded by love,
Wanting to own beauty,

Where the moon sheds her white blood,
Desiring strangeness,

And we become hastening flames
Left over from the animal brain.

Here I am a skirt walking.
I am a figure with beautiful hair.

Tonight I go outside
Where the air is cold as an assassin's heart,
Where the sky is unclear like the future,

And the hills are the black
Of waking up in a box.

BARBARA SMITH

Apple Pie Dying

How I wish I had been with her
As she measured the flour and the salt,
Cut in the shortening
And sprinkled on water,
Balling the dough,
Rolling it out, lifting it—
Peeling the apples, slicing them,
Spicing them and crimping the crust,
Listening to Paul Harvey or Cokie Roberts
Or Oprah in the background,
Mopping the floor and changing the beds,
Filling the birdfeeder while the pastries were baking,
Then cooling, then being basketed and backseated
And on to the church.

Oh, with her as she delivered, them,
Two pies to the women saying, "Bless you!"

With her as she closed that door and opened another,
Falling past the pavement and onto green grass
Which cushioned her clean slacks and blue shirt,
Her last breath trembling a lavender impatiens
Which her own pie fingers had planted just one week
    before.

Oh, to have been there,
    to have been there,
        to have been there,

To have learned how to die.

Lines

Anchoring, I watched him climb,
His legs still smooth, his ringless hands
Grasping, inching at the cliff,
His eyes turned upward toward my own,
My own smiling downward at my son,
Trying not to look beyond
At what lay a thousand feet below.
We climbed, he climbed, his hair blown wild,
His fear clenched tight between his teeth,
Our courage on raw fingertips.

And then a piton went. He fell
Into the space that welcomed him
And toward the rocks that waited.
My hand, not knowing, reached far out,
Reached empty into empty air.
The mountain turned him upside down,
And then the falling stopped.

He dangled there—

A diver diving half a sky,
His body limp,
Suspended on a nylon line
Drawn taut, mere twisting from his waist
To mine, from which that life,
Now saved, now caught,
Now breathing far beyond my own,
Had come.

The Omen

They say, back down beyond where my Will was born,
That if you're wise you'll go by the signs,
Like when to plant and when to try for babies,
When to can tomatoes and put on a roof.
They say that smartness can't be got out of books.
No writing yet has said some things I been told,
Like what happened before the big war broke out
And why for truth corn prices will fall.
I'll tell you one thing. I was right there
When them two white horses come along the fence.
I heard the neighing, and I saw them come,
When my brother Randall and them other five men--
Them Norrises and two Postens and a cousin named Mayle
Carried my Willie's coffin out of that door.
Them two white horses that never'd been out of the woods
Come fast that day, watching every blessed move
Like they wanted to take him up on their backs,
Up into the woods where he'd found them.
Never did know for sure where they come from nor went.
Now, I can't begin telling you what it all signifies.
I ain't no seer and I ain't no saint,
But I don't allow nobody'll ever persuade me
Other than they was pure omen.

Transplant

I think it has healed
The scars
Of my transplant
From the hills I love
But every spring
The wound aches
And trembles
When I see
The small blossoming trees
Of the city
When I remember
The flowering mountains
I know
          No city
        Can ever be
        My home

Roots

Way back
Somewhere
All of us came
Running
    for riches
Running from
    being hungry
    being hunted
    being hung
    being done wrong
Or
    snatched up
    enslaved
    enshackled
        then had to give them a song
Way back
Somewhere
All of us
    Except our red brother
    Except our bled brother
Have roots
In some other soil

Bitter Herb

It grows again, crowding out the lilies,
though we try to root it out every fall,
leaves dark green, so dark for early spring.
Chow-chow, your mother's name for it,
your black-garbed mother from the old country.
Tough, bitter weed, leaves shaped like swords.
She chewed it, spat it out,
laced it with vinegar.
Weed that forces its way through my flowers
turns up every spring, sure as sorrow.

Summer Twilight Along the Ohio

The iron handle of the pump behind the house
Hangs, a filigree of rust.
An iridescent beetle shoulders its way
Into the heart of Grandmother's perfect rose.
In the pounded dirt floor of the foundry
Your ring finger has turned to dust. A train slices
    the town in half.

Barefoot children ride down the hard wheels
Of the cannon mounted in the town square.
From the river with the mist rising
Sound the deep low tones of barges easing into the bend.

The metal box under your bed is empty.

Across the street at the skating rink, the mirrored globe
    hurls rainbows across the spinning floor.

Linoleum: Camouflage of the Absolute

I found your name written in an old hymn book:
some heathen called you "Hot Pants"
right above "The trumpets are a-sounding"

well you won't last long respectable
that's one thing I'll say by God
for I know how you are

you're like the flowers on linoleum
God-awful to have in the church house
But T-total-perfect for all night dancin

Poem to my Grandfather

My grandfather argued
With bugles of phlegm,
Said gurgle a gurgle a gurgle:
No one could win with him,
He was so full of whiskey
and the sweet juice of human meat.

He could gargle up a bubble
Of the cold wind whistling
On a poor man's knife:
He made wine out in the open
In the foreign part of town
Where the cops were scared to go.

Just before he had to quit drinking
Old granddad got a split-tongued crow
And he taught it socialism:
Well sir, they used to sit up drinking in the kitchen,
The crow saying all men are brothers,
The old man gurgle gurgle, yes yes.

Aubade

if thieves come baby and steal the chairs
we wont get up   wont go nowheres
leave the cops and robbers to their own affairs
if thieves come baby and grab them chairs.

ill push you down to China if your dreams are bad
so roll on up and kiss me and don't be sad
and think and just think of all the fun we had
to fall clear down to China when a dream goes bad

so wind flame diamond from the final fleece
down down dropping in the deep hearts peace
outside theyre nervous   theyre calling police
but wind flame diamond and the final fleece.

COMFORT ME WITH HYSSOP

in soft pencil my great grandmother Caroline
underlined all the most pessimistic parts
of her cheap littleprint 1880s Bible
how like a flower we spring up in the morning
are cut down by evening: no wonder

what with Lloyd's lifelong whiskey habits
Eva her youngest dreadfully burned to death
while stirring the kettle of family clothes
not to mention the vast screendoor boredom
of dingly West Virginia cattle farming

wonder at her finding the inside outside
in the giant void growing on Mill Creek
found her way into the quiet mineral grass
how many keys there are to heaven's rooms
but a broken heart's the axe to every door

TOUCH AND TIME

You are steeped in moonlight, breath simple
and baroque as rising flights of goldfinches
or woodsparks snapping as they consume the air.
You are drenched in moonlight
and this is my hand in your hair.

I know from the moon's example
that distances may be breached
by light. But touch decays like radium.
What has no fingers leaves clearer fingerprints.
Sleeping, you pursue some faint trail.
What is it? White stag deer-path through cornstalks?
Woman with bare shoulders?
Room with all your dead in it?

Time elongates, condenses, sweeps everyone in.
Somewhere in condensed time
when you are not yet
your father sings your mother flesh-songs.
In the instant of retrieval
something crucial happens:
the mouths of all your ancestors
are kissing you.

I am not yet made
but I know from the moon's example
that distances may be breached by light.
I am there like a moth at the window.
Your mother presses her belly
as if to touch you sooner.
My father not yet a father
remembers me as something he will make.

Yet touch decays, as its fruits.

Time elongates, condenses, drags everything in.
Goldfinches flash like woodsparks in the leaves.
My mother, a schoolgirl, lays her hands on her belly.
Your mother looks up at a moth at the window.
This is my hand in your hair.
~~Something crucial is happening~~
but you will not remember.

KNOT IN THE LIVING

What tie wrenched tight in the quick
when loved one's flesh
casts lots for stones? What knot in the living
binds the feet of the dead
that they may step no further away?
That ligature (pivot of healing,
whetstone of breath) made of braided
love and sinew
      (And we sing this wintry

carol, chorale of ice
bobbing up from the bottom, pieces
breaking free to twirl in blood-
black undertow
until the right ship's seamless hull
wholly appears. The weight of it
the shining weight of it continually
asking, How deep?
      (And we sing this hoarse

chord where wounds and music twine
in placental isolation growing
full-bodied, thickening.
Those sewn to us by love
Those sown to us by love
a rowboat drifting

sutures drawing redly wetly apart
as that crucial voice thins, pause
in Quiet's long sentence
       (And we sing this panting
       (And we sing this panting

song, we, the quick, the living,
our throats gone rigid, savaged by that cord
drawn tight as piano wire.
Whatever is godlike goes mute.
Whatever is human gasps
       (And we sing this falling rhythm

LEARNING THE NAMES OF GOD

When will the streaked bones rise
screeched into wakefulness
by the hiss of the world's hydraulics
stopping? We learn slowly
here at the crux of revelation
and distance is the least of our problems.
In the shook-up vat of fermenting nations'
froth and foam
I think your name must be Blood.

But you have other names, and many silences:
Leaf-shudder, Ant-scuttle, Touch-me-not,
Flesh. Hearing these common names, I remember
how much overlaps. Wine water blood
fills the mouth of the dark, a red prayer
to cancel the spilling.

And so I am reading this scrapbook you left me,
afraid of my ignorance.
Do I dare call you Murderer or Jester?
Are you Quake and Flood?

Yes, but also the creek's wet Pebble,
the Exponential Integer, the cleansed Slate
unmarked between far-flung suns.
If You are Suture, are you also Faultline?
You are Plus and Minus, cough and hiccough.

But surely you have short names and long ones.
If a speckled fish leaps, it is one syllable.
And if a man touches his wife's hair or eyelids,
how many volumes have been filled?

Ash-marrow, Cedar-tang, Grief—can you hear me?
What honor do you milk from my stuttering?
I am trying to learn. Have I paid enough?
Even by accident, I say your names:
the eloquent, the unspeakable.
Will you now say mine?
Thorn-jab, Waterfall, Love-maker, Thief—
I ask and ask.
Remember, Highlander. I am small.

Letter to My Sister

It is dangerous for a woman to defy the gods;
To taunt them with the tongue's thin tip,
Or strut in the weakness of mere humanity,
Or draw a line daring them to cross;
The gods who own the searing lightning,
The drowning waters, the tormenting fears,
The anger of red sins...
Oh, but worse still if you mince along timidly—
Dodge this way or that, or kneel, or pray,
Or be kind, or sweat agony drops,
Or lay your quick body over your feeble young,
If you have beauty or plainness, if celibate,
Or vowed—the gods are Juggernaut,
Passing over each of us...
        Or this you may do:
Lock your heart, then quietly,
And, lest they peer within,
Light no lamp when dark comes down.
Raise no shade for sun,
Breathless must your breath come thru,
If you'd die and dare deny
The gods their godlike fun!

THE BIRDBELL CAFE

H
   a
n
     g
i
   n
g
  in
an old
oak tree,
the Birdbell
Café crazily
swings to and
fro—for all to
see—a welcome
sight for flocks
in flight—looking
for a place to light
and fill their bellies
for the night. First to
stop and get in line, small
songbird sparrows start to dine
at the salad bar—then from afar—
a motley crew of cockatoos choose not
to queue but chew and spew until they rudely
bid adieu. Next we see wee chickadees clinging
tightly in the breeze, black-caps bobbing up and down,
clownlike nibbling upside down. Our next guest wears a
crimson vest, to match his crest, and his request is some
thing simple to digest—like sweet cracked corn—or a sun
flower seed, which happens to be the favorite feed of a tufted
titmouse with beady eyes—who looks surprised—as he drops
down from the skies above—and swipes a seed from a mourning
dove. Next we hear a raucous caw, as a blue-jay spies the furry
paw of an uninvited would-be guest, who tries to sneak in from
the west, to nab himself a tasty treat—and nuts and seeds
are NOT his meat. The party seems to be getting rough
and the birds believe they've had enough—so loudly they
scatter this way and that, leaving behind a hungry cat
and the Birdbell Café, of great renown,
lowers its blinds
and closes
d
o
w
n
!

BLACKBERRY WINE

One evening I was sitting on the front porch
when a man walked up the driveway carrying
a suitcase. "Hello!" he said with a big smile.
"I'm Ernest Butcher from Kingsport, Tennessee."
"Friend, come in and sit a spell," I told him.
Resting, he said, "I'm a preacher of the Gospel.
I travel on foot, the way Jesus did."
"That's a mighty fine calling," I remarked.
"Have you been saved?" he asked. "Yes," I replied.
We talked for a good while and then he ventured:
"Do you suppose I could stay here overnight?"
"Of course you can. I live by my lonesome
and so have plenty of room to put you up.
It will be an honor to have you stay."
I excused myself and went to the kitchen.
I came back with two four-ounce glasses nearly full.
"This is homemade blackberry wine," I told him.
"Made right here by yours truly. Nothing better."
"Oh no," he said. "I never touch alcohol."
"Our Lord and Savior drank wine," I reminded him.
"Well, all right, then. But just this one."
To his I had added sugar and a generous dollop
of Mama's narcotic sleeping potion,
which luckily I had not thrown away.
I rescued the glass as he fell asleep.
The cards in his wallet identified him
as Robert L. Johnson of Ashland, Kentucky.
The suitcase was locked but I found the key.
Clothing, a Bible, toiletries, a sharpened
beer-can opener, an ice pick, a switchblade,
a coil of rope the color of dried blood,
and a thick packet of paper money held
with a rubber band. My hunch had been right:
I was dealing with a serial killer.

I had followed the crimes from their beginning.
There were all torture murders, the worst kind.
And I was to have been his latest victim!
I dug a grave by moonlight at one corner
of the garden, within the high paling fence.
The work was backbreaking and seemed endless.
When the pit was ready I buried him
alive, snoring, along with his hat and suitcase.
I kept the money. I figured I deserved it,
considering all the trouble he had put me to.
No one ever came looking for him.

THE BEER GARDENS
OF LOGAN COUNTY

Southern West Virginia circa 1940

A neon sign or one carefully painted
particularizes the establishment.
SYCAMORE GROVE. THE GOLDEN EAGLE.
COZY OAKS. THE BLUE GOOSE.
They serve short orders and very cold beer
brought by deft, muscular waitresses.
Strictly speaking these places are not beer gardens
since they do not serve beer out-of-doors,
with trees around, as the term was understood
in the age of Queen Elizabeth and Shakespeare;
but that is what everybody calls them.
If you want beer you must go to a beer garden,
by twenty-one or older, and drink it on the spot.
For a nickel you can have a song played
on the glowing jukebox. In busy periods
there is constant music, loud and lively.
Now and again couples dance on the open floor.
A man may bring his wife or girlfriend in
for a few beers, in the afternoon or early evening.

Boldly painted ladies of the evening
arrive singly, depart with a man or singly.
The men sit on stools or in booths and drink.
They gain relaxation and a sense of well-being.
They eat sandwiches to prolong their drinking.
In time they become intoxicated, lustful, mean.
The room becomes a kind of arena
with irritable disputants and contenders.
Insults. Women are fought over. Curses. Threats.
A man may have brought along a knife or a pistol.
Three or so men are killed every weekend
at beer gardens in Logan County.
Except for their families, no one much cares.

Star Disc

Warm greetings. We are unhappy.
Our lot, the solar system, darkens urgently.
Fair is foul, our world not enough,
escape our only wish. Where you arise
we call the heavens. Will you come down?
Coordinates to follow. Advance directly.

Perhaps as you, we are upright,
bilateral, fluid within slow flame
called skin. We animate by wondering,
scatter electron volts, and love
last laughs. Star struck,
we cannot naturally fly. Help us.
We deserve better. By this disc
are we delivered, our two figures
etched naked, waving. Keep it,
for platinum outlasts.

Born singly, we dance a turn, die
apart. Opposing digits overdo the planet.
Imagine the answer machine, artificial
flowers. Picture windows, bridges,
a flying disc. Yet incomplete, we probe
the sky for illuminati. Hello?

We give our word, our sun is young.
Come. At the edge of your known
universe, a milky region on the charts,
no one but us. No tricks. Hope
charges us from within, doubt
from without. A nervous system.

The Incomplete Is Unforgiving

Split a rock right. To a sharp
eye, it takes the lay of the landscape
from which it was lifted. Man,
have a lighter hand on that
fragment of the world.

Fault lines the inner life, as any
soul could see. A skull
will not break clean
like an antler under the hand
of a cutter of arrowheads.
But it will break.

Use a flint blade older than shale,
harder than steel. If with one blow
you send concordant waves
through a seam of layered faces,
holding the wedge with a little
lateral give, you will have yourself

a second weapon.

Aerodynamic

Wrist broken, a man on a veranda
watches the lowest, bluest range of sky.
He thinks he sees white vultures cruising,

a plural idea. They spiral in elevator
updrafts longer than any scavenger
ever would, when at last the man

understands they are gliders
with men inside, so far off that, head-on,
they vanish briefly between the grids

of his resolution. Then, banking against
fall sun: white wings, sheer airfoils—
apparently aloof. The man counts five.

He likes them better as gliders. Vultures,
white or not, might sooner touch down
close enough to mind, and all for one.

A KISS

Far be it from me
To imagine the crowning
Of the Queen of Heaven:
Angels in charge of tornadoes
Bowing and whispering obeisance
To a maiden lady
Whose presence is almost absence,
Behind the scene usually,
Not center stage.
It is too much for me.
I try, while driving this back road,
To see her more simply
Brushing a tear from Jesus' cheek
Replacing it with a kiss.
Imagine a kiss from the Blessed Virgin Mary!
My eye falls on a single April daffodil
lighting the grassy edge of a wood.

IN THE TROUGH

I live in the trough of huge waves.
There is the past; it slid under me
Just a moment ago carrying my childhood.
    Little Billy afraid of the boogie man
    Hiding under the dining table
    Because a rock he threw from the porch
    Banged on a windshield below.
Carrying the tanned vanity of age fifteen
And all the ruck of parttime jobs
    Bagging a peck of potatoes at Blood's
    Peddling papers Sunday at the Square
    Shoveling snow back onto a no-pay driveway

Renting pillows or loading luggage
    on a bus to Machias
Shivvying a feminine foot into a shoe
    at Thom McAnn's
All sports I could I played with forever friends
    Football dodging cow patties
    Baseball in a league with uniforms
    Basketball on triumphant teams
    Skiing with crazy George
    Bowling, swimming, golf et al,
    Et all my sparest time off book and job
College matched perceptions with the faculty's
    The historian who would have gone dumb
    without the river metaphor
    The scholar-esthete who found poem readings
        "brilliant"
    The plain redhead who said Phi Beta Kappa
        disappointed because it admitted <u>her</u>—
        A lovely insight made her lovely forever
Later the Navy. Solo, loops, wrestling champs
    deck apes, boot camp again, holster on hip
    TacRadar School, then out to sea to see the sea
    Hear a few explosions, SP in Nagoya, home again
School, orals, skeptics mining for intellectual gold
A career of forty years gone by like suds
Retirement golf with the walking wounded
Dire surgeries that ended pain
The second childhood age evolves
Children bringing children home

The future looms above the transom
Wisdom—I missed it somehow—
may be some lighthouse below the horizon.

PEARL

Celebrated the Fourth by
Hanging red white and blue panties
On her front porch clothesline.
Would shake and shimmy
Like someone on stage
If you looked her way.

She didn't just walk;
She strutted, about to prance,
Energy abounding,
Caught glances like a juggler.
It was easy to believe
She trouped in a circus
On a bareback horse.

Once we had tall tulips
That drew her finest compliment,
"How exclusive!"

We never knew for sure
Where she came from
What her life had been
Or even her last name
Her stories changed
She had to fib a little
Or a lot.

When the man she lived with
Died, his grown children
Disowned her and she
Left our neighborhood
And became a walker.

You know the kind.
They walk the main streets

Endless hours as if
Hoping to meet companions
With welcome in their voices.

Her walking lately became listless
Drifting along some current
Of city air, head drooped
Though her shoulder
Still flew a brave bandana.

This morning I read
How a woman named Pearl
Seventy-eight, about her age,
Was seen wading the Ohio
At 4:40 a.m., and soon after
Her body was found drifting.
She had left her keys ashore.
Everyone liked her, said her landlord.

Remember her gaiety instead—
The luminous boots, fur collars,
Gloves, and fluorescent scarves
That left Salvation's Army drab
Behind her, that Eveready showgirl smile,
Her need for others to see her life enchanted.
Ophelia. The Lady of Shalott. Pearl.

GHOST STORY, MANASSAS

When twilight comes, doe-eyed,
And fog hangs in patches
Like smoke from Jackson's guns
He comes back here to the Deep Cut,

One of those who fired
His forty cartridges, scrounged
More from comrades who
No longer needed them

Then, when those were gone,
Chunked rocks at the blue-coats
Who stood where we're standing now

　　　　　　　　　　　　　—There!
　　　　　　What startled those quail?
　　　　　Watch, boy. You'll see him.

Man like that, death's too
Inconvenient to be tolerated long

So when twilight comes, doe-eyed,
And fog hangs like cannon smoke
He hefts his musket again, comes
Back to his place in the line.

TEXAS, 1935

You should have seen it when
Grass was more than a memory,
Before the dust. We ran some
Cattle here, let me tell you.
If you'd seen this place then,
Maybe you'd understand.
　　　　Maybe.

What magazine did you
Say you're working for?

The place never was much, I
        guess.
Not like the King Ranch—
I expect you've heard of that one.
Here in the Panhandle
It was always hard scrabble,
Root, hog, or die.

But it was mine, by God,
Every cactus, weed, and stock
        tank.

Still is.
        Still is.

Over where the fence posts are
        sticking up —
You can just see the tops
Poking out of the dunes —
We killed the biggest damn
Rattler you ever will see.
Eight feet if he was an inch.
That was the summer I broke my
        arm
Fixing the windmill.

Your readers want to know
Why I stay?
Hell, boy, I—

Tell 'em if they could have
Seen it before,
When grass was more
Than a memory.

You tell 'em that.

SESTINA

I.

Let muses mutter in thickets on Gilmer County's hills.
Transcribing their whispers, poets scribble in valleys.
Fern fronds rustle, water drips from rocks,
Clashing clouds scatter shadows on maple wood.
Sunlight speckles fawn's back; and white-tailed deer,
Alert in hemlocks, catch at phrases poets write.

II.

Like druids, muses circle oaks in ancient rite.
Their moss and lichen songs bombard the hills,
Stir to polkas fawn, doe, and antlered deer.
While bards of summer pen iambics in the valleys,
Windblown cacophonies echo from the wood,
And waterfalls shake sparkles over wrinkled rocks.

III.

In shale ledges: coal, petroleum ("oil of rocks"),
And runic petroglyphs—verses muses write.
Poets finger these inscriptions as they would
Interpret Braille on tombs half buried under hills.
Ghostly, seething winds sweep through brittle valleys;
Icy shards are mirrors glazing eyes of deer.

IV.

Let dancing muses trace the hoofprints left by deer
On greenbrier paths tangling sumacs near the rocks.
A silent snowfall fills crevasses in our valleys,
And every fox and titmouse believes it has the right
To tiptoe past retreats of poets built on hills,
Where window candles ray out circles in the wood.

V.

Ground moles, fieldmice, shrews in snowy heaps, where wood
Meets stone, avoid the hawks that soar above the deer.
One raptor's feather slowly spirals down the hills,
Drifts along the ridges, out to panthers' rocks.

The poet picks it off a spruce and with it starts to write,
While muses float on fogs that, wraith-like, numb the
valleys.

VI.

Let spring approach now, dispensing flavors in the valleys
Of dogtooth violets, bluets, fringe of yellowwood;
No muse instructs the slugs and snails in how to write
Their shimmering poems on grassy pastures grazed by deer.
The poet can only stare and clamber over rocks,
Unable to describe the green and golden hills.

Envoy

Barn owls hooting in valleys softly comfort deer;
Flickers drumming on wood scatter chips on rocks;
Poets try to write; and muses haunt the hills.

INCANTATION

    In the evening by the moonlight,
    Firelight, starlight;
    Read the faces in the June night,
    Owl light, tree light;
    See the traces of the sky light,
    Rock light, river light;
    Hear the stories in the twilight,
    Smoke light, ghost light;
    Smell the shadows in the moonlight.

ARLINE R. THORN

Elegy for My Brother Joe

1

The road follows the creek, Broad Run,
past the farm where we grew up.
Shadowed in trees, running between the fields,
rippling easy between the amber pools
banked with Joe Pye weed
bugs striding the blue surface
crawdads hiding in the green deeps
the creek flows toward the river, unhurried, deliberate.

Vultures lift on currents of air
as if death never interrupted.

Where does the creek begin?
I think somewhere on Union Ridge
where they are singing hymns and holding revival
at the campground in the pines.

2

I know where the creek empties
laden with clouds and floating leaves
into the powerful, gentle Ohio—
not far from a place in some ragged pines
where you emptied out your own life's blood.

A white plume floats up
from the power plant on the river to join
white veins of cloud in the opaque
blue stone of summer sky.

Far up the stream, in high open fields
perched on the steel tower
a young red-tailed hawk screams.

3

Clouds of Queen Anne's lace
bloom in your great-grandfather's fields
all around the home place you will never inherit
where the children you will never father
would be riding your powerful shoulders.

Shoulders and chest of a blacksmith
but couldn't hammer the darkness
Hand and eye of a locksmith
but couldn't unlock the pain
Skill of mechanic, you couldn't make it run
You couldn't climb on it like a motorcycle
and ride it where you wanted to go.

4

Mom is weeding the bright green lettuce
in the garden planted after the cold wet spring
where the sweet corn will never ripen.

Dad is watching the men drill a well
where the apple trees have already been cut down
and the beehives have been taken away.

They find water a hundred feet down
in the ancient white sands
on top of a thin seam of coal.

5

What is the source, brother,
of the power in the stream?

Could you not swim easy from ripple to pool
from river to cloud to rain?
Where is the water of life to be found
and how do you drink it?

For you, the roadside cornflowers
a pair of goldfinches picking the white-winged seeds
the deep blue lobelia, spray of blackberries
and sumac clusters like the flames of pentecost.

The Idea of the Table

begins in the tree —
ingrained by a branch
the stress, old scars and knots
interrupting straight and true
He tells me about the wood
the shape in it
cutting it
He works, constructs
the forms that are there
and the image in the brain
the shape in the hand
the acts of eye and nerve
making the table of an idea
& we finish it together
The poem of the table
that began in the tree
working always, still with the grain—
The dream of the table
is figured in the wood

Exploring the Poles

You my South Pole—together
we traverse the farthest ice sheets
skirting the edge of
the crevasse—

sheltering in a frail tent
from howling storms—
my upside-down continent.
Quiet nights you enchant
me with polyphonic colors—
          aurora australis.
And I your Alaska
of volcanic ranges
terrible white bears
wandering caribou
salmon rivers
and short, brilliant summers—
          eider and curlew.
Exploring each other's map
writing the names of rivers, bays
camps and unknown peaks—
tasting strange berries, moss, meats—
We will be fishers
hawks, hunters
          fat in fall, lean in spring.

The Old Family Album

Here are forgotten faces; my grandsire
Clad in smart uniform and forage cap;
Grandmother (her first baby on her lap)
With hoop-skirts wide and other quaint attire;
My mother next, in satin bridal gown
And veil adorning her sweet girlish grace,
Her hand on father's shoulder; his young face
Be-whiskered like some statesman of renown;
Those aunts in basques and bustles; and that elf
In frilly frock and sash—my first sweetheart;
Who is this dimpled infant? With a start,
I recognize him as my long-lost self.
These pages are not for the jester's eye;
I close the book and gently lay it by.

The Still, Small Voice

If you could shut your mouth for a few minutes
you might be able to hear it.
And if you can hear it, maybe you can figure out
just what it's all about.

It's about the moaning sound of
ice breaking up on the river,
It's about finding panther tracks
in the chicken yard of a morning,
It's about losing three brothers
in three days
to Typhoid Fever.

It's about the lonely beauty of
a crisp September dawn.
It's about not knowing where
the old stories end and the new ones begin.
It's about working the best you can,
playing the best you can,
remembering the best you can.

Listen for the rhythm, for the lilt
in those old-timers' voices; sweet
like a banjo tune and lonesome
like a fiddle.

A Beautiful Jar of Jelly
for Dwight Diller, Kirk Judd and David Morris

I grew up with people who made music, and made sense.

Rogue uncles and button-shoed aunts,
who'd come to Sunday dinner

in their proud brown coats
sewn on the treadle machine,
and fastened with mismatched buttons
rescued from other coats
that could no longer be patched.

Crow-eyed bachelor men
who lived on the hillside and smelled
of fried potatoes and machine oil,
men who shaved on Sunday and
always brought by a loaf of bread
or a sack of tomatoes when they
walked past the house
on their way into town.

Stern-faced baptist ladies who'd tell us
"I know your mama"
whenever we got caught
where we shouldn't have been.
Women who'd always ask after your granddaddy,
who'd say things like *"he ain't got a lick of sense"*
or *"what a beautiful jar of jelly."*

Old fiddlers who had to toss their whiskers
over their shoulder so
they wouldn't get
caught up in the bow,
and the older-still women
who sang murder ballads while they
swept off the back steps or
cut out biscuits with a tin can.

The finest times at our house
were summer evenings on the front porch.
I'd fall asleep on my granny's broad lap
listening to the bullfrog plunk of the banjo
and the katydid fiddle sing.

Father

I remember how I first saw my father.
He was a big man, with big hands.
He staggered a little.
Dressed in a dark suit, crisp white shirt,
and wide tie.
Always wore a wide-brimmed fedora,
Cocked to one side.

Cowering, small, I hid in the shadows,
To me, he was a giant.
Loud-voiced, slurred speech,
Curved over my little mom.

Hiding together, I comfort my baby sister.
Shhh, don't cry, he'll see us,
Shhh, soon he'll be gone,
Gone down the road again.

Turnings

She talks to trees of late
in mental rustlings, a half-
speech bright with musings,
just this side of summer. Days
trail with fruit in memory, opulent,
and a lazy hum returns to drowse
in circles round a full-blown rose,
like scented music from two rooms
away, while late warm days spin
their dusty yellow over afternoons.

The trees answer her, trembling. Their
leaves, sensing a change, hoard green
like gold. With dry mouths they shape
a prophecy peculiar as landscapes seen
by moonlight, when familiar paths turn
shimmering strange and sidewalks, grass,
melt into silver pools. But first they
will gather the rose's red, the sunny
orange, the purpling plum, and scatter
them on the wind like colored notes.

White Witch of Moss Creek
In Memory of Ann Hudak

Mrs. Hudak summoned me next door
innumerable days, *Come here, honey, will ya?*
Mud-pie dirty, shaking a bit from eagerness
to please, or hearing in my head the warning
not to tell our business ever, I'd lean
against her belly, grab a bunch of housedress
for support, let her wipe my face with her hem.
There now. See how pretty? Yes, Sugar, yes.

Croons soft as cream, incantatory, fed an ache;
hands grown wise wrestling life cupped
and steadied mine, pressed in one a shiny nickel.
A pound of minced ham, okay? A loaf of bread.
And tell Agnes put it on the new two weeks.
(an emphasis, a testing measured pace I later learned
we use on high-strung children, or some luckless witness who,
stunned insensible had fate been kind, stays keenly conscious).
She held my eyes, turned hers to mirrors, then set me free
to seek in errands a self beyond the smoking dumps of boney.
Magic mute, I bowed to portals, washhouse, giddy with belief,
and saw behind the company store, in water, a castle's shadow.

But that was long ago—some forty years. Last spring
her son, her daughters—noble grieving masks—
received her tributes. I tried to tell her power,
how once she caught me, falling, with her eyes,
and sent me, dancing, jeweled, erect, to meet my life.
They seemed confused, uncomprehending. Or perhaps
they guessed I never told her.
                    Outside, the stars were white
as doves in darkened choir lofts, waiting to sing.

HOG KILLING

It's hog killing time in the mountains.
The chill is short-legging it
Up and down the hillsides,
And the six men around the fire
Are talking in winter's code.

They stand, breathe, and listen to
The blood drip from out the hog.

    The hog stands on tiptoes
    Ten inches off the ground
    Reaching for a sky
    That's no longer there

Some of the guts lie
Twisted & knotted in a
Wheeling Steel washtub.
Its handles, thin galvanized loops on
A ten cent coffin, stick out
Waiting the pall
Bearers.

    Cars fly by on 52,
    Few see the life-sucking gash
    Up the hog's middle

But every now and then, before the curve
Steals them back, someone points.
It is interesting.
Even if we have eggs
We can't fry eggs and bacon, or
Eggs and sausage, if we don't have
Hogs gutted and hanging by the roadside.

Hog's guts in washtubs. Men standing
in the cold — freezing and dreaming
Of eggs.

It's hog killing time in the mountains

New England Light

Yeh Mr. Coal Man
I see you comin home
Weavin round ruts
In your rusty Dodge

And I watch you get out
Spit a stream brown
As a shined shoe
On Sunday

Walk up to the house
Slow, gatherin breath
Like you're a tourist
Never seen it before

Never seen the old lady
Or the dogs, the creek
Sycamores speckled and
Stretching over fast water

The earth has an eager
Early taste of you
The hoot owl calls
In the black of night

Your kids run the roads
Burnin gas like it's youth
The Tee-Vee News seems

Far away as atom bombs
Hittin on Pigeon Creek
Still your E-Z Boy satisfies

Sometimes Saturday night's
Honky Tonk hot dogs
George Jones & Falls City
Must seem a fair reward
For them eight hours or
Doublebacks in the hole

But that top'd just
Soon fall as not
And no matter your color
You're colored coal
Every seam in your body
Is stitched black as rich dirt

Your life's hot coal, fired
As the whites of your eyes
Gums shinin pink, teeth white
As New England light

DIARY OF A MAD BOMBER
(or: Martin County Is a Blast)

I mean
   if you woke up
   one
   day
Boulder in your
   mobile home bed
Both parents
   young but older
than your 2-1/2 years
    dead

& Billy Edd's
        Jed
Jethrodaiseymae
Burley-Q says,
amongst farts & fishin,
        "I never thought
it would happen, now that
it's happened,
        ain't no use
        to
        worry
        about it"

then
 you'd
        make damn sure
        THE sheriff
        didn't catch you
        blackstrap molassin
them earth strippin
        machines
them deer drivin
        sigh-reens
jack still rippin
        my dreams
them
earth mother
muckers

It was the Wind

It was the wind,
The laughing voice of the wind
Playing on the strings
Of memory
With the little fingers
Of the pine trees
Above my head...

I thought it was you--
But it was the wind,
Playing with memory--
Memory as futile
As the grasping of
The little fingers
Of the pine trees
On the rumbling wind...

There'll Be a Tomorrow
(For Clifton and Mary Bryant)

In all my wanderings
I've gone most to the poor
who are adept at hiding pain.
Sometimes the mountain man
does it stolid, ox-like,
revealing scant emotion.
But I know there is a cry inside
a flute song hungering for words
and maybe a curse...

On Cabin Creek I eat and sleep
in the makeshift home

of a disabled miner.
Hurt lies heavy on the house
but the deepest hurt is still unworded.

There is a today on Cabin Creek—
ghost town mining camps
miners who sit idle
drawing DPA checks
while machines drag coal from under the mountains
and bulldozers tear the mountains down
mixing with cesspool creek filth—
a today swallowed in poverty's greedy gullet.

There was a yesterday on Cabin Creek
Paint Creek, Matewan, Logan—
yesterday with heroes, heroines and hope—
Mother Blizzard, Mother Jones
and women ripping up rails and crossties
that the Baldwin Felts armored train
might not pass,
a yesterday with Bill Blizzard
and a hundred others indicted for treason
by courts doing corporation bidding,
a yesterday with Steve Mangus shot dead
and the long march to Logan.
Seven thousand Kanawha Valley miners
with rifles, shotguns and pistols
on the long march to Logan...

Woods Colt

Walking between low mountains
In the poolroom's yard of brown beer glass
Broken as the coal was
Broken into pebbles of dissipated
Texture, I stepped contented.

Only jungle cats could
Walk more softly and more proud,
More tenderly strong, following
The code of never-afraid.
Following the clean way of temptation.

The seed was planted
By lowbrow benchers carrying
Past to present in vulgar whispers.
"Whose daddy are you, young gentleman?"

Head high to the black purse
I looked above and the
Carrier mother put me at guard.
"You've no call to play
With bums, with asking fools."

At what untelling age I
Comprehended and at what
Reversed meanings I know not now.
The bench birth of truth
Put me at question and at limp.

From which loin and tree
Sprang the never proud, the
Nervous walker, the drying me?
I ask the lone companion bee,
Heaven and the symmetry.

Going for Cows

Maybe you have gone barefoot
For cows at dawn, sucking in moon
Mist rising as out of sleep
In icy grasses, and slapped the heavy
Shadows of bone to raise hind-first
And stood on dry-warm spots where they
Have lain mooing in a field of dew—

Well, so you understand.

The going out for and bringing in
Of cows may be bewitching.
This shadow hopping from spot of warmth
To spot was from the larger cold
My game, and largely self imposed.
So when I hear complaints of sweat
Turned blood, a world turned ice, and hearts
Rare islands of warmth and few between,
I think that folks are driving cows
Before them to the barns they choose
And could, if cold enough, wear shoes.

SILENT MOUNTAINS

What it was was never much, I know
A camp, the hills—only the fallen snow
Could flatter what every other day
Saw fading bare and oily grey.
But it was home.
It was a place to go.

The noise was closer than the air it rode
From coal car and tipple—it was sewed
In the ear, as if it were a fly

Pushing against the glass and wanting by.
It ached inside
The car. It's aching still.

It is not that I mourn my youth that's lost
Or grow weary at how the years get tossed
One on one in this fumed memory of mine.
Sad would be the word. I say be kind
To one who cannot prove
He was a boy

By pointing to a tree, a house or creek
And saying from behind a rutted cheek
"It was this world I was born into.
My father carried off this hill on his shoe
Into the house.
My mother swept it out."

Now the town itself is swept away.
The grey and crumbling houses are the whey
Of three hundred lives, as near as many broods
Who had to bide the mountain and its moods.

The mountain stands
Silent now, biding other mountains.

CHRISTMAS IN COALTOWN

Tonight the men lift pokes instead of coal.
Their backs are puzzled by the lack of weight
And wish it were as easy lifting slate.
This work is play and good for a miner's soul.

They ride in the company truck by every door
Opening as they approach from the house below.
The fire spreads across the bluish snow
Tinting bearers of gifts from the company store.

And not a man but wishes these light sacks
Of nuts and candy and sweet tangerines
Were costlier gifts to suit the children's dreams,
Toys, and clothes to wear upon their backs.

But the men laugh. They laugh and they spread cheer
To the kid who takes a bag and darts back in
Behind the window, sending out his grin.
They may not laugh again the rest of the year.

THE CRAFT SHOP

"If you like somebody treatin' ye quaint,
You wait on 'em. I tell ye I ain't
About to be exhibit A
For snobby tourists hunting a way
To color their trip along the edge
Of our mountains. Let's see you wedge
A dollar out of their deep pockets.
They gawk till their eyes pop the sockets,
But buy? No, they're eyeing you
Mostly, glancing to see if one shoe
Matches the other. You love Mankind,
Or so you talk. See if you find
One thing to love about city folks
That figure us for dumb slowpokes.
Ah. Lordy!"
    It was my brother's defense
Which bowed daily to his business sense
And put him through the curtained door
With: "Howdy, and what can I do-ye-for?"

I never saw more genuine ardor
Or humor in a mountain martyr.

Cardinal Singing   *July 7, 1998*

"Do not sit by my grave and weep,
I am not there, I do not sleep…"
—Excerpt from American Indian death song

This morning at dawn my father came,
red feathered, singing the cardinal song.
His death, one year gone, and I am anointed again
with his attendance pulling me into the day;
His celebrations slip silently into my spirit.

There are hayfields waving,
others turn in the sun,
give up their back-throat bouquet;
Scythes wait for the rhythm of his sweep,
the grace of his stance
reflected in lanky country boys
shirtless at the afternoon roadsides;

There are grease-covered hands
lathered with Lava, waiting to dip
into galvanized buckets of spring water,
come up, palms pink,
nails and cuticles smudged and dark.

Somewhere gardens wait at the top of farms
their pale red dirt, dry and anxious for the crunch of hoe,
the dip of spade into potato hills;
Onion patches and cucumber vines
whisper his presence, give up the taste memory,
and I rejoice in the rich yellow offering of peaches.

There are tools expecting to be hung in garages
on pegboards made of plywood and nails;
to be clunked and clanked, used daily
and wiped with the rags of old white undershirts;

Waiting to be borrowed and returned,
borrowed and not returned.

Old songs hang thick in the air each Saturday;
Jeannie and her light brown hair, *Clementine*
and *Buffalo Gals*, come 'round the mountains
and drop from tenor voices which drift
over cowboys dropping roses on graves;
Tunes which glide and hum unexpectedly,
enter my mind with the turn of morning light.

Water and weeds, packs of plump unfiltered cigarettes;
Bicycles, wagons, wheelbarrows, posthole diggers,
linoleum, doors and windows moved so pianos
and music can move into the lives of daughters
who wait to write over and over
the story of their life made lucid by his.

No ending to the celebration
passed from his life to mine,
the wisdom of wind, the promises made
in rain and echoed by thunder.
I come to his grave ready to wail
but laugh, touch grass and grain,
lift song and thanksgiving toward each shape
he conjures now, to touch my life.

Manassas, Virginia (1861)

In, to the syrup of sleep I turn
and pray that if I wake
it be a hundred years hence
when the graves
of the boys and men
have grown smooth with grass,
when this meadow no longer
smells of blood and powder,

but has grown ripe
with corn and hay.
Let me wake after
the farmers have tilled
and cleared away
all shot and cannon balls
all severed arms and legs.
Only cicadas screaming in this valley
only rain falling
only men singing
and sleeping with women.

Like Patent Leather Shoes

When I was a child my father sold linoleum.
He knew the right design to make any place
look like patent leather shoes.

He could lay linoleum, make the patterns match,
curve it around the door sill so it wouldn't
curl and nothing could catch or trip.

He picked the perfect one,
installed it so that a double red line
split the room I shared with my sister;
gave us a single neutral square at the door
to enter or exit in young anger
when we tried to divide our lives.

Before the first grade he taught me
to spell the word, to say the word,
to enjoy the way it fills the mouth.
He let the alliteration of it push me into poetry.

Linoleum has always been
one of my favorite words.

Tongue to the pallet "li,"
the calming mantra "nou,"
tongue to the pallet again "li,"
pleasure hummed in the throat "em."

Linoleum.
Billy Greenhorn took that word,
made it his girlfriend, his
"T-total-perfect for all night dancin" girlfriend.

Oh Bill, how I miss you. If I had known you,
you could have helped me make a new word,
a new ship slip pattern on the floor word,
a word I can use to tell your friend
in the old brown, under the street lamp hat, that
his name in my mouth is better than linoleum.

Estate Auction
Corner Cupboard, circa 1840

I don't know hardly nothin'
about that corner cupboard,
'cept she said it was her momma's.

I always thought it strange,
how she kept it in the front room.
Had that straight back arm chair always on the left,
her knittin' or crocheting on the floor.

I know she felt it special though,
every Sunday after service
she'd get the bee's wax out and work on it.
Only chore she'd do that day.

Never knew for sure what she kept inside.
But they tell me them auction men

found nothing, 'cept her Herbert's wedding band,
the jar of wax, a tin-type of her mom and dad,
a postcard of a hotel in Edinburgh—
only thing that one could read was her name
everything else had been erased...
oh yes,   and a baby gown.

I remember back that spring
when her little Ella died. I'd stop by real regular
and no matter when I'd come, she'd be there
sittin' right in front of that cupboard,
like it was a person, sometimes crying,
sometimes talking, sometimes just sitting.
Did that, way up into fall. Took that death real hard
but who wouldn't, their only child and all.

I remember a couple of times later,
when I'd be there and she'd be talking,
usually 'bout something sad,
she'd make a point of walking by,
touching it, right up there where the molding
joins the door just beside the hinge.

And when her husband died so quick last winter
I one time saw her napping on the floor
curled up against the base.
A woman her age got no need for sleeping on the floor.

Suppose since she was so young
when her mother died, she felt
that cabinet held some power, some comfort,
some way of keeping her momma with her.

Don't know who'd want to buy that cupboard
that old wood, carrying all that pain
deep in its grain.

Remembering

The moon wore a sleeve of blue silk
the night we drove back
from the reading at Wesleyan College.
You pointed through fog to a splash
of lightning between two hills
and said you wished the ride would never end.
My sleepy eyes watching your fingers
massage the steering wheel,
I wanted to say the same thing—
but just kept talking
about cartoons and old music.
Between us,
we said, we knew
every important song of the last 30 years.
And realizing we had sat
on living room carpets
at different ends of the continent
and blinked seven-year-old eyes
in the same shows' flicker,
we rode on slowly
and sang along with the radio.

MOUNTAIN WRITER

Words flow like sunlight
to hill top,
like fragrance
from a mountain bloom.
Through his miles of upward climb,
years of listening to the voices
of mountain people,
he has become one with the hills.

No man can write
of more than he is.
No depth of writing bubbles
from the shallow life.
Wrap life around you
like a winter coat.
Words jerked from the brain
like carp pulled from a muddy stream
spoil fast. No one can write
of more than he knows,
believes in,
or dreams about.

CALL ME BAD

I'm not going to be a good girl
in my next life.
Especially, I'm not going
to love everybody.
Like that old son-of-a-gun
preacher who told her
she wouldn't be depressed
if she had more faith—
thought positive and prayed.

Warned her against psychologists,
told her to pull herself up
by her bootstraps
and get more faith—faith—faith.

Well, I've got the faith
to tell you
I'm not going to be a good girl
in my next life.
I'm gonna grab up
that old son of a hawk
and if I have to walk
every step of the way
I'm dragging him to the Grand Canyon
so I'll have a good place
to throw him over.

I'm going to snatch him up
by his long oily tongue
whirl him around my head three times
and sling him over.
Then, I'll lean over that rim
and send words THUNDERING
into the canyon.
"Think positive, brother.
Grab a bootstrap. Get more
faith—faith—faith."
Words will bounce off those walls,
echo, and follow him
all the way to the bottom.

I'm going to be a bad girl
in my next life
and it occurs to me
maybe I better start practicing
a little bad right now.

To Lone Wolf

There we were, all hundred and fifty or so
Standing at our seats like stalks of corn in windless rows,
And I planted on the left corner of the last
Had perfect view from below the shoulders
Of most suits and showy dresses
Ahead of me, it seemed for miles,
And all across the room they stood.

When from the corner of my diagonal self
smoke arose and spread, fanned and floated by the feather
Across the front, above the heads it rode the air
And began beautifully smelling its way to me
Down the side, just beside and then behind
Gracefully gone along the back and up the
Far side to meet its circling self.

Thus Lone Wolf, the Apache brave, the Brave Apache
Purified the class, the room, by sage and rose
The spirit knew what mind could not explain.
In an instant our world was changed,
And heavy air hovered there.

I could SEE the power of prayer.

Prayer for Prayer

Solitude so perfect it's not lonely:
grant us, merciful God/dess, this sense
just once of satisfying prayer
— each of us Your one and only
supplicant. We'll bat across the back fence
dark things difficult to share.

We'll need new words. Nothing off-the-shelf
can quite express our urgent need
simply to confess, unburden, and unbind.
Most prayers turn out like talking to oneself
even with the spirit up to speed
and quiet mollifying the mind.

Accept our words and thoughts as psalms
— or merely our most pitiful candle lamp
that quavers toward the author of desire.
Admit their doubt. And more, admit my qualms.
I feel like a monkey creeping into camp
to worry embers from your fire.

Remedio Farms the Sonoran Desert

I have been thinking about this many nights now
— when I leave here and go, no more on this Earth —
that I should begin to prepare for that.

I'm working today to make a new field
and a shrine nearby. See,
my mind has been going this way
— that I should be planting things,

leaving little green things growing up.

Gathering the smoothened arroyo stones
for a shrine—*That's* how I want to be remembered
by my grandchildren, and for the live things
that will just keep growing.

Tend the Earth and help the desert yield its food—

Remedio was leaning on his shovel
looking out over the desert
talking to me as if *listening*
for the things he wanted to say

for their meaning to rise out of the desert and come to him.

Acid Rain

Upriver, handymen sell their houses back to Strout Realty.
Eyeball enough un-plumb jambs and rolling floors
and you can sniff apocalypse some distance off.

Here in the floodplain, sandbags sell dear.
Fishermen line their boats on rings that slide
up and down tall poles struck deep to the river's bed.

Reverend Osgood preachifies that apocalypse
is the launching pad of good theology. Even so,
they know the river's rising. They know
you'd best get yourself to higher ground.
Even the earthworms have started clearing out, Salamanca says.
Let them that have eyes to see, see.

The reverend tries to teach the kids to whistle up
the separate syllables of *eschatology.*
"Put it all together later," he says.
Salamanca says, no way. They think it's just

one more spitball needs ducking in this life.
Let them that have ears to hear, hear.

Letitia McBride tells Salamanca last night's warm winds
blew from the wrong direction. Evil, she says. Such winds.
They enter your barn door and lift the whole shebang
clean off the ground. Letitia suspects
that wasn't what Malachi meant—was it?—about God
flinging open heaven's windows. Salamanca says, "Repent.
It's the tenth portion that anchors your barn."

BOONE COUNTY BOUNTY

from The Appalachian Suite

"What's fer ya?" spit the cook in my direction.
Spaghetti proved to be my predilection.
The setting was a "greasy spoon" in Boone.
I'd hit the town of Madison a trifle after noon.

A continental cuisine I was fed —
French dressing for my salad, Grecian bread.
With pie and coffee added to the order,
The damage came to four bucks and a quarter.

The sauce was spicy, laced with local gossip...
The pasta fair...The salad was a tossup...
But with the gay abandon of the trip,
I left a brand-new dollar as a tip.

My coal-town host appeared to claim my bill,
And as he scooped my six bits from his titillated till —
"A most delightful repast, sir," I lied.
"And how'd ya like yore dinner?" he replied.

PETER ZIVKOVIC

IN THE NAME OF THE SON AND THE HOLY GHOST

He crawled out of my loins
when I was just a careless
kid myself.
Raised him as my own
for two years
of weekends and furloughs
bought groceries and shelter.
He was handsomer than
the son I had in later wedlock.
Lively kid. Bright.
Lying in the crook of my arm
his dreams woke me from mine...
When I left his hot country
for my own, I received
from his mother
letters with love in them
and pictures and I—
I answered with money:
a year of guilt tithes.

"He is a good boy, I am proud.
He wears coins on chains
around his neck.
He has too many girlfriends
but he treats them gently.
He is a good boy. I am proud."

I dreamed of trees
in the rolling snow, branches
burning in winter sunshine,
angels washing away sins. I
bought meat and milk and insurance
for my family,

earned raises and promotions,
attended club meetings, even
coached a little league team.

"He is a good boy.
You would be proud and you
would love him."

But I do love him, I remember!
"He wears money in pouches
on chains around his neck.
His is handsome and everybody
loves him. Everybody."

And I dreamed of dark children
clawing a way into an unfinished
world made by strangers,
lively little boy faces
and wrong names.
I paid taxes and dues
right on time
for three eternities.

"He has turned brutal I don't know why.
He is coming to America,
believe me I tried to slap him.
Beware. He has learned somewhere
to use weapons. He is lean and
has the hard eyes of his father."

Yes, and around his neck
are chains, chains with money
and everybody loves him,
everybody, and he is coming
to claim the father he never had
coming hard
with money around his neck
and a gun in his boot

and now I see him.
He has found me
and I see him coming and
he is Jesus,
Jesus coming at me
with a knife in his teeth
and his bones showing.

THIEF

"Who are we, anyhow?
What do we belong to?
Are we a we?"
     — Anne Sexton, from *Protestant Easter*

Damn you're a fine one
to call her a thief!
All these people
sticking their heads in idle cars
and live, unlit ovens,
jumping off January bridges and
blowing away their heads
and stuff. And you,
you talk about "a dumb prayer," and
"with your mouth into the sheet."
Ha! You talk!
"Perjury of the soul indeed."
You who purged the world
of your words
you "damn bitch."
How I wish I'd been there
when you sucked
that garageful of fumes—
I'd have kicked your sweet poetic ass
all the way to that hell
you ordained for yourself,
you classic faker without

even the guts of your own guilt.
Remember when you said
"I keep right on going on?"
What happened? Where did you go
after you didn't write to me again
that time in Boston?
You keeper of the pure purple
did you sit comfortably
or get down on your knees and
breathe deeply for quickness?
"Death's a sad bone; bruised, you'd say."
I didn't march to your funeral,
damn you, and
they closed the lid too soon
and too slowly, too, to suit me.
I didn't tug my hair out either
or bang on wash tubs. Instead
I hid my face for a week
and went back into your words.
Particularly the ones that go
"....Live, Live because of the sun,
the dream, the excitable gift."

SPECIAL BUCK OF MINE

        Boy this buck
bulled past high timber in mid-morning,
blurred white burr of a tail brushing
through thickets, lurching
as he sensed me
        A numb salt of joy
lumped in my throat: I knew as well as he
where he'd come out of that pattern.
I ripped around trees, over briars,
lungs catching anticipation.
I loved that buck already — for being mine.

Through tangled sedge, now leaping
the barbed fence, leaping like Olympians
but proud that it was only a minor
accomplishment, leaping then and
pouncing to one knee there
at the clearing's edge, knowing within ten yards
where my buck would come bounding out
of the bullrush, knowing,
    sure in knowing.
Half an instant before I expected,
he came. Ready as life, I laced
that bullet into his shoulder
more perfect than dreams, the earth
breaking his heart instantly, gluing
his neck to the sudden ground, tumbling
over his flash of pain, hugging the land.

Even after I bled him, he was heavy
to heave to my back. Nice the way
blood seeped around my neck, trickled
down my chest, that proud warm
thickness, final trace of life.
But then—then—he sighed on my shoulders.

It was no guilt indifferently arranged
by Gods and nations; it was that buck,
    sighing.

There was the proud and primed alert
specimen, me, and there was merely
a buck deer floating through forests
hoping he'd never have to sigh dead on
strong young bloody shoulders.
    When
I put him down on the smokehouse
floor, I kissed his eyes and wept.

Wild Sweet Notes

Publishers Place, Inc. is a nonprofit consortium. Our mission is *to encourage, promote and elevate the quality of the publishing arts in West Virginia for citizens of all ages.*

Thank you for your support through purchase of Publishers Place, Inc., products and through sponsorships.

INDEX

OF THE POETS AND THE POEMS

BIOGRAPHICAL INFORMATION

WILMA STANLEY ACREE has published in several journals including *Appalachian Heritage, Crazy River,* and *West Virginia Medical Journal.* She has read her work in various venues, including the Columbus, Ohio, "Poetry in the Park" series. She has presented writing workshops nationally as well as regionally. Her chapbook *About Bee Robbing and Other Things* was published in 1995 by Tantra Press. She is an active member of West Virginia Writers, Inc., and The Ohio Valley Literary Group.

GAIL GALLOWAY ADAMS has had stories and poems published in *The American Voice, The Georgia Review, The North American Review,* and elsewhere. Her collection of short fiction, *The Purchase of Order,* won the Flannery O'Connor Award and has been reissued in paperback. She is on the permanent workshop staff at Wildacres Writers Conference in Little Switzerland, North Carolina, and in 1991 was the McGee Professor in Creative Writing at Davidson College. She is now on the creative writing faculty in the English department at West Virginia University. She was named West Virginia Professor of the Year by the Carnegie Foundation for the Advancement of Teaching in 1995. She is completing a novel and continues to write short stories.

JEAN ANAPORTE-EASTON is associate professor of English at West Virginia State College. Her work has appeared in *The Anthology of Magazine Verse* and *Yearbook of American Poetry, 13th Moon* and *Mid-American Review.* She is the editor of *Breathing from the Belly: Etheridge Knight on Poetry and Freedom* (University of Michigan Press). She has taught poetry in universities, prisons, and mental health facilities.

COLLEEN ANDERSON is the author of *The New West Virginia One-Day Trip Book.* She has had stories and poems published by the PEN Syndicated Fiction Project, *Redbook, Embers, Kestrel, Carolina Quarterly, The Sun,* and other periodicals. Her songs have been featured on Public Radio International's "Mountain Stage" and "The Folk Sampler." She lives in Charleston, West Virginia.

MAGGIE ANDERSON spent most of her growing-up years in Buckhannon, West Virginia. Her new and selected poems, *Windfall,* has just been released from the University of Pittsburgh Press. Her previous volumes include *A Space Filled with Moving* and *Cold Comfort.* She is the editor of *Hill Daughter: New and Selected Poems by Louise McNeill* and co-editor of *A Gathering of Poets* and *Learning by Heart: Contemporary American Poetry About School.* Anderson teaches at Kent State University where she directs the Wick Poetry Program and edits the Wick Poetry Series through the Kent State University Press.

BOB HENRY BABER, a native of Richwood, West Virginia, has migrated back and forth across time and distance to reclaim his Appalachian heritage. A prolific poet and essayist, he once ran for governor of West Virginia. He has a Ph.D. in creative writing from The Union Institute and is a Kellogg fellow. He earns his living doing residencies in writing in the schools, most recently in Loraine, Ohio.

LOUISE S. BAILEY, a Florida native, joined the Marshall University English department in 1961. Now retired in Huntington, she continues her interest in poetry, which began with her first published poem at age nine. She has won prizes and honorable mentions from Ohio Poetry Day, West Virginia Writers, and *Writer's Digest* annual contests. She has published poems in *Lucidity, Summerfield Journal, New Voices, ESC! Magazine, Poet, Z Miscellaneous, Hill and Valley, Guyandotte Poets I, Innisfree,* and others. She also writes dramatic monologs.

MELISSA BAILEY was killed February 28, 1986, at the age of 21 in an automobile accident in Key West, Florida. A native of Pineville, West Virginia, she graduated from Pineville High School and studied writing at George Mason University and Mary Mount College of Virginia and Concord College of West

Virginia. Melissa traveled widely, visiting China and the Far East and the North American continent from coast to coast. She authored a novel and several short stories and essays, as well as many poems, collected in the volume *From the Beyond.*

JOSEPH BARRETT (1950-1990) was a West Virginia native. He was born in Montgomery and went to high school in Richwood, at the southern end of the Monongahela National Forest. He attended Bethany College and studied at Oxford and in the Middle East. He was internationally published, his poems appearing in literary journals in Japan, France, and Australia, as well as the U.S. In 1988, he co-edited VENUE, a literary anthology. He published two poetry collections, *Roots Deep in Sand* and *Periods of Lucidity,* and had completed a third, *Blue Planet Memoirs,* at the time of his death.

JOE BASILONE grew up in Virginia and moved to West Virginia in 1967 after discharge from the Marine Corps. He studied writing under the late Ray Rohrbaugh at West Virginia Wesleyan College. He lived in Randolph County and was active with the Cheat Mountain Poets in the 1970s. In 1986 he moved to James City County, Virginia, where he still resides. He has a second home on Hatteras Island, North Carolina, where he is a contributor to *The Island Breeze,* a monthly magazine. He is seeking a publisher for *The Tides of November,* a novel about West Virginians fishing at Hatteras. He is married to the former Bonny Bibb of Charleston; they have two sons.

JEAN BATTLO, writer and educator, is a lifelong resident of McDowell County, West Virginia, where she is currently at work on a commissioned drama based on the murder of Sid Hatfield and Ed Chambers at the Welch County Courthouse. The play, whose working title is "Terror of the Tug," and her musical "Life/A Celebration" are scheduled for production in summer 2000. Besides writing poetry, she has also written articles on historical subjects.

LAURA TREACY BENTLEY is from Huntington, West Virginia. Her poems have appeared in *Poetry Ireland Review, The New*

York Quarterly, Art Times, Blue Violin, Eureka Literary Magazine, Small Pond, Controlled Burn, Pine Mountain Sand and Gravel, and *Grab-a-Nickel,* among others, and in three anthologies, *Getting the Knack: Twenty Poetry Writing Exercises, A Gathering at the Forks: The Guyandotte Poets I,* and *Weeping with Those Who Weep.* In 1994 she won a Fellowship for Literature from the West Virginia Commission on the Arts, and her poetry collection, *Elemental,* won second place at the West Virginia Writers, Inc., state competition in 1998.

ELAINE BLUE, poet, playwright, author, was born and raised in West Virginia. She has molded the minds of children by being an elementary school teacher, a counselor, and a community organizer. Now living in Huntington, she graduated from Marshall University and is an activist for children and female rights. She reinforces the value of African American culture and the family in the world. She has written and published four books of poems. Currently, she is working on another book of poems and a novel. She has written several plays which have gained her awards and national recognition. Her plays have been performed throughout West Virginia, Ohio, and Kentucky in women's prisons, at culture centers, on university campuses, in night clubs, and in public forums. Her poetry speaks of life.

EVERETT F. BRIGGS, a retired Roman Catholic priest, has published poetry since his late teens. After being interned as a P.O.W. in Japan, he served as professor of Japanese in the U.S. Navy V-12 Training Program. He has written Haiku poems published in Japanese journals. His English poetry has been published in American reviews since 1925. A collection of some 650 of his poems, *Across the Bridge,* was published in 1996. Of his twelve books of poetry, six were written in Japanese. He currently is administrator of a nursing home in Monongah, West Virginia.

JOSEPH BUNDY was born in Bluefield, West Virginia, where he now resides. He is a graduate of Marshall University. He is a performer, writer and the founder and artistic director of the Afro-Appalachian Performance Company. Since 1990, he has been a contracted History Alive Scholar for the West Virginia Humanities Council. His literary works include three plays, *In the Pink, Banns,* and *To Do His Will*; two volumes of verse, *Freedom and Love: A Dream for Blues People,* and *Springs Eternal,* and one essay, "Why Are We Free."

ELEANOR BUSH, of Philippi, West Virginia, is an amateur botanist and has published scientific articles in botanical journals. Her poems have appeared in *Bird Digest, Grab-a-Nickel, Pokeberry Days,* and *Bird Verse Portfolios #9,* the Audio-Visual Poetry Foundation, and elsewhere.

MICHAEL E. "Jim" BUSH is a native of Gilmer County, West Virginia, and holds a B.A. in English and speech from Glenville College and an M.A. in English Literature from Marshall University. He has taught in the public schools and community colleges since 1965 and has been publishing poems since his undergraduate years. The winner of more than three hundred poetry awards around the country, he currently lives in Ripley, West Virginia, and serves as editor of *Laurels,* the quarterly journal of the West Virginia Poetry Society.

EDWARD J. CABBELL is, in his own words, "an African-Appalachian." Born and raised in a McDowell County coal mine and railroad community, he founded the John Henry Memorial Foundation and Festival, which has been a black Appalachian cultural voice since the late 1960s. He was the first black to receive a master's degree in Appalachian Studies as a result of his discovery and documentation of the black experience in Appalachia. He currently lives in Morgantown, where he writes short stories and nonfiction as well as poetry.

JOSEPH W. CALDWELL, an attorney in Charleston, West Virginia, has published one chapbook, *Sabbatical on Winifrede Hollow* (Trillium Press, 1993). He won a writer's fellowship in 1992 with the West Virginia Commission on the Arts and is a past participant in the Breadloaf Writers Conference.

SHIRLEY YOUNG CAMPBELL, recently of Charleston, West Virginia, has been writing "words shaped like poetry" for many years, beginning before 1950. Her published writing includes fiction, nonfiction, poetry and drama. Much of it reflects life as she knew it while living in a West Virginia coal camp. She enjoyed editing and publishing *Hill and Valley* magazine for seven years and says this activity almost equaled the joy of being the mother of five children.

boyd carr, a longtime resident of West Virginia, recently returned to his native Virginia. boyd graduated from the University of Virginia in 1957 with a bachelor's degree in aeronautical engineering. After serving as a Cold Warrior in the United States Air Force, he was a commercial traveler and a corporate officer of Blue Ridge Optical Company, Inc. boyd became a full-time artist and writer in May of 1979. His line drawings and short poems have appeared in many venues. In 1999, his book, *my.th,* was published on the internet.

GRACE CAVALIERI is the author of ten books of poetry and numerous produced plays. She has written texts and lyrics for opera, stage and film. She teaches poetry workshops throughout the country and is on the poetry faculty of St. Mary's College of Southern Maryland. She produced and hosted "The Poet and the Poem" weekly on National Public Radio from 1977 to 1997, presenting two thousand poets to the nation. She now produces this series once a year from the Library of Congress via NPR satellite. She has received the Pen-Fiction Award, the Allen Ginsberg Poetry Award, The Corporation for Public Broadcasting Silver Medal, and awards from the National Commission on Working Women, the West Virginia Commission on Women, and the American Association of University Women, among others. She received the inaugural Columbia Merit Award for "significant contribution to poetry." She also received the inaugural playwriting award from the West Virginia Commision on the Arts. She writes full-time in West Virginia, where she lives with her husband, sculptor Kenneth Flynn. They have four grown daughters.

BARBARY CHAAPEL is a sailor come home to Buckhannon and the West Virginia mountains of her birth. Her poems have been published in journals and anthologies. She won an award in the 1999 West Virginia Writers competition for her poetry collection *No Name Harbour.*

LINDA MANTINI CHRISTEN is a practicing herbalist and co-owner of an herbal company in Monongalia County, West Virginia. With her husband, David, and their four canine pets, she lives on a mountain ridge in peaceful country.

LENORE MCCOMAS COBERLY was born and raised in Lincoln County, West Virginia. She holds degrees from West Virginia University and the University of Pittsburgh. She has worked as a writer and a teacher in Madison, Wisconsin, since 1964. She was a workshop leader at the Green Lake Writers' Conference for twenty years. She returns to Hamlin, in Lincoln County, West Virginia, once a year. She is married to Parkersburg native Camden A. Coberly.

In her collection, *Take One Blood Red Rose,* **MARY JOAN COLEMAN** said of herself, "My writing is enriched by my Appalachian heritage, but not limited by it. Mine is blood art; I slash at the arteries of social, personal, ethnic consciousness—not as a violent political convert, but as liberator of those elements vital to the spirit of endurance. My life has been hard, and often my lines are, too. But neither my life nor my work is defeated...."

DEBRA CONNER of Parkersburg has recently published an essay in *Teaching Writing from the Writer's Point of View,* published by the National Council of Teachers of English. She works as a writer in residence for the Ohio Arts Council and performs in-character as the poet Emily Dickinson. She has received fellowships from the National Endowment for the Arts and the National Endowment for the Humanities.

LAWRENCE COTTRELL was born and still lives in Kanawha

County, West Virginia. He holds a B.A. degree from West Virginia State College. Although he didn't begin writing poetry until around the age of 40, he has authored close to 3000 poems.

RICHARD CURREY is the author of the novels *Lost Highway* and *Fatal Light* and two story collections, *The Wars of Heaven* and *Crossing Over: The Vietnam Stories*. A recipient of West Virginia's Daugherty Award in the Humanities, he has also received two National Endowment of the Arts fellowships, in poetry and fiction, and many other awards and fellowships. His work has been published in eleven languages and more than twenty editions.

ED DAVIS, born in Princeton, West Virginia, ended up migrating to Ohio, where he teaches at Sinclair Community College in Dayton. He is the author of three poetry chapbooks, *Appalachian Day* (Samisdat Press), *Haskel* (Seven Buffaloes), and *Whispering Leaves* (Great Elm). He now writes mostly fiction and recently completed a novel tentatively titled *Danny Be Good* and a young adult novel, *Bird-Man and the Rat*. His fiction and poetry have appeared in *The West Virginia Hillbilly* and other magazines and in the anthology *In My Life*, which collected writings about the Beatles.

JULIA DAVIS was a prolific writer: a novelist, playright, and poet. The author of more than twenty books, she published her poetry in a number of journals. She had one play, *The Anvil*, that enjoyed a successful off-Broadway run in New York.

LLOYD DAVIS, a native of Charleston, graduated from West Virginia University and completed graduate work at Vanderbilt. He then taught for 37 years at West Virginia University. His chapbook, *Fishing on the Lower Jackson*, was followed by a longer collection, *The Way All Rivers Run*. The latter book won an Annex 21 prize. His work has appeared in such literary vehicles as *The Ohio Review, The Georgia Review, Kansas Quarterly, Foxfire, Southern Poetry Review,* and *Three Rivers Poetry Journal*.

MARY LUCILLE DEBERRY grew up in Harrisville, West Virginia, but has lived for more than three decades in Morgantown, where she is a producer-director for West Virginia Public Television. While in high school, she worked a couple of summers for *The Ritchie Gazette* before attending West Virginia University to major in speech and drama. Later, she earned her master's degree at The University of Iowa. She taught theater and directed plays at Alderson-Broaddus College for two years and studied acting for a year at the Yale University School of Drama. She has published nonfiction in *Goldenseal* and poetry in *Appalachian Journal, Appalachian Heritage,* and *Grab-a-Nickel.*

MARK DEFOE chairs the English department at West Virginia Wesleyan College, where he has taught literature and writing since 1975. He has read and published widely, his work appearing in *Poetry, Paris Review, North American Review, Poetry Ireland Review, Kenyon Review, Sewanee Review, Christian Science Monitor, Michigan Quarterly Review, Black Warrior Review, Mississippi Review,* and many others. He has published three chapbooks, *Bringing Home Breakfast* (Black Willow, 1982), *Palmate* (Pringle Tree Press, 1988), and *AIR* (Green Tower Press, 1998).

CHERYL DENISE grew up in Elmira, Ontario. After college she did two years of voluntary service through a Mennonite organization as a nurse for a public health agency in the rural Hispanic community of La Jara, Colorado. She now works part-time for a health department doing cancer screenings for low-income women. Recently she and her husband, Mike Miller, built a timber-frame home in the Shepherd's Field Community in Philippi, West Virginia.

VICTOR M. DEPTA was born on Buffalo Creek in Logan County, West Virginia. He served in the U.S. Navy, then took a B.A. in English from Marshall University. He followed that with an M.A. in Creative Writing from San Francisco State University and a Ph.D. in American Literature from Ohio University. He has published five books of poetry and a novel. Currently, he is Professor of English at the University of Tennessee at Martin and co-editor of Blair Mountain Press.

MURIEL MILLER DRESSLER, who died shortly before this anthology went to press, published *Appalachia, My Land* in 1973 through Morris Harvey College, now known as the University of Charleston. Poems in this collection previously appeared in such publications as *Poems from the Hills, Appalachian Journal, Poems on Parchment,* and *Wild, Wonderful West Virginia*. The essay with which she introduces her book is a soaring tribute to her native state. A phrase from her poem "Appalachia" — *wild sweet notes* — serves as the title of this anthology.

CHARLES O. ("OSCAR") DUBOIS III, D.D.S., was born in Belgium. As a teen he came to America with his family, eventually settling in West Virginia. He worked for over forty years as a cutter in various window glass plants in Clarksburg and Morgantown. He spent about thirty years refining a group of poems that formed a single published book, *Lichen and Moss*. He died June 21, 1989, ten weeks shy of his 110th birthday.

EDNA SMITH DUCKWORTH has written extensively of the neighborhood in which she grew up in Huntington "lower 10th Avenue and Bruce and Douglas Street." Education was extremely important to her family. Her parents having died when Edna was very young, her sister became her surrogate parent. A community activist, Mrs. Duckworth has belonged to many organizations aimed at improving the lives of African Americans and the economically deprived.

HELEN ELLISON, a long-time resident of Morgantown, was a loyal member of West Virginia Writers, Inc., and attended every annual conference while she was able. Quiet and modest, she was well loved and highly respected by her writing colleagues. Her work was published in such journals as *Grab-a-Nickel, Appalachian Heritage,* and *Wonderful West Virginia*.

HARRIET EMERSON moved to West Virginia in the 1960s from the Philadelphia area. She has an undergraduate degree in literature from Davis & Elkins College, where she helped produced *The Adum*, the school's poetry journal. She lived in Elkins for twenty-five years and belonged to The Cheat Mountain Poets. In 1998 she won a West Virginia Division of Culture and History fellowship for fiction and a West Virginia Writers' award for a children's book. She holds an M.S. in journalism from West Virginia University and has worked as a writer and editor for the university since 1991. She lives in Morgantown with her son, Justin Emerson Long.

ROBYN EVERSOLE was born in Harrison County, West Virginia, and attended Bridgeport High School and the Interlochen Arts Academy in Michigan. Her graduate degrees were achieved at McGill University in Canada. Since being an exchange student in Australia, she has lived there and in the Dominican Republic, Canada, and Bolivia. In addition to being an established poet, she has published four children's books, one of them bi-lingual. She lives in New York City.

CAROLYN SUE FERGUSON is a native West Virginian, born at Green Sulphur Springs, Summers County. She is an avid writer of poetry, short stories and articles and has won many awards. She has been published in local, state and national journals. She has been an active member of West Virginia Writers, Inc., and Wyoming Writers, as well as of Authors Link of Wyoming and St. Albrans Writers of West Virginia. A realtor for almost thirty years, she and her husband, Pete, live on a farm near Hurricane, West Virginia. Their two grown sons and five grandchildren all live in the Hurricane area.

ETHAN FISCHER edits *Antietam Review* and teaches English at Shepherd College. His recent work has appeared in *Potomac Review, Free State, Ruby, The Dogwood Tree, Antietam Review, Mountain Pathways,* and *Sans Merci,* among others. He is creator of the "Johnny Dime, the Poet of Crime" radio series.

KITTY FRAZIER is an associate professor of English at West Virginia State College. Her poetry and prose have appeared in regional publications. She spearheaded a poetry project in Wheeling, West Virginia, involving persons affected by MR/DD, and edited a 1979 compilation of West Virginia women writers. A former long-time member of the U.S. Archery Team, she has competed nationally and internationally in Olympic style archery.

DREAMA WYANT FRISK was born in her grandmother's house on McCanns Run, Jane Lew, West Virginia. During World War II she moved with her parents to Oak Hill. Her father worked at the Alloy Plant near Gauley Bridge. She graduated from West Virginia University and the University of Virginia. In West Virginia she taught at Morgantown and Montgomery High Schools. She now teaches history in the Adult Education Program in Arlington, Virginia. She and her husband, who is from Oak Hill, live in Arlington. She has published collected poems in a book, *Ivory Hollyhock*, and has published a variety of poems in small journals.

WINSTON FULLER coedited *Trellis* in the 1970s with Irene McKinney and Maggie Anderson. He has taught creative writing at West Virginia University for twenty-five years. His work has appeared in *The Ohio Review, The Indiana Review,* and *The Laurel Review,* among other publications. He is at work on a book about descriptive poetry titled *The Body of the World.*

BILL GARTEN is the winner of the Emerson Prize for Poetry and the Margaret Ward Martin Prize for Creative Writing. He has been anthologized in *And Now the Magpie* and *What the Mountains Yield.* His poetry has appeared in over 100 literary journals, including *Poet Lore, Pudding, Sow's Ear, The G.W. Review, Piedmont Literary Review, Birmingham Poetry Review, The Laurel Review* and *Wayne Literary Review.*

JOSEPH GATSKI was born in Fairmont, West Virginia. He attended high school in Grafton, West Virginia. He has published two volumes of poetry, *Promontory* and *Annie's Stick.* He is an avid outdoorsman and mountain hiker. He is also an artist, singer-songwriter, musician and gardener.

ROBERT S. GERKE taught English and American literature at Marshall University for some 30 years. He earned his Ph.D. at Notre Dame University, specializing in medieval studies. In addition to publishing scholarly articles on poets both medieval and modern, he published his own poems in journals such as *Southern Humanities Review*, *Laurel Review*, and *Poet Lore*. With Marshall colleagues William Sullivan and John McKernan, he helped found The Guyandotte Poets, who continue to meet monthly after 20 years of existence.

MABEL D. GILMORE was born in Hundred, West Virginia. She earned degrees at West Virginia University and George Peabody College for Teachers, Nashville, Tennessee. She taught high school for thirty-four years, dividing her time among biology, science, art, and physical education. Her publications include two books of poetry, *Poetic Potpourri* and *Poetic Digs*.

ROY LEE HARMON, born in 1900, was a native of Boone County. He served for many years as the Raleigh County Member of the West Virginia House of Delegates. A graduate of Morris Harvey College, he was a freelance writer, newspaper-man, and member of the Raleigh *Register* editorial staff. The founder of the West Virginia Poetry Society, he was the State's Poet Laureate three separate times, serving a total of 23 years.

JAMES HARMS has published three books of poetry with Carnegie Mellon University Press: *Modern Ocean*, *The Joy Addict*, and *Quarters*. His poems have also appeared in *The American Review*, *The Kenyon Review*, *Gettysburg Review*, *Poetry*, and *Kestrel*, among other journals. Born in Los Angeles, he holds a bachelor's degree from the University of Redlands and an M.F.A. from Indiana University. He is Director of Creative Writing at West Virginia University.

MARC HARSHMAN lives in Marshall County, West Virginia, where, until recently, he taught in the Sand Hill School, one of the last of the three-room country schools. His poetry has been published in *The Georgia Review*, *Wilderness*, *Shenandoah*,

Passages North and *Outposts (UK)*. He is also the author of seven children's picture books, including *The Storm*, a Parent's Choice Award recipient and Smithsonian Notable Book for Children. He has children's titles forthcoming from Marshall Cavendish and Harcourt Brace. His poems are included in the recent anthologies *Wildsong: Poems of the Natural World* (University of Georgia Press, 1998) and *Learning by Heart: Contemporary American Poetry About School* (University of Iowa Press, 1999). His new collection of poems is *Rose of Sharon* (Mad River Press).

VERA ANDREWS HARVEY was born in Cedarville, Ohio, in 1875. She attended Cedarville College, graduated from Western Reserve University, and obtained an M.A. from Columbia University. She taught at Marshall University and served as West Virginia's Poet Laureate in 1960-1961. She was a past president of the West Virginia Poetry Society and was for many years active in the Huntington Chapter of West Virginia Women's Clubs.

EMMETT HEASTER was born and raised in Greenbrier County. He became a school teacher but worked later as a farmer, a mail carrier, and a carpenter. Father of four children, he returned to teaching when he was sixty years old. Writing was far more than a hobby, but he was never able to pursue it as a career. He died in 1995 at the age of 98.

MONA KAY HELPER now lives in Manassas, Virginia. She is originally from Cross Lanes, West Virginia. She attended Nitro High School, West Virginia State College, and Northern Virginia Community College. Her work has been published in *Central Appalachian Review, What the Mountains Yield, Now the Magpie, Hill and Valley, Mountain Ways, Kanawha Review,* and *Goldenseal.* Currently she serves as financial officer for Osbourn High School and is very active in community theater and has been an extra in four feature films.

TERRANCE HILL was born in South Charleston, West Virginia. He coauthored *This Ain't Sex* with Michael Pauley. He was on the editorial staff of the illustrated *Appalachian Intelligencer* and has had poems published in *West Virginia Magazine*, *Hill and Valley*, *Poets' Corner*, and *Grab-a-Nickel*, among other journals. His work also appears in the anthology *Venue*. He currently lives in Edmonds, Washington.

CHARLEY HIVELY was born and raised in Nitro, West Virginia. His poetry collection *Looking into the Dark* took first place honors in the West Virginia Writers, Inc., open poetry competition in 1997. He is the reference librarian at the Clarksburg-Harrison Public Library and adjunct instructor of English and literature at Fairmont State College. He makes his home in Clarksburg with his Siamese cat, Desdemona.

RON HOUCHIN was raised in Huntington and has taught public school for 29 years in southeastern Ohio. His work has appeared in various journals, such as *Poetry Ireland Review*, *Sycamore Review*, *The Southwest Review*, *Antietam Review*, and many others. His first collection was published in 1997 by Salmon Publishing of Ireland. The same press will bring out his second collection in 2001.

DAVID JARVIS was a native of Hurricane, West Virginia. His poetry reflects his love of nature and pride in his Appalachian ancestry. His volume of poetry, *The Born Again Tourist*, was brought out in 1995 by Trillium Press.

ROBEN JONES was born in Hansford, West Virginia. She attended Marshall University but has had no formal training as a writer. She currently lives in Gallipolis, Ohio.

NORMAN JORDAN was born in Ansted, West Virginia. His family moved from Ansted to Cleveland, during which time he attended Cleveland public schools and then served in the U.S. Navy. Returning to Ansted in 1977, he enrolled in classes at West Virginia University. He earned a B.F.A. in theatre. Later he took an M.A. from The Ohio State University. His poetry has been anthologized in 35 books of poetry, the most recent being *Make a Joyful Sound: Poems for Children by African-American Poets* and *In Search of Everywhere: A Collection of African*

American Poetry. His plays have been staged in San Diego, Cleveland, Texas, Atlanta, and New York. He holds a United Nations Playwright's Award and participated in the 1967 U.N. International Playwright's Workshop. He has taught African American Literature at West Virginia University and Glenville State College. He is also director of the West Virginia African American Arts and Heritage Academy and the African American Heritage Family Tree Museum in Ansted. He is president of the United African American Artists of West Virginia.

KIRK JUDD, co-editor of this anthology, helped found West Virginia Writers, Inc., and is the co-founder and co-director of *Allegheny Echoes* (with Sherrell Wigal and Mike Bing). A graduate of Marshall University, he has a strong dramatic reading style that has gained him wide recognition as a performance poet evoking, sometimes to musical accompaniment, the Appalachian experience. He has published two volumes of poetry, *Field of Vision* (Aegina Press) and *Tao-Billy* (Trillium Press). His work has appeared in regional publications such as *BOGG, Then and Now, The Sow's Ear, Grab-a-Nickel, Down Home, Hill and Valley* and the anthologies *Down the River* and *Kestrel*. He has been featured three times on National Public Radio's "The Poet and the Poem," hosted by Grace Cavalieri.

EARL KEENER lives in Bethany and works as a track repairman on the railroad at Weirton Steel. He is also a singer-songwriter and part-time dollmaker. His wife, Pamela, is founder of the Moon Lodge Art Group in Bethany.

LYNN KERNAN has recently been living in Shepherdstown, and previously had lived in Martinsburg. Having suffered a stroke two years ago, she has made a remarkable recovery. Though she lost the use of her writing hands, she has ingeniously switched to speaking her poems into a tape recorder.

SHIRLEY KLEIN, born with cerebral palsy, has acheived success as a writer and as an information representative for the West Virginia Dept. of Vocational Rehabilitation, working as a full-time employee. She received four hours a week homebound instruction in Beckley, West Virginia, to complete her early schooling, but entered college in 1968, earning a B.A. degree in English from Marshall University and later continuing her education at West Virginia State College. *Of Bitter Choice,* her first volume of poetry, was published by Mountain State Press in 1983.

ANN KRUEGER is an artist and writer who lives with her husband, Al, on four acres in the Monongahela National Forest in Randolph County. She has been a public school teacher and also has worked in the mental health field. A member of both Barbour County Writers' Workshop and West Virginia Writers, Inc., she is now retired and writing poetry. She also is at work on a book of short stories about her 20 years on the family farm in Barbour County and on a narrative about the adoption of her twin sons. She has been published in *Grab-a-Nickel, The Lucid Stone, The Organic Harvester, The Shaver Fork River Coalition* and in two anthologies of poetry.

P.J. LASKA has published seven collections of poetry, including *D.C. Images*, a National Book Award nominee in 1975. In his latest book, *The Mason-Dixon Sutra* (Igneus Press, 1999), he reunites his work with that of Joseph Barrett and Bob Snyder, two poet friends who died in the 1990s.

CLETA M. LONG, author, poet, and historian, is a lifelong resident of Tucker County, West Virginia. Among his publications are the books *Pass with Care* (Augusta Heritage Books), *Across the Bridge* (McClain), and *The History of Tucker County* (Tucker County Community Endowment Foundation). He has also published in *Appalachian Log, The West Virginia Hillbilly,* and *Grab-a-Nickel.* In 1992 he was named Poet Laureate of Tucker County. He is a member of West Virginia Writers, Inc. He has appeared on West Virginia Public Radio's "Mountain Stage" and on "CBS Sunday Morning," as well as at the Augusta Heritage Festival and the Jackson's Mill Storytelling Festival.

PAT LOVE, of Charleston, a long time contributor to the state literary scene, is a native West Virginia poet, father and grandfather. He is past president of West Virginia Writers, Inc., and past president of The Appalachian Literary League. He has three books in print, *Street Scenes, Bridges Over Reality,* and *The Chronicles of Lincoln County,* and is currently Assistant Editor of *Goldenseal* magazine.

PETER MAKUCK is Distinguished Professor of Arts and Sciences at East Carolina University, where he has edited *Tar River Poetry* for 20 years. He is the author of a collection of short stories, *Breaking and Entering* (University of Illinois Press), and five volumes of poetry, the latest being *Against Distance* (BOA Editions, Ltd.). His essays, poems and stories have appeared in such journals as *Virginia Quarterly Review, The Southern Review, The Sewanee Review,* and *The Hudson Review.*

JEFF MANN grew up in southwest Virginia and southern West Virginia. He holds degrees in English and forestry from West Virginia University. He has published in *The Laurel Review, Poet Lore, Appalachian Heritage, The Hampden-Sydney Poetry Review, Spoon River Poetry Review* and *Prairie Schooner.* His collection of poems, *Bliss,* won the 1997 Stonewall Chapbook Competition and was published in 1998 by BrickHouse Books. He teaches Appalachian Studies and creative writing at Virginia Tech.

RUSSELL MARANO was born in Clarksburg, West Virginia. He graduated from Northwestern University with a degree in philosophy. He also did graduate work there. Although he left the West Virginia hills, the people and the landscape were never far from his heart. He published two books of poetry, *Poems From A Mountain Ghetto* and *Pockets of Love,* and his poems and short stories appeared in many literary magazines and several national anthologies.

ROSEMARY MARSHALL, poet, feature writer, and ragtime pianist, was born in Bonne Terre, Missouri. As a teenager she wrote a column for her hometown newspaper. She put away writing for many years while she raised a family of six children with her husband Marvin, who worked for the U.S. Forest Service. The Marshalls moved to Elkins, West Virginia, in 1967, and she began to write again. She was a member of the Cheat Mountain Poets and also returned to her love of writing newspaper feature stories.

SANDRA MASHBURN teaches writing at West Virginia State College and has served as editor of the campus magazine, *Kanawha Review,* for over twenty years. She was a 1994 recipient of a Creative Writing Fellowship from the West Virginia Division of Culture and History. Her poems have appeared in national publications and have been collected in two chapbooks, *Controlled Flight* (Alms House Press) and *Undertow* (March Street Press).

LEE MAYS, who was a resident of Ripley, West Virginia, authored many volumes of poetry, including *Child of the Hills* (1953), *The Return to the Hills* (1955), *Echoes From the Hills* (1957), *Epic of Creation* (1965), *Worse Torse Vorse* (1967), *Philosophy of the Hills* (1968), and *Ramble in the Hills* (1969), and a work of fiction, *Maid of Magdala* (1967). He was a longtime member of the West Virginia Poetry Society, The National Federation of State Poetry Societies, The Mark Twain Society, The Filson Club, and Kiwanis International.

MICHAEL MAZZOLINI has lived in the Elkins area for the past twenty-five years. He is founder and past editor of *Backcountry*, a literary tabloid. His collected poems were published under the title *Hot Knives, Greasy Spoons, & All Night Diners*. He currently teaches at Davis & Elkins College.

BARBARA McCULLOUGH is a West Virginian currently living in Marietta, Ohio. Her poetry has appeared in several regional publications. She was editor of *Confluence*, a literary magazine, from 1990 to 1996. A teacher by training and profession, she has been a bridge builder between the arts and communities of education.

MARGARET MCDOWELL *no biographical data available*

GEORGIA LEE McELHANEY lives in Shepherdstown. She has published poetry in *Antietam Review, Athanor, Pivot,* and in several anthologies and exhibits of poetry, including having three poems published in *A Controversy of Poets,* eds. Paris Leary and Robert Kelly (NY: Doubleday, 1965). In 1982 she won first place in the Virginia Poetry Society's annual Edgar Allen Poe poetry competition for her poem "Theodore Roosevelt's Island." She edited *Pivot* from 1984 to 1985. In Shepherdstown she has run a bookstore, worked as town clerk and been director of the Housing Authority. Now semiretired, she co-edits a monthly poetry column for *The Shepherdtown Chronicle* featuring poems from The Bookend Poets, of which she is a member.

BONNI McKEOWN grew up spending winters in Philadelphia, Pennsylvania, and summers at her family's 200-year-old summer resort in Hampshire County. There she later served as manager of the land, farm, and history. During the 1970s and 1980s she worked for newspapers in Beckley and Charleston and on the staff of Congressman Ken Hechler. Her book *Peaceful Patriot: The Story of Tom Bennett* was published in 1980 by Mountain State Press. She co-published *Some Poems by Some Women* in 1975 and published her own collection, *Pieces,* in 1978. A citizen-activist, she has led campaigns to save "The Cardinal" passenger train through southern West Virginia and to stop the proposed Corridor H highway and instead improve existing roads in the state's eastern highlands. A 1971 graduate of the West Virginia University School of Journalism, she is the mother of a daughter and lives in Hampshire County.

JOHN McKERNAN was born during the Second World War in Nebraska. He was educated at schools in Omaha and graduated from the University of Omaha. He earned an M.A. in English from the University of Arkansas, an M.F.A. in writing from Columbia University, and later a Ph.D. at Boston University with a dissertation on Shakespeare's sonnets. He has taught at Marshall University since 1967. From 1968 to 1980 he was editor of the literary journal *The Little Review.* He has won fellowships from the Benedum Foundation, the Marshall Research Board, Boston University, the West Virginia Humanities Council, the National Endowment for the Humanities, and the National Endowment for the Arts. His poems and translations have appeared in *The Atlantic, The New Yorker, The National Review, Antaeus, Snerd, Paris Review, Field, Virginia Quarterly Review, Ironwood, Agni Review* and elsewhere. He is the author of two books of poetry, *Walking Along the Missouri River* and *Erasing the Blackboard*, and several college textbooks. He is working on a third book of poetry and on a textbook anthology titled *Forms and Themes in Poetry*.

LLEWELLYN McKERNAN, a native of Arkansas, has lived in West Virginia longer than anywhere else. Here she has written and published two poetry books, *Short and Simple Annals* and *Many Waters*, and four children's books, *More Songs of Gladness, Bird Alphabet, This is the Day,* and *This is the Night*. She holds an M.F.A. in writing from Brown University and has taught English at Marshall University. She is an active member of The Guyandotte Poets. Her poetry has appeared in *The Kenyon Review, Southern Poetry Review, Antietam Review, Potomac Review, Poet & Critic,* and *Appalachian Journal*.

IRENE McKINNEY, Poet Laureate of West Virginia since 1993, still lives on the family farm in the Talbott Community near Belington. She has published four collections of poetry—*The Girl with the Stone in Her Lap, The Wasps at the Blue Hexagons, Quick Fire and Slow Fire,* and *Six O'Clock Report*. Another collection is due out soon. Having earned a Ph.D. at the University of Utah, she is a member of the faculty at West Virginia Wesleyan College.

DEVON McNAMARA is Associate Professor of English at West Virginia Wesleyan College. She has spent innumerable years in poet-in-schools programs in many states. She has been published in *The Christian Science Monitor*, among other publications, and lives in a farmhouse built before the Battle of Little Bighorn, located in Barbour County, West Virginia.

LOUISE McNEILL was born in West Virginia in 1911 on the farm where her family has lived since 1769. Her first major collection of poems, *Gauley Mountain*, was published in 1939, with a foreword by Stephen Vincent Benet. Other poetry books include *Paradox Hill* and *Elderberry Flood*. In addition, she published poems in many prestigious national journals. After her retirement from teaching in 1972, She wrote her memoirs, *The Milkweed Ladies*, considered by many to be her masterpiece. She served as Poet Laureate of West Virginia from 1979 to 1993.

C.A. MEADE was born in Fairmont, West Virginia, attended Dunbar High School, and holds degrees from West Virginia State College and The University of Toledo (Ohio). She is currently employed by the Marion County Public Schools, teaching eighth-grade language arts at Monongah Middle School. She also directs the choir at Trinity United Methodist Church in Fairmont.

NANCY MERICAL, poet, writer, speaker, photographer, artist, and workshop director, has had nearly 300 publications in various markets. She has won over 80 awards ranging from local to international. Her first book, *Just for Kids* (Lillenas Publications), appeared on the religious market in 1999.

DORIS MILLER was born in Wayne County. Educated at Marshall University and West Virginia University, she taught school in West Virginia for many years and worked as a reporter for the Huntington Publishing Company before retiring in 1972. She published two volumes of poetry, *Desert the Mirror* and *Who Burnishes the Lamp*, and wrote the *Bicentennial History of Huntington* in 1971. She was a longtime member of the Huntington Poetry Guild and the West Virginia Poetry Society.

PHYLLIS WILSON MOORE considers herself a literary historian and an occasional poet. Her research and poems may be found in *Traditions: A Journal of Folk Culture and Educational Awareness*, the official journal of the West Virginia-Virginia Folklore Center at Fairmont State College. Her essay "Yes, We Have

Authors" was reprinted by the West Virginia Humanities Council as part of the 1996 Circuit Writers Program. She was one of 70 authors selected by the West Virginia Library Association for inclusion in their 1999 *Celebrating 100 Years of West Virginia Authors*. Her best known poem, "We Have Some Writers," summarizes the state's rich multicultural liteary heritage and is a readers' theater piece in Harrison County Schools. The poem was also incorporated into a WNPB-TV literary history program "Live and on the Line," hosted by Mary Lucille DeBerry.

LINDA LAULIS MOSHER *no biographical data available*

LENORE MYERS *no biographical data available*

DON NARKEVIC comes from Ambridge, a steel town in southwestern Pennsylvania. He has lived in Philippi, West Virginia, for the past 20 years with his wife and children. His play "The Interview" was to be produced in Chicago in the Year 2000.

VALERIE NIEMAN, a 1978 journalism graduate of West Virginia University, is an editor with *The News & Record* newspaper in Greensboro, North Carolina. Her second novel, *Survivors*, was due out this year from Van Neste Books. Her short stories have appeared in *The Kenyon Review* and *Antietam Review*. Her poetry has been published in *Poetry, West Branch, New Letters* and other journals. She has received a National Endowment for the Arts fellowship in poetry, and grants for fiction writing from the West Virginia Commission for the Arts and from the Kentucky Foundation for Women. Most recently, her fiction won the 1998 Elizabeth Simpson Smith Award and her poetry the Greg Grummer Award at Phoebe.

CHRISTINE LAMB PARKER, a native Californian, lives in Morgantown with her husband and two children. Currently she is working on a memoir of her two years in Malaysia at a leprosy colony. She earned a master's degree in Creative Writing from San Francisco State University and has received various awards and citations, including a Browning Prize in poetry and a West Virginia Writers, Inc. poetry award. Her poems have appeared in *Yankee Magazine, The Seattle Review, Antietam Review, Calliope,* and elsewhere.

MICHAEL JOSEPH PAULEY (1950-1992) was a widely published poet, fiction writer and historian. A native West Virginian and former president of West Virginia Writers, he worked as a historian for the state. Much of his professional work and writing was in the field of historic preservation.

E.D. PENDARVIS lives in Huntington, WV, and teaches writing in the School of Education Marshall University. Her poems and essays have appeared in *Antietam Review, Café Review, Grab-a-Nickel, Louisville Review, Now & Then, Phoebe,* and *Zone 3,* among other journals. Her poetry collection, *Joy Ride,* is published in *Human Landscapes* by Bottom Dog Press.

JAYNE ANN PHILLIPS is the author of *Black Tickets, Fast Lanes, Machine Dreams, Shelter* and a delightful little book of poems titled *Sweethearts.* Her work has been translated into fourteen languages. She is a recipient of the Sue Kaufman Prize from the American Academy of Arts and Letters, a Bunting Institute fellowship, a Guggenheim fellowship, and two National Endowment for the Arts fellowships in fiction.

CALISA PIERCE, a wife and mother of three children, lives in southern West Virginia, where she was born and raised. She is Director of Developmental Studies for Southern West Virginia Community and Technical College and organist at First Baptist Church of Logan.

DAVID B. PRATHER, a native of Parkersburg, was raised and educated in the isolated terrain of Wirt County. He received his B.A. in English from West Virginia University and his M.F.A. from the Warren Wilson College Program for Writers. He attended the accelerated summer program for actors at The National Shakespeare Conservatory. He is an active member of The Ohio Valley Literary Group and West Virginia Writers. He currently teaches English and creative writing at West Virginia

University at Parkersburg. In 1998 Naomi Shihab Nye nominated his work for a Pushcart Prize, and she subsequently included his work in her 1999 anthology *What Have You Lost?* (Greenwillow Books). His poems have appeared in *Seneca Review, Prairie Schooner, Colorado Review, The Literary Review, American Literary Review, Santa Barbara Review, Poet Lore, Potomac Review, Borderlands, Texas Poetry Review,* and others.

BONNIE PROUDFOOT is originally from New York City and has lived in West Virginia since 1979. She holds an M.A. in Creative Writing from Hollins College and an M.A. in English from West Virginia University, and is finishing a Ph.D. in Creative Writing at Ohio University. Her stories and poems have appeared in *The Gettysburg Review, Kestrel, The Lyric, The Potomac Review, The Best of West Virginia Writers,* and *The Hollins Critic.* Her awards include prizes in poetry and fiction from West Virginia Writers and a 1994 Literary Fellowship from the West Virginia Commission on the Arts (for Novel in Progress).

CHARLES RAMPP is a retired Lutheran clergyman who lives in Harper's Ferry, West Virginia. He grew up in Appalachian Ohio. He has published over 600 poems—Appalachian, lyric, and religious—and 23 short stories.

TIM RUSSELL was born in Steubenville, Ohio, but was raised in West Virginia. He has spent most of his life within a mile of the Ohio River and currently lives in Toronto, Ohio. Educated at West Liberty State College and the University of Pittsburgh, he has been employed for many years at Weirton Steel, primarily as a boiler repairman. His first full-length book, *Adversaria,* won the Terrence Des Pres Prize for Poetry.

SUSAN SHEPPARD is a native of Doddridge County, West Virginia, but has lived much of her adult life in Parkersburg. Her work has been published in *Nimrod, The Ohio Review, Negative Capability,* and several Pennsylvania reviews. She has published one book, *The Phoenix Cards,* and another on astrology, listed by Book-of-the-Month. In her spare time she guides a ghost tour around Parkersburg. Her online poetry and fiction magazine can be found at http.//home.wirefire.com/pooka.

BARBARA SMITH, co-editor of this anthology, is a freelance writer and editor and former chair of the Division of the Humanities and Professor of Literature and Writing, Alderson-Broaddus College, Philippi, West Virginia. She has published over 200 poems, stories, and journal articles in, among other places, *Antietam Review, Potomac Review, Tar River Poetry, English Journal,* and *Goldenseal.* She has also published one novel and seven books of non-fiction. Most recently she was a contributing editor for the poetry anthologies *Weeping with Those Who Weep* and *Coming Together.*

MARY CARTER SMITH was born in Birmingham, Alabama in 1919. Orphaned at the age of four, she was raised by relatives and graduated from Coppin Teacher's College in 1942. She was a teacher and librarian in the Baltimore City Public Schools from 1942 until 1973. An internationally known performer as well as a widely published poet, she is a founding member of Big Sisters International and co-founder of the National Association of Black Storytellers.

ANNA EGAN SMUCKER is the author of two books for children, *No Star Nights*, winner of the 1990 International Reading Association Children's Book Award, and *Outside the Window*, a bedtime story (both published by Knopf). Her *History of West Virginia*, a work written for adult new readers, was published in 1997 by the West Virginia Humanities Council. Her poems have been published in *Now and Then, A Gathering at the Forks,* and *The Best of West Virginia Writers.* She has been a teacher, a children's librarian, and a writer-in-residence. She lives with her family in Bridgeport, West Virginia.

BOB SNYDER (1937-1995) grew up in St. Marys, West Virginia, on the Ohio River north of Parkersburg. He attended West Virginia University on a General Motors scholarship and went on to graduate school in Cincinnati, where he began publishing poetry. After serving as director of Antioch College Appalachia in Beckley, he entered Harvard's Graduate School of Education, where he completed his Ph.D. In 1977, after he had published widely in literary journals, his collection *We'll See Who's a Peasant* appeared under the pen name "Billy Greenhorn." At the time of his death, he had completed a second collection, *Milky Way Accent.*

LEANNE SNYDER is a lifelong resident of West Virginia, now residing in Colliers. Her poetry has appeared in *West Branch, Snake River, Tar River Review,* and *Pulpsmith.* She has been a guest writer at Bucknell University in Lewisburg, Pennsylvania, and has done readings and workshops near home, at Bucknell and elsewhere.

ANNE SPENCER was born in Martinsville, Virginia, but grew up in Bramwell in southern West Virginia, and later taught school there. She later returned to Lynchburg, where her house is on the national registry. She was an early leader of the NAACP, and a close friend of Langton Hughes and other well-known African-American poets. Her poetry has appeared in several of the Harlem Renaissance anthologies and is still considered exemplary of the African-American culture.

MARY V. STEALEY is a native of Clarksburg, West Virginia. After retiring from the federal government, she became a charter member of W.R.A.P. (Writers, Readers, Authors & Poets) and is also a member of West Virginia Writers, Inc. She has had stories published in *Goldenseal* and *Good Old Days* and was a second-place winner in the 1998 West Virginia Writers, Inc., Annual Writers Competition, in the category of novel.

PAUL CURRY STEELE was born in Logan, West Virginia, in 1928. He studied at Virginia, Harvard, and Iowa. His *Anse on Island Creek and Other Poems* was brought out by Mountain State Press in 1981. He lives in Charleston, West Virginia.

A.E. STRINGER earned the B.A. in English from Ohio University, where he graduated with honors in General Studies and was elected to Phi Beta Kappa. He earned his M.A. in English at Colorado State University and an M.F.A. in Creative Writing from the University of Massachusetts. He published collected poems as *Channel Markers* (Wesleyan University Press) in 1987. His work has appeared in *The Nation, Antaeus, Ohio Review, Poetry Northwest, Denver Quarterly, Ironwood, New Virginia Review* and elsewhere. He is a Professor of English at Marshall University, and a former department chair. He teaches creative writing, American literature, and composition.

WILLIAM SULLIVAN was a U.S. Naval officer during World War II, serving in the Pacific. He received a B.A. and an M.A. from Tufts University and a Ph.D. from Columbia University. His field of scholarship was British and American literature. An avid reader and long-time poet, he taught at Rockhurst, Fordham, Stephens, McNeese, the College of St. Rose and, finally, at Marshall University in Huntington, West Virginia. In 1977, with Robert Gerke, he founded the still-active Guyandotte Poets (Huntington area). He died October 15, 1997.

GERALD D. SWICK is a freelance writer living in Clarksburg, West Virginia. His weekly history column, "Once Long Ago," appears each Sunday in *The Clarksburg Exponent-Telegram* and has e-mail subscribers across the country. He received a literary fellowship in 1998 and is presently writing a history of the family of Mary Todd Lincoln. He is a consultant for a PBS special about the Lincolns.

BARBARA W. TEDFORD is the author of scholarly articles on such writers as Eudora Welty, Flannery O'Connor, and Henry James. She has won prizes for her poetry and for 14 years was advisor to the literary magazine *Trillium* at Glenville State College. She graduated from Maryville College and holds the M.A. in English from the University of Tennessee and the Ph.D. from the University of Pittsburgh.

ARLINE THORN, born in New Haven in Marshall County, did her undergraduate work at Marshall University and earned an

M.A. and a Ph.D. in Comparative Literature at the University of Illionois. Her poetry has been published in such vehicles as *Pikeville Review, Southern Humanities Review,* and the anthology *Weeping with Those Who Weep.* Owner and editor of Trillium Press, she is one of the founders and a current member of the Guyandotte Poets.

JESSIE TRESHAM was a teacher in the Ritchie County Public schools for 54 years. She held a B.A. and M.A. from Ohio University at Athens, and also did a year's graduate work at West Virginia University.

DOUGLAS VAN GUNDY is a writer and musician living in Pocahontas County, West Virginia. He has performed and taught fiddle and poetry workshops throughout the eastern United States. His poems have appeared in the *Gullwater Review, Kestrel, Negative Capability* and the anthology *Connected Writers of the Information Age.* A 1996 M.F.A. graduate of Goddard College, he lives in Marlinton with his wife, Melissa, and dog, Hickory.

TWYLA S. VINCENT has been a lifelong resident of Harrison County, West Virginia. She and her husband, Harold, have three children and six grandsons. She graduated from Salem College with an Associate Degree in Nursing and later earned her B.S.N. from West Virginia University. A member of West Virginia Writers, Inc., she has published in *Appalachian Journal, Grit Magazine, Big Beautful Women, West Virginia Medical Journal, The Journal of Nursing Jocularity,* and in several local newspapers.

SANDY VRANA teaches composition and literature (including Appalachian literature) at Alderson-Broaddus College. A member of Barbour County Writers, she is the editor of *Grab-a-Nickel,* published jointly by Alderson-Broaddus and Barbour County Writers.

JIM WEBB is a poet, playwright and swarper, whose days and writings have been saturated by Mingo County, the Tug Valley, and the Great Appalachian Flood of 1977. He is infamous for "Poultry Where?" the first Appalachian Poultry Designer T-shirt (now in its sixth edition, which features his epic poem "Get in Jesus.") He lives atop Pine Mountain in Letcher County, Kentucky.

DON WEST, controversial poet, folklorist, professor, minister, activist, and union organizer, founded the Appalachian South Folk Life Center near Pipestem in Southern West Virginia. He authored thousands of poems, essays, and articles and vigorously supported literary activities throughout West Virginia and Appalachia.

BILLY EDD WHEELER was born and raised in Boone County, West Virginia. He graduated from Berea College and went on to graduate studies in playwriting at Yale University. He has authored more than 20 plays, including the long-running *Hatfields & McCoys* at Beckley, West Virginia, and *Young Abe Lincoln* at Lincoln City, Indiana. He has published two volumes of poetry and five best-selling books of humor, four in collaboration with Loyal Jones. Besides poetry, Wheeler's first love is song writing. His several hits include "Jackson," recorded by Johnny Cash and June Carter, Nancy Sinatra and Lee Hazlewood; "Coward of the County," recorded by Kenny Rogers; "It's Midnight," recorded by Elvis Presley; "The Coming of the Roads," recorded by Judy Collins. He also wrote and recorded "Ode to the Little Brown Shack Out Back." He has finished a first novel, *Star of Appalachia*, as yet unpublished. He and his wife, Mary, have two children and live in Swannanoa, North Carolina.

SHERREL R. WIGAL is a native West Virginian, currently living in Parkersburg. Her work has been published in *Gambit, Now and Then, Appalachian Heritage,* and *Best of West Virginia Writers.* She also performs some of her work with traditional old-time West Virginia musicians. She has held various offices in West Virginia Writers, Inc.

RANDY WILKINS grew up in Clarksburg, West Virginia, where he attended Washington Irving High School. Upon graduation he joined the Navy and served as a machinist's mate for six years. While studying at West Virginia University, he published several poems in *Calliope*, the English Department's annual literary journal. His poem *"Vivre en Poesie"* won an Honorable Mention in the 1998 West Virginia Writers, Inc., contest. He is a member of the Morgantown Writers Group.

JEANNE WILSON has had stories and poems published in many venues and has garnered awards. Children often surface in her writing. In addition to raising her own children, she has worked as an elementary school teacher, the principal of a primary center, and a leader for scout, 4-H and church youth groups.

BARBARA YEAGER was born in Huntington, grew up in St. Albans, and now lives in Dunbar, West Virginia. She was educated at Kanawha County schools, Charleston Catholic High School, Wheeling Jesuit College (B.A. in writing and speaking arts), Marshall University (M.A. in English), and at Virginia Polytechnic and State University (Ed.D. in curriculum and instruction). She has taught in the Humanities Department of Morris Harvey College/University of Charleston for 36 years. Her research interest is Appalachian literature. She is the current president of Mountain State Press and has helped produce The Appalachian Arts Festivals and the Young Writer's Day programs at UC since 1969. She enjoys her five children and her year-old grandson.

ED ZAHNISER has been living and writing in the Eastern Panhandle of West Virginia since 1977. He is the author of two books of poems, *The Way to Heron Mountain* and *A Calendar of Worship,* and three chapbooks, *The Ultimate Double Play, Someone Stole My Guru's Voice,* and *Sheenjek & Denali: Alaska Poems.* He is the editor of *Where Wilderness Preservation Began: Adirondack Writings of Howard Zahniser.* He is an associate editor of *Antietam Review,* contributing editor for the arts of *The Good News Paper,* and a columnist for *The Shepherdstown Chronicle.* He was curator and editor of the exhibit catalog anthology of poems *Public Hanging!* for the Boarman Arts Center in Martinsburg, West Virginia. He lives in Shepherdstown, West Virginia, with his wife, Christine Duewel, and two sons.

JACK ZIEROLD, a past president of West Virginia Writers, Inc., is a resident of Weirton, West Virginia. He has gained fame not only as a poet, but also as a playwright and lyricist. His works have been produced in West Virginia and in other states. He has won numerous awards, both in state and out of state.

PETER ZIVKOVIC served in the Army Security Agency during the Korean War and earned degrees from the University of Illinois (B.A., M.A.) and the University of Iowa (M.F.A.). He played college football and professional baseball (with the Detroit Tigers' minor league chain). He has published over 100 poems and stories in various reviews and quarterlies, a novella, three chapbooks, and a collection of poems, *Belly and Bone* (Timberline Press). He teaches at Fairmont State College.

Unless noted, permissions to reprint poems were granted by authors holding the copyrights. Acknowledgements are nonetheless made here to honor the periodicals and books in which the poems originally appeared. Every effort has been made to obtain publication rights from both living poets and the families of deceased poets. In a few cases no literary heirs of deceased poets were located. Similarly, the publisher was unable to locate photographer Vincent James Vendolini or his kin. Publishers Place invites artists or heirs to make themselves known.

Acree, W. – Elegy for My Father – *Best of WV Writers 1991-1995, About Bee Robbing and Other Things*-Tantra Press 1995; At Honanki – *Blackbirds, About Bee Robbing and Other Things*-Tantra Press 1995; **Adams, G.** – Three Women On a Porch – *American Voice*; **Anaporte-Easton, J.** – The Seabed – *Washout Review* Vol IV #2, May 1986; Red Dress – *13th Moon* #15, *Groundswell* 2 #1, Winter 1986; **Anderson, C.** – Bob Thompson at the Piano – *Kestrel* Spring 1993; Huckleberries – previously unpublished; Great Aunt Margaret – *New Voices* Fall/Winter 1993; **Anderson, M.** – Querencia – *Years That Answer;* Cucumbers – *Years That Answer*; Long Story – *A Space Filled With Moving*; A Place with Promise – *A Space Filled With Moving,* Courtesy U Pittsburgh Press.

Baber, B. – West Virginia Lowku – *Wonderful West Virginia* Magazine; **Bailey, L.** – Interlocking Circles – previously unpublished; The Artist's Wife – previously unpublished; Breakfast in the Big Scrub – *New Voices* Fall/Winter 1993; **Bailey, M.** – City Darkness – *From the Beyond* – Gull Publishing, Pineville, WV 1986; Home – *From the Beyond* – Gull Publishing, Pineville, WV 1986; Iron Curtains – *From the Beyond* – Gull Publishing, Pineville, WV 1986; Family Dinner – *From the Beyond* – Gull Publishing, Pineville, WV 1986; **Barrett, J.** – An April Exultation – *The Mason-Dixon Sutra* – Igneus Press, Bedford, NH 1999; Everything's Arranged – *Best of Hill & Valley*; John Berryman's Bridge – *Periods of Lucidity* 1978; Mars on a Vivid Night – previously unpublished; **Basilone, J.** – For Sale – *White Noise*; -30 – *White Noise*; Allegheny RFD – *White Noise*; **Battlo, J.** – Memorial to My Father – *Mountain Review*; First Song of Dulcinea – *Bone and Flesh*; **Bentley, L.** – Downstairs: 5:30 A.M. – *Eureka Literary Magazine*; Postcards – *Small Pond*; sibylline – *Eureka Literary Magazine*; **Blue, E.** – The Show – *A Million Dreams;* In Spite of All Odds – *A Million Dreams;* Old Woman – *A Million Dreams;* **Briggs, E.** – Senryu – *Across the Bridge* – Apostrophe Publishing, Sykesville, MD 1996; Heart to Heart – *Across the Bridge* – Apostrophe Publishing, Sykesville, MD 1996; Flowing Waters – *Across the Bridge* – Apostrophe Publishing, Sykesville, MD 1996; **Bundy, J.** – Contradiction – self published; Swing and Sway – self published; 95-65-95 Militant – self published; **Bush, E.** – On Giving Voice – *Grab-a-Nickel*; The Girl in the Feed-Sack Dress – *Grab-a-Nickel*; **Bush, J.** – 11/22/63 – *The Reach of Song* 1996; Showing the Buyer – *California Quarterly* 1995; The Estate Sale – *NFSPS Prize Poems* 1996

Cabbell, E. – Activist – *Life and Work, Now and Then* Vol 7 #3 1990; Appalachia: An Old Man's Dream Deferred – *Now and Then, A Southern Appalachian Reader*; An Appalachian Dilemma – *Now and Then* Vol 3 #1 1986, *Hill and Valley, Black Diamonds*; **Caldwell, J.** – Getting the Mail on Mud Lick Branch – previously unpublished; Bells on Parchment Creek – previously unpublished;

Sabbatical on Winifrede Hollow – *Potato Eyes*, courtesy of Nightshade Press; **Campbell, S.** – The Executive Director of the Coal Community Y – *Still No Theme* 1992; Men Sitting at Mahogany Tables – *Grab-a-Nickel*; **carr, b.** – untitled – previously unpublished; marginal figures of eight – *my.th*; **Cavalieri, G.** – Letter – *Artworks*; Give It Up – *Voice as a Bridge*; The Protest – *Voice as a Bridge*; You Can't Start the Spiritual Journey – *Nimrod*, WPFW Anthology; **Chaapel, B.** – Her Face, My Face – previously unpublished; The Ancient Art of Shape-Shifting – *Grab-a-Nickel*; **Christen, L.** – That Girl with Pre-Raphaelite Hair – previously unpublished; Cora Two-Moons – previously unpublished; **Coberly, L.** – There Would Come a Day – Fireweed Press; Take an Old Cherry Table – *Christian Science Monitor*; Reminds Me of a Beach – *Christian Science Monitor*; **Coleman, M.J.** – Dandelions of April – *Take One Blood Red Rose* – West End Press 1978; Noah Totten – *Take One Blood Red Rose* – West End Press 1978; Golden Gloves – *Take One Blood Red Rose* – West End Press 1978; **Conner, D.** – Saturday Night Jamboree – *Antietam Review*; Cold Light – previously unpublished; Fifth Grade – *Ohio Schools*, *The Maine Educator*; **Cottrell, L.** – All That August Knew – *Vandalia Mistress* 1996; Windlestraw Days – *Shanties* 1996; Benediction – previously unpublished; **Currey, R.** – Here are the facts of the matter – *Crossing Over* – Clark City Press

Davis, E. – He Could Write – *Poetpourri* Vol 6 #2 Fall 1992; Haskell and the Widder Woman – *New River Free Press* Vol 8 #4 May-June 1990; Humanities 297 – *S. Coast Poetry Journal* 1987; **Davis, J.** – Seasonal – *Harvest – Collected Works*, Arts & Humanities Alliance of Jefferson County, Charlestown, WV 1992; Old Age Is Not for Sissies – *Harvest – Collected Works*, Arts & Humanities Alliance of Jefferson County, Charlestown, WV 1992; **Davis, L.** – Farmington No. 9 – *Three Rivers Poetry Journal*; Panic on the Lower Jackson – *Fishing the Lower Jackson* 1974; **DeBerry, M.** – Death of a Black Dog – *Tantra Press* Vol 1 #2 July 1993; Gift from Joe Gluck in July – previously unpublished; **De Foe, M.** – 13 Ways of Eradicating Blackbirds – *The Brand -X Anthology of Poetry*; Applewood Books 1981; Mantle's Knees – *Tulane Review* 10 #1, Fall 1988; Late Winter Snow – *Christian Science Monitor* Vol 91 #56 Feb. 1999; Street Dance: WV – *The Chowder Review 7*, 1976; **Denise, C.** – The Relief Sale – previously unpublished; Heaven and Things – *Gospel Herald Magazine* Dec 1997; God and Farmers – previously unpublished; **Depta, V.** – Minor Gods in the Coal Fields – *The Silence of Blackberries* – The Blair Mountain Press, Martin TN 1999; A Man on a Cloudy Day – *The Creek* – Oberlin Printing 1973; Well Somebody on Buffalo Creek – *Appalachian Journal*/Appalachian State University 1973; **Dressler, M.** – Sing Appalachia – *Appalachia: My Land* – Morris Harvey College 1973; Appalachia – *Appalachia: My Land* – Morris Harvey College 1973; I Was a Fool – *Appalachia: My Land* – Morris Harvey College 1973; I Am Not Weaned – *Appalachia: My Land* – Morris Harvey College 1973; **Dubois, O.** – Potato Roast – *Lichen and Moss and Other Poems* – McClain Press, Parsons, WV 1976; **Duckworth, E.** – Age? How do we equate it? – *Ramblings of a Scorched Soul*

Ellison, H. – China Tour – *Best of Hill & Valley*; **Emerson, H.** – the journey – previously unpublished; Side of Beef on Third Street – *Back Country*; Greyhound Blues – *Back Country*; **Eversole, R.** – How – previously unpublished; At War – previously unpublished

Ferguson, C. – Changeling Child – previously unpublished; **Fischer, E.** – Young Gods – *Shepherdstown Chronicle*; Apple – *Wonderful West Virginia* Magazine; **Frazier, K.** – The Conversation – *The Laurel Review*; The Fire Chief – *Old Wounds, New Words*; **Frisk, D.** – Iced Tea Recipe – *Ivory Hollyhock* – 6 July

Old Wounds, New Words; **Frisk, D.** – Iced Tea Recipe – *Ivory Hollyhock* – 6 July Press; **Fuller, W.** – The Season – previously unpublished; Defeat – *Indiana Review*; Not Now – previously unpublished; Darwin's Wife – previously unpublished

Garten, B. – At Four – *Samisdat*; Putting a Patent on Hope-Part 1 – *Bottomfish*; Putting a Patent on Hope-Part 2 – *Parnassus*; Last Night – *Black Buzzard Review*; **Gatski, J.** – Earth Time – *Promontory* – Greenmont Company 1995; **Gerke, R.** – New Year's Eve, 2000 – previously unpublished; Frostbitten Memories – previously unpublished; Depending on Trees – previously unpublished; **Gilmore, M.** – Green Lace – *Poetic Digs* – McClain Press, Parsons, WV 1997, My Treasure Chest – *Poetic Digs* – McClain Press, Parsons, WV 1997

Harmon, R. – A Summer River – *Roses in December (Poems of a Mountaineer)* – Harlo Press, Detroit, MI 1978; **Harms. J.** – Copper Wire – *The Missouri Review*; Photo – *Kestrel*; Mother to Daughter – *The Missouri Review*; **Harshman, M.** – Them – *Equinox*; There Will Be Dancing – *Shenandoah*; Oxford – *The Georgia Review*; Checking the Spring – *Poetry Now*; Clark Hill – *Mother Earth News, Pembroke Magazine*; **Harvey, V.** – Vandals – *Touching the Stars* – Banner Press, Emory University 1954; Wheat Fields – *Touching the Stars* – Banner Press, Emory University 1954; Touching the Stars – *Touching the Stars* – Banner Press, Emory University 1954; **Heaster, E.** – Right Up to Now – *Limericks and Lyrics from Deep Rhododendron Thickets* – McClain Press, Parsons, WV 1973; **Helper, M.** – Our Separate Days – *Our Separate Days* – Rowan Mtn; **Hill, T.** – Zero Point Energy – *Two Heart Mountain* – Silver Pen Press, Seattle, WA 2000; **Hively, C.** – Vespers – previously unpublished; Early Menopause – previously unpublished; Before David Died – previously unpublished; **Houchin, R.** – The ghosts of dogs – *The Stinging Fly*, Ireland; New night for Lazarus – *Poetry Ireland Review*; My dog's tongue – previously unpublished; How sound gets into dream – previously unpublished; The possibility of magic – previously unpublished

Jarvis, D. – Ancestry – *Best of Hill & Valley*; Untitled – *Best of Hill & Valley*; Dark-haired Boy – *The Born Again Tourist* – Trillium Press, St. Albans, WV 1995; Mr. and Mrs. Death – *The Born Again Tourist* – Trillium Press, St. Albans, WV 1995; **Jones, R.** – Song for an Accidental Traveler – previously unpublished; Disinherited – previously unpublished; **Jordan, N.** – How to Sprout a Poem – previously unpublished; Hometown Boy – previously unpublished; **Judd, K.** – The High Country Remembers Her Heritage – *Kestrel*, Issue 1, Spring 1993; Voyager – *Field Notes*, Vol.35 # 2, June 1993; The Campfires – *Now and Then* Vol 7 #3 Fall 1990

Keener, E. – Jeopardy – *Antietam Review*; Shadow Play –*West Branch* – *The Sandburg-Livesay Anthology*; **Kernan, L.** – The Gift – *Pivot*, 1985; Manhattan Street Scene: November – *Potomac Review*, Spring 1997; In the Garden – *Remington Review*, Oct 1976; **Klein, S.** – Untitled – previously unpublished; **Krueger, A.** – Twenty-Six Steps – previously unpublished; Movin' On – previously unpublished

Laska, P.J. – The Moon over Morgantown – *atelier 3* Boston; Extra Munction – *The Day the Eighties Began* – Igneus Press, Bedford, NH 1991; The Race of the Century – *Appalachian Journal*; The Squab Woman – *The Sow's Ear*; **Long, C.** – Tryst of Elements – Riding the Shaving Horse – *Hagerstown Almanack* 1997; **Love, P.** – Rejection – *Street Scenes* – Phoenix Press, Charleston, WV 1992; Cabin Fever – *Street Scenes* – Phoenix Press, Charleston, WV 1992; **Makuck. P.** –

Where We Live – (BOA Editions, Ltd, 1982); Nights – *Where We Live* – (BOA Editions, Ltd, 1982)

Mann. J. – Tomato Stakes – previously unpublished; Dilly Beans – *Appalachian Heritage*; Digging Potatoes – *Confluence*; **Marano, R.** – Boys' Dreams – *Poems from a Mountain Ghetto* – Back Fork Books, Webster Springs, WV 1979; The Gardens – *Appalachian Heritage, Poems from a Mountain Ghetto* – Back Fork Books, Webster Springs, WV 1979; The 'Numbers Runner' – *Nitty Gritty, Poems From a Mountain Ghetto* – Back Fork Books, Webster Springs, WV 1979; **Marshall, R.** – Circa 1935 – *Backcountry*; The Burning Ground – *Backcountry*; Sale Today at the Harper Place – *Backcountry*; **Marshburn, S.** – Clock – *Midwest Quarterly, Undertow*; Travelers – *Potomac Review*; **Mays, L.** – Twilight – *Idylls of the Hills* – Nortex Press, Quarale, TX 1975;
Mazzolini, M. – Wild Bill's Garage – *Backcountry*; Millhunk – *Backcountry;*
McCullough, B. – Voyeur – previously unpublished; **McDowell, M.** – The Child's Song – *Our Song, Too* 1974; Traveling Song – *Our Song, Too* 1974;
McElhaney, G. – Snow Bird – *Pivot* 1983; Under the Volcano – *Pivot* 1981;
McKeown, B. – Coal Miners Off Duty – *Pieces*, 1978; Labor – previously unpublished; **McKernan, J.** – Someone Lived Through That Famine – *Prairie Schooner*; The Funeral of Death – *The Virginia Quarterly Review*; The Dawn – *The Atlantic Monthly, Walking Along the Missouri River*, Lost Roads Press, 1977; The Shadow Beneath My Corpse Is Always – *The Paris Review*; **McKernan, L.** – Churn – Federation of State Poetry Societies, *1994 Anthology of Winners*; The Girl in the Black Leather Raincoat – *1983 National Poetry Competition Anthology of Winners, Many Waters*; Swimming in Greenbo – *The Kenyon Review, Many Waters*; **McKinney. I.** – Visiting My Gravesite – *Six O'Clock Mine Report*; Deep Mining – *Six O'Clock Mine Report*; Sunday Morning, 1950 – *Six O'Clock Mine Report*; Viridian Days – *The American Voice*; Fodder – *Artful Bone*; Twilight In West Virginia – *Six O'Clock Mine Report*; Courtesy U Pittsburgh Press
McNamara, D. – That Green Fuse – *The Hiram Poetry Review*; Bison Trace – *The Rickshaw*; Fossil Fuel – *Trellis 79*; **McNeill, L.** – The Long Traveler – *WV and Regional History Collection*, WV University Libraries; Faldang – *WV and Regional History Collection*, WV University Libraries; Mountain Corn Song – *WV and Regional History Collection*, WV University Libraries; Martha MacElmain – *WV and Regional History Collection*, WV University Libraries; Hill Daughter – *WV and Regional History Collection*, WV University Libraries; Poet – *WV and Regional History Collection*, WV University Libraries; Corner Tree – *WV and Regional History Collection*, WV University Libraries; **Meade, C.** – Who Is My Neighbor? – previously unpublished; **Merical, N.** – The Nazarene Carpenter – *Warner Sunday School Bulletin*; **Miller, D.** – April's Moon – *Desert the Mirror* – The Dierkes Press, Eureka Springs, Ark. 1957; **Moore, P.** – Haiku – *A Gathering at the Forks*; On the Eighth Day – *Appalachian Heritage*; On the Hard Drive – *Whetstone*; **Mosher, L.** – The Visit – *Going Home* – Norwood Press 1992;
Myers, L. – Two Cinquains – *Verse and Worse* – Torrance Company, Philadelphia, PA 1969

Narkevic, D. – Marigolds – previously unpublished; Ivy – previously unpublished; the new river – *Standing Wave*; **Nieman, V.** – Pissing in the Woods – *Fresh Ground*; Above Dunkard Mill Run – *How We Live*; How We Live – *How We Live*

Parker, C. – Four Year Old's First Test – *Yankee Magazine*; Older Brother – previously unpublished; The Community of Women – previously unpublished;
Pauley, M. – Stones – previously unpublished; street-lit jesus on jackson street –

Pauley, M. – Stones – previously unpublished; street-lit jesus on jackson street – previously unpublished; retribution – previously unpublished; **Pendarvis, E.** – Augury – previously unpublished; Mixed with the Piping – *Grab-a-Nickel*; Sequoyah – *Grab-a-Nickel*; Crazy Quilt – *Joy Ride* -Bottom Dog Press; **Phillips, J.** – SnowCloud – *Sweethearts*; Shaping – *Sweethearts*; Cheers – *Black Tickets* – Dell-Doubleday; **Pierce, C.** – Reunion – previously unpublished; **Prather, D.** – Ignominious – *Potomac Review*; Remission – *American Literary Review*; Genesis in the Uncut Field – *Kestrel*; **Proudfoot, B.** – These Winter Evenings – previously unpublished; Amesville Flood, 1996 – previously unpublished; Silver Trumpet, Satin Cap – previously unpublished

Rampp, C. – emergency – previously unpublished; fatherwood – *Phoenix, Poets' Guild*; **Russell, T.** – Steel Mill Ornithology – *The Possibility of Turning to Salt* 1987; In a Nutshell – *The Possibility of Turning to Salt* 1987; The Possibility of Turning to Salt – *The Possibility of Turning to Salt* 1987; In Extremis – *Lousiville Review, In Dubio* – State Street Press Chapbooks 1988; In Rem Versum – *West Branch, In Dubio* – State Street Press Chapbooks 1988; In Loco Citato – Yarrow, *The Possibility of Turning to Salt* 1987

Sheppard, S. – Through Which Things Are Watched Harshly – *Nimrod*; Here – *The Ohio Review*; **Smith, B.** – Apple Pie Dying – *Limestone Circle*; Lines – *Aethlon*; The Omen – *Appalachian Heritage*; **Smith, M.** – Transplant – *Heart to Heart* – Fairfax Press; Roots – *Heart to Heart* – Fairfax Press; **Smucker, A.** – Bitter Herb – *A Gathering at the Forks*; Summer Twilight Along the Ohio – previously unpublished; **Snyder, B.** – Linoleum: Camouflage of the Absolute – *We'll See Who's a Peasant* – Mountain Union Books, Beckley, WV 1977; Poem to my Grandfather – *We'll See Who's a Peasant* – Mountain Union Books, Beckley, WV 1977; Comfort Me with Hyssop – *The Mason-Dixon Sutra* – Igneus Press, Bedford, NH 1999; **Snyder, L.** – Touch and Time – *West Branch*; Knot in the Living – *Mountain Pathways*; Learning the Names of God – *Blue Unicorn*; **Spencer, A.** – Letter to My Sister – *American Negro Poetry* – Hill & Wang 1974; **Stealey, M.** – The BirdBell Cafe – previously unpublished; **Steele, P.** – Blackberry Wine – previously unpublished; The Beer Gardens of Logan County – previously unpublished; **Stringer, A.** – Star Disc – *Kestrel*; The Incomplete Is Unforgiving – *Ohio Review*; Aerodynamic – *Kestrel*; **Sullivan, W.** – A Kiss – previously unpublished; In the Trough – previously unpublished; Pearl – previously unpublished; **Swick, G.** – Ghost Story, Manassas – previously unpublished; Texas, 1935 – previously unpublished

Tedford, B. – Sestina – previously unpublished; Incantation – previously unpublished; **Thorn, A.** – Elegy for My Brother Joe – *Weeping with Those Who Weep*; The Idea of the Table – *The Guyandotte Poets*; Exploring the Poles – *Southern Humanities Review*; **Tresham, J.** – The Old Family Album – *The Collected Works of Miss Jessie Tresham* – Daughters of American Pioneers, Thomas Ritchie Chapter 1975

Van Gundy, D. – The Still, Small Voice – *Kestrel*; A Beautiful Jar of Jelly – *Kestrel*; **Vincent, T.** – Father – *Appalachian Journal*; **Vrana, S.** – Turnings – previously unpublished; White Witch of Moss Creek – previously unpublished

Webb, J. – Hog Killing – *Appalachian Journal*; New England Light – *Pine Mountain Sand and Gravel*; Diary of a Mad Bomber – *Laurel Review*; **West, D.** – It Was the Wind – *O Mountaineers* – Appalachian Press, Huntington, WV 1974; There'll Be a Tomorrow – *In a Land of Plenty* – West End Press 1982;

Wheeler, B. – Woods Colt – *Song of a Woods Colt*; Going for Cows – *Song of a Woods Colt*; Silent Mountain – *Song of a Woods Colt*; Christmas In Coaltown – *Song of a Woods Colt*; The Craft Shop – *Song of a Woods Colt*; **Wigal, S.** – Cardinal Singing – previously unpublished; Manassas, Virginia (1861) – *Poke Berries and Chicken Feathers* – Tantra Press 1995; Like Patent Leather Shoes – *Dickensonian*; Estate Auction – previously unpublished; **Wilkins, R.** – Remembering – previously unpublished; **Wilson, J.** – Mountain Writer – previously unpublished; Call Me Bad – previously unpublished

Yeager, B. – To Lone Wolf – previously unpublished

Zahniser, E. – Prayer for Prayer – *Odd Angles of Heaven*, Anthology, Harold Shaw Publishers, Wheaton, IL; Remedio Farms the Sonoran Desert – *The Other Side Magazine*; Acid Rain – *Amicus Journal*; **Zierold, J.** – Boone County Bounty – *Hill & Valley*; **Zivkovic, P.** – In the Name of the Son and the Holy Ghost – *Of Belly and Bone* – Timberline Press, Fulton, MO; Special Buck of Mine – *Of Belly and Bone* – Timberline Press, Fulton, MO; Thief – *Of Belly and Bone* – Timberline Press, Fulton, MO